W9-AAW-102

The Gulf Wars and the United States

The Gulf Wars and the United States

Shaping the Twenty-First Century

Orrin Schwab

PSI Reports

PRAEGER SECURITY INTERNATIONAL

Westport, Connecticut · London

Library of Congress Cataloging-in-Publication Data

Schwab, Orrin, 1956–
   The Gulf wars and the United States : shaping the twenty-first century / Orrin Schwab.
    p. cm.
   Includes bibliographical references and index.
   ISBN 978–0–275–99754–0 (alk. paper)
1. Persian Gulf War, 1991. 2. Iraq War, 2003– 3. United States—Foreign relations—1989– 4. United States—Military policy—20th century. 5. United States—Military policy—21st century. I. Title.
DS79.72.S544 2009
956.7044'2—dc22   2008033714

British Library Cataloguing in Publication Data is available.

Copyright © 2009 by Orrin Schwab

Library of Congress Catalog Card Number: 2008033714
ISBN 978–0–275–99754–0

First published in 2009

Praeger Security International, 88 Post Road West, Westport, CT 06881
An imprint of Greenwood Publishing Group, Inc.
www.praeger.com

Printed in the United States of America

The paper used in this book complies with the Permanent Paper Standard issued by the National Information Standards Organization (Z39.48–1984).

10 9 8 7 6 5 4 3 2 1

To future peace in the Gulf and to the memory of the fallen

Military arrangement and movements in consequence, like the mechanism of a clock, will be imperfect and disordered by the want of a part.

George Washington,
letter to the President of Congress,
December 23, 1777

We shall not enter into any of the abstruse definitions of war used by publicists. We shall keep to the element of the thing itself, to a duel. War is nothing but a duel on an extensive scale.

Carl Von Clausewitz, *On War*

Contents

Preface

The idea for this book came out of my earlier works on the Vietnam War and a general synthesis for U.S. international history during the twentieth century. The Gulf Wars of the late twentieth and early twenty-first centuries were bookends to what looks like a generational war with characteristics similar to both the Vietnam conflict and the larger Cold War. For U.S. military and diplomatic historians, the Gulf Wars have been a reconstruction of those earlier conflicts, demonstrating similar processes and events that shed light on the continuing development of U.S. national security institutions.

Having said this, I do recognize that, for most historians, it is far too early to think about let alone write about these connected conflicts as history. For most practitioners, more than a few years in the case of the Iraq War, or a decade and a half in the case of the Gulf War, is sufficient time to conceptualize these complex phenomena as historical subjects. Only with reluctance, have I discussed the postwar events of the Second Gulf War. This was because the war termination phase for the 2003 conflict had not ended as of spring 2008, and the complexities of those events, not to mention the hard emotions of the times, argued against an attempt at writing about them. Nonetheless, the topic is so rich and important to contemporary political thought and analysis that I decided they should be included, even if my analysis is too contemporary to be historical.

Another advantage in waiting a generation or two would be the availability of primary sources. I believe I have overcome this obstacle for my purposes. There are in fact, huge source materials of greater importance that are within the public domain for both Gulf Wars and for the intermediary period of the Clinton administration. Since my level of analysis includes most importantly that of the international system, I am less handicapped that I would have been if my approach depended more on the trail of diplomatic and political documents that await declassification some decades hence. This work is not only intended as a comprehensive history of U.S. foreign relations but also an interpretation on the two recent wars of global importance.

The first chapter sketches my original concepts for analyzing U.S. foreign relations and modern international relations and how they relate to the Gulf Wars. Chapter two contextualizes the First Gulf War as a part of the final stage of the Cold War and the first moments of the post–Cold War international system. The third chapter interprets the origins of the First Gulf War within the context of both U.S. Cold War and Iraqi history. The chapter covers the chronology of 1990–91, emphasizing institutional and political as well as military aspects of the war. The fourth and fifth chapters explain the evolution of U.S.–Iraqi relations from the end of the First Gulf War through the end of the Clinton administration and the transformative events of September 11 during the second Bush administration.

The final chapters bring all the themes of this monograph together. The concept of the technocratic state, neoconservative doctrine, the nature of scripts in national cultures, foreign policy, and leadership systems are all taken into account as are the tectonic forces of globalism on the nature and course of international wars. The author accepts full responsibility for the text its concepts, explanations, and interpretations. All mistakes written or otherwise have been my own.

Acknowledgments

I would like to thank Gary Sick and the Gulf 2000 discussion list for their insightful comments and educative resources they have been supplied to me since I joined the list in 2006. The list has been a wonderful source of ideas about the Gulf region, its contemporary politics, diverse cultures, societies, and histories. As an American historian, I must always be forced to take myself out of the framework which I have inherited from my profession and my own culture that remains unashamed in its nationalist ideology. Seeing the world from perspectives that are often diametrically at odds with one's own can be distressing but more importantly invaluable to learning and understanding the intuitive aspects of international history.

The Regenstein library at the University of Chicago was as always a helpful resource for books and electronic materials. I would also like to thank my colleagues at Carriage Hill Partners, who it should be noted, have made this book possible. My family as always deserves credit for admiring my work as an independent scholar and encouraging me in that regard.

Finally, Heather Staines and Adam Kane, editors at Praeger Security International deserve thanks for giving me the opportunity once again to publish a work in my field, of my own choosing, so confident they and their editorial board have been in my scholarship.

Orrin Schwab
April 2008, Aurora, Illinois

1 ————————————————————————————

The Gulf Wars and American Foreign Relations

There is general recognition in the Middle East, as elsewhere, that the United States does not seek either political or economic domination over any other people. Our desire is a world environment of freedom, not servitude.

Dwight Eisenhower[1]

The Americans on their part showed no great desire to search for oil far away in the Middle East until the end of the first World War when they realized the importance of oil for the military machine and saw how much of the American oil supplies had been consumed by the war. From then until the end of World War II, and even afterwards, a continuous struggle has been carried on between the United States and Great Britain for the exploitation of the oil resources of the Middle East.

Benjamin Shwadran[2]

At the very end of the Cold War, the world was surprised by the invasion of the oil-rich sheikdom of Kuwait. At the beginning of August 1990, in the blazing heat of the Persian Gulf, the tank divisions of the Iraqi army swept across the Iraqi-Kuwaiti border capturing the Kuwaiti capital in a matter of hours. The Kuwaiti royal family and other members of the government escaped to neighboring Saudi Arabia while Saddam Hussein jubilantly announced the capture of Kuwait and its incorporation into the Republic of Iraq. Iraqi claims to Kuwait predated the despotic regime of Saddam Hussein and indeed the creation of the modern state of Iraq from the British Mandate. This mattered little to most of the world, including Iraq's neighbors, who viewed the invasion with extreme alarm. Hussein's impressive Soviet-supplied armor was within easy striking distance of the largest and most important oil fields in the world. Saudi Arabia, a country that did not have a modern army, lay helpless before the Iraqi armored divisions save for the interdiction of the Saudi's essential allies, the United States and Great Britain. The lead article in the *New York Times* of August 3, 1990, summarized the gravity of the situation in its first sentence:

> Iraqi troops stormed into the desert sheikdom of Kuwait today, seizing control of its capital city and its rich oilfields, driving its ruler into exile, plunging the strategic Persian Gulf region into crisis and sending tremors of anxiety around the world.[3]

For the United States and the administration of George H. Bush, the Iraqi invasion and occupation of Kuwait was shocking but not completely unexpected. In conversations with the U.S. ambassador to Iraq, senior Iraqi officials indicated their grievances against Kuwait.[4] The country was accused of "stealing" Iraqi oil from disputed land on the Kuwaiti frontier. Further, several islands at the mouth of the Tigris–Euphrates river system were claimed by Iraq and deemed vital to its national security. To remedy the situation, the Iraqis had indicated a possibility of an armed attack. In this event, the consequences for U.S. national security of an Iraqi invasion were plain. In less than a day, Iraq had captured one of the largest reserves of oil in the Gulf region and the world. They now controlled the Kuwaiti oil industry in its entirety, and with their large force of Soviet-built tanks and battle-hardened troops, threatened the independence of the other oil-rich Gulf states. Before any U.S. ground forces could be deployed, a powerful Iraqi army now threatened Saudi Arabia, the world's largest oil supplier, critical to the energy needs of Japan and Western Europe and therefore, a vital and irreplaceable strategic ally of the United States.

Between August 1990 and April 2003, the United States deployed and fought two major regional wars against the regime of Saddam Hussein. The first conflict, fought by a coalition of several dozen nations, expelled Hussein's army from Kuwait, destroyed substantial parts of Iraq's military-industrial infrastructure, and in its war settlement imposed a strict containment regime on Iraq. The Second Gulf War, initiated by President George W. Bush, entailed the invasion of the Iraqi state, occupying the country and destroying the Ba'athist regime that had controlled Iraq since 1968. The end of the second war resulted in a period of anarchy and active insurrection against the occupying forces of the United States and Great Britain, producing a deadly civil war that at the time of this writing remains without a definitive conclusion.

Already, a large literature exists on the First Gulf War, in American parlance also known as "Operation Desert Storm." The interregnum of the 1990s, which included the eight years of the Clinton administration, was a period of de facto war between Iraq and the West. U.S. forces imposed a strict containment policy on Iraq, controlling the export of Iraqi oil, demanding weapon inspections, and imposing "no-fly zones" on the Iraqi air force to protect Kurdish and Shia Arab populations who faced genocidal practices by Saddam's military. There also exists a significant literature on the interwar period. Finally, a significant number of books and primary documents have become available for the origins of the Second Gulf War, which related to the September 11 attacks, and the birth of the GWOT (Global War on Terror). Indeed, the Gulf Wars and the GWOT have been part of the same underlying historical process that has gripped the Middle East and its relationship to the world in the last decades of the twentieth and the beginning of the twenty-first centuries. The combined subjects are so broad and controversial that it is hard to point to a coherent literature on the idea.[5]

The purpose of this narrative is to explain the Gulf Wars of 1990–91 and 2003 as products of U.S. foreign relations. The origins and conduct of the wars relate to the dynamics of American power in the contemporary world. In earlier books, I have discussed the idea of the American technocratic state and the rise of the liberal technocratic order in world history during the twentieth century.[6] In this analytical monograph, I will use those terms and the conceptual framework of the technocratic state and order to interpret the U.S.-Iraqi conflict. In important ways, the Iraq wars bare resemblances to earlier American interventions in the Third World, including the Vietnam War. While the Vietnam conflict was fought in the radically different terrain of rain forests and swamps, the structural characteristics of the national security system that the United States used in Vietnam were those of an earlier form of the technocratic war machine that entered the Persian Gulf in 1990 and continued through the first decade of the twenty-first century.[7]

THE STATE

Since the Second World War, the most salient characteristic of U.S. foreign policy has been institutional. Large and complex national security institutions have developed and implemented military, diplomatic, and economic policies in every corner of the world. Indeed, the modern national security state or system was characteristic not only of the United States during the second half of the twentieth century, but it had significant counterparts among major world powers, including the Soviet Union. There exists a significant literature on the institutional aspects of U.S. national security. The scholarship presents a broad picture of technological and doctrinal development over the range of U.S. foreign policy interests.[8]

For the Gulf Wars, one of the most salient ideas relates to the progressive development of U.S. national security institutions, before the First Gulf War of 1990–91 and beyond the end of the Second Gulf War of 2003. From the first years of the Second World War, U.S. strategic doctrine has been premised on the concept of dominance. American national security, as defined by both civilian and military thinkers, was a global idea. To assure the national security of a country with global interests and dependencies, global military dominance was required. For a society as rich, dynamic, and as ambitious as the United States, the notion of global military superiority was not grandiose but an appraisal of national interests and capabilities that appeared possible and, for some national security thinkers, desirable.[9]

From the Second World War, through the Korean and Vietnam wars, and then the 1980s, the Reagan era which coincided with Soviet communism's denouement, the institutional, technological, and intellectual foundations for American power grew, even accelerating in its potential to project strategic domination to all the corners of the earth. While there were clear limits to American power, which Truman found in Korea, Johnson found in Vietnam, and Carter and Reagan found in the Middle East, the structural determinants of national strength increased over time, a function of the ongoing rapid technocratic transformation of First World civilization.

INSTITUTIONAL SYSTEMS: PUBLIC AND PRIVATE AXIS

The national security state can be best understood as a complex of interlocking institutions, both public and private, that provide a means for formulating, communicating, and executing national security policy. The American national security state is a general concept that includes not only the NSC, Department of Defense and State, and their associate intelligence agencies but also many well-funded private centers of important intellectual production, including the Rand Corporation, the Brookings Institution, and the American Enterprise Institute. The state also includes a vast number of private corporations that supply the state with products and services essential to the vast responsibilities for global U.S. national security.[10]

U.S. national security in the last decades of the twentieth century and the first of the twenty-first involved the development of a large array of technologies to observe and control the global security environment. The technologies included means for advanced electronic intelligence as well as the weapon systems required to achieve U.S. military superiority on the battlefield, in the air, outer space, and on all the world's oceans. In quite literal terms, U.S. global security was defined since the Second World War as the universal dominance of U.S. military forces everywhere in the world. Accordingly, the national security state evolved a military and political establishment that recognized the centrality of this mission, and produced technologies, doctrines, and advanced weapon systems that matched the national mission.

INTERESTS

Another diffuse but essential concept is "interest." A state's interests are by definition very broad, encompassing the particular interests of the groups, ethnic, political, and economic, that are part of any modern nation-state. Beyond the general concept of dominance, U.S. national security policy has always been related to particular group and institutional interests. To produce a coherent response to a threat, national interests must be articulated at local and regional levels. The interests must be related to distinct areas of vital concern to both local and national constituencies. Broadly, national interests fall within three domains: strategic, political, and economic.

STRATEGIC

During the Cold War, strategic interests were relatively easy to define. The United States defined strategic interests with respect to the containment of the Soviet Union. The Persian Gulf was a vital strategic interest when Soviet power threatened to expand into the region and to control its petroleum resources essential to the functioning of the world's economy. The Carter doctrine enunciated in 1980 in response to Soviet expansion into Afghanistan established a military protocol to defend the Gulf and the vital strategic interest of Persian Gulf oil:

> The region which is now threatened by Soviet troops in Afghanistan is of great strategic importance: It contains more than two-thirds of the world's exportable oil. The Soviet effort to dominate Afghanistan has brought Soviet military forces to within 300 miles of the Indian Ocean and close to the Straits of Hormuz, a waterway through which most of the world's oil must flow. The Soviet Union is now attempting to consolidate a strategic position, therefore, that poses a grave threat to the free movement of Middle East oil.

> This situation demands careful thought, steady nerves, and resolute action, not only for this year but for many years to come. It demands collective efforts to meet this new threat to security in the Persian Gulf and in Southwest Asia. It demands the participation of all those who rely on oil from the Middle East and who are concerned with global peace and stability. And it demands consultation and close cooperation with countries in the area which might be threatened.

> Meeting this challenge will take national will, diplomatic and political wisdom, economic sacrifice, and, of course, military capability. We must call on the best that is in us to preserve the security of this crucial region.

> Let our position be absolutely clear: An attempt by any outside force to gain control of the Persian Gulf region will be regarded as an assault on the vital interests of the United States of America, and such an assault will be repelled by any means necessary, including military force.[11]

The Carter doctrine remained in place after the Cold War. The Persian Gulf remained a central strategic asset for the United States, even without the threat of the Soviet Union and the bipolarity of the Cold War international system.

The First Gulf War, which coincided with the end of the Soviet-American rivalry, triggered U.S. strategic interests within hours of the Iraqi invasion of Kuwait. The First Gulf War triggered an automatic response to defend Saudi Arabia and the smaller emirates from Iraqi invasion. The strategic interest was conflated with the economic interest in protecting the Gulf's oil supply, in aggregate estimated in 1990 to be two-thirds of the world's recoverable reserves.[12] In strategic terms, control of oil by Saddam Hussein would have magnified his power exponentially, turning Iraq into a Middle Eastern superpower in every sense of the word. Neither the United States nor other members of NATO, nor the moderate Arab states, and the world community in general, would allow Iraq's dominance of the Gulf, including the occupation of Kuwait, by itself an economic and strategic asset of tremendous value to both Saddam Hussein and his many adversaries.[13]

POLITICAL

American political interests in the Gulf were hard to extricate from economic and strategic interests. Domestic political interests had to do with two distinct areas of concern. First, access to Gulf oil had enormous bearing on the world price of crude petroleum, which in turn determined the cost of gasoline and heating oil to hundreds of millions of American consumers. Second, Iraq's power, military, political, and economic threatened the State of Israel, a country whose unique influence in U.S. foreign policy made any threat to it a significant domestic political interest for any American administration.

While domestic political interests were compelling in themselves, the international political interests associated with Gulf security were of equal importance. Since the Gulf's energy resources were critical to the global economy, ensuring the safety and supply of those assets had to be a vital strategic, economic, and political interest for U.S. international interests. In regional terms, the political stability of the Gulf was of direct importance to the stability of the entire Middle East and Southwestern Asia. The delicate balance between the opposing branches of Islam, Sunni, and Shia was held in control by the Gulf region's state system. The altering or collapse of that regional balance-of-power system, involving Iraq, Syria, Saudi Arabia, Iran, and Turkey, was a compelling regional and international political interest of the United States. In his memoirs, Bush's Secretary of State, James Baker, discussed the regional political dimensions of the First Gulf War:

> In managing the regional implications of the crisis, we needed to consider a host of major players in the region besides the Saudis: Turkey, a country where civilian government had often been weak and which had genuine concerns about Kurdish nationalism undermining national stability; Syria, where President Assad hated Saddam but was loath to give comfort to Israel; Egypt, the primary voice of Arab

moderation in the region; Israel, which could have undermined the coalition at any moment by moving preemptively against Saddam; Iran, whose enmity for Iraq was surpassed only by its hatred of the United States; Jordan, whose King pursued a policy of equivocation to keep from alienating his stronger neighbor, Saddam; the Palestinians, whose support for Saddam threatened our hopes for forging an anti-Iraq Arab majority; the Gulf states, whose sheikhdoms were Saddam's next dominoes; and Yemen, whose support of Saddam splintered anti-Saddam Arab solidarity.[14]

ECONOMIC

Economic interests exist at many different levels of analysis. The Gulf's extraordinary resources in oil and natural gas, some two-thirds of the world's proven reserves at the start of the First Gulf War, represented an essential economic interest for the global economy. It was a critical interest for the advanced industrialized economies, Japan, West Germany, France, and others, in addition to being of extraordinary significance to developing and middle-level economies that were dependent upon oil imports. For the United States, economic interests in the Gulf were coterminous with strategic and political interests. The oil shocks of the 1970s had raised the world price of oil from less than $2 per barrel in 1970 to a peak of nearly $40 on the world spot market in 1980.[15]

In the United States, electoral politics were intricately tied to the condition of the national economy. A president's approval rating was directly correlated with the overall health of the economy. Economic health, in turn, was predicated on stable and affordable energy. The massive rise in energy costs in the 1970s was a principal cause of the high inflation, high unemployment, and declining living standards experienced in the United States during the latter half of the 1970s and the first years of the 1980s. In practical terms, the security of Gulf oil was vital to the political survival of governing coalitions in the United States and other energy-dependent liberal democracies.

In American politics, the security of the Persian Gulf from the Nixon administration of the 1970s into the twenty-first century demonstrated the confluence of strategic, economic, and political interests. The Gulf combined the parochial concerns of state and local officials, with the strategic issues of successive presidential administrations, which simply could not get past the basic arithmetic of oil dependency.[16]

IDEOLOGIES

Interests, national, institutional, and local, informed the political milieu of the nation-state in the late-twentieth century. With interests came belief systems that expressed their particular groundings in group, institutional, and national cultures. Coincident to competing interests, American foreign policy was informed by a number of competing ideologies. Most decision-makers were influenced by all of the principal ideological systems that were grounded in the institutional and historical scripts within American society. Five major modes of understanding, or policy ideologies, were dominant. Political realism was favored by conservative diplomats such as Richard Nixon's Secretary of State and National Security Adviser, Henry Kissinger, George H. Bush's Secretary of State James Baker, and many others. Progressive internationalism, took two forms, neoconservative, identified with many members of the second Bush presidency, and a liberal progressive internationalism most clearly associated with the Democratic Party and the presidential advisors for presidents Jimmy Carter and Bill Clinton.

In addition to these three political ideologies, the internationalist framework associated with the armed forces was grounded in classic military doctrine. In previous books, I have termed this Clausewitzian internationalism or military realism. Finally, the ideological system for foreign policy distinct from both political and military modes of thought, I have termed managerial or technocratic internationalism. The managerial ideology had to synthesize the institutional and group interests embodied in the American state, organizing the foreign policy system to function domestically and internationally. These often conflicting world views and doctrines frequently resulted in incoherence and broad dysfunction in the conduct of American statecraft and military operations. Yet, the history of any complex society, democratic or not, suggests discordant public policy as a general characteristic of its complexity.[17]

POLITICAL REALISM

Political realists define national interests as the achievement of national political objectives. Fundamental national interests require a matching of national resources with attainable objectives. George Kennan, widely regarded by U.S. diplomatic historians as a principal architect of the concept of "containment" during the Cold War, defined American national interests with respect to an effective policy of balance of power. To preserve American national security against international communism, Kennan assumed American dominance of at least three centers of power in the world system. To contain the postwar Stalinist Soviet Union, the United States needed control of at least two out of three nation-states that he believed determined global dominance. These were Great Britain and the defeated Axis powers, Germany and Japan. In Kennan's paradigm, maintaining a stable balance of power in the world system was the most realistic and effective strategy to protect the United States after the end of the Second World War.[18]

The realist tradition was continued throughout the Cold War, with Henry Kissinger as its most important exponent during the Nixon and Ford administrations. Kissinger's realism, which emphasized dispassionate and politically defined national interests, was a major frame of reference for George H. Bush and his key advisors, NSC Director Brent Scowcroft and Secretary of State James Baker. The First Gulf War was fought and settled in a manner that reflected the ideology of political realism. This mode of thought limited the war to only the liberation of Kuwait. It also premised intervention on the construction of a vast international coalition, thereby maximizing the use of political capital in international affairs.[19]

CLAUSEWITZIANISM

Clausewitzianism or military realism was the strategic ideology of the American military. Both U.S. strategic and operational doctrines of all four branches of the armed forces emphasized fundamental principles of war first articulated by the German military strategist, Eric Von Clausewitz during the Napoleonic era. Military realism, in contrast to the political form of the ideology, defined international relations in military terms. A military commander's view of the utility and necessity of the use of force in world affairs most often differs from the political views of diplomats. This divergence in perceptions, grounded in different professional training, experiences and institutional memories, as well as political orientations, created conflicts over policy throughout the Cold War and the post–Cold War. The schism was most evident during the Vietnam War, when the senior officer corps preferred the use of overwhelming military force in Indochina, while diplomats, fearful of the consequences of such an aggressive course of action, saw the war from an entirely different point of view.[20]

By 1990, the American officer corps was led primarily by junior field officers from the Vietnam era. Both Colin Powell, Chairman of the Joint Chiefs of Staff during the First Gulf War, and Norman Schwarzkopf, the Commander in Chief of U.S. Central Command and theater commander during the war, were Vietnam War veterans. The orientation of the commanders who shaped the operational and strategic doctrine for the First Gulf War was Clausewitzian, but it was a military ideology defined by the lessons of the Vietnam conflict. Colin Powell's "doctrine of invincible force" was premised on classic military principles. To execute an effective war plan, maximum resources had to be applied to the campaign to ensure that no matter what tactics were employed by the enemy the massive application of military power would defeat any possible means of defense.[21]

The Powell doctrine, a true form of modern military realism, established the framework for the military's ideological participation in the First Gulf War. The institutional leadership of the U.S. armed forces did not want to repeat the disaster of the Vietnam experience. Although Joint Chiefs of Staff Chairman Powell preferred containment of Iraq over military assault, he went along with the political determination that Kuwait had to be liberated by military force. The military was willing to support a national objective to defeat the regional enemy of vital U.S. national interests. The Joint Chiefs were committed to evict Iraq from Kuwait to restore the balance of power in the Persian Gulf. The only proviso that the professional military had was that it be given the means to accomplish its mission.[22]

After the First Gulf War, which was a great victory for the allied coalition, the U.S. military's role was subjugated entirely to the political interests of the White House. From March 1991 through the Clinton administration, the second Bush administration, and the Second Gulf War, the classic strategic view of power, based upon a professional understanding of military threats and deterrence was surpassed by the political and technocratic modalities that dominated the civilian departments of the executive branch. Historically, this was usually the case. Constitutionally, the American military's view of the world must always defer to civilian authority. Civilian control in a democratic state always incorporates the political issues related to the use of force. In the modern national security context, this has meant invariably the domination of a managerial or technocratic protocol in the conduct of international war.

PROGRESSIVE INTERNATIONALISM

Besides political realists who tended to be diplomats and lawyers, American elite culture had two idealist forms of foreign policy ideology. One group of idealists who followed the liberal internationalism of Woodrow Wilson, Franklin Roosevelt, Adlai Stevenson, and John F. Kennedy supported the liberal progressive vision of American internationalism. More in favor of diplomacy than military power as a method of conflict resolution, they championed human rights, foreign aid, and multilateral institutions as instruments to achieve the goals of American internationalism. In the late twentieth century, the liberal progressive internationalist ideology energized the left wing of the Democratic Party. The liberal progressives opposed both the first and second Gulf wars as foolish adventures in militarism motivated by corporate capitalism's addiction to oil and the recalcitrant jingoism of the American right.[23]

The other form of American progressive internationalism, whose most salient ancestor was Theodore Roosevelt, synthesized progressive beliefs in nation building, democracy, and liberal institutions, with the conservative and nationalist creed that extolled military power and strategic interests. American conservative progressive internationalism became a dominant ideological force in American foreign affairs during the administration of George W. Bush. The famous "neocons" who were active in Republican administrations and conservative think tanks from the 1970s into the twenty-first century formulated a new foreign policy ideology, with elements of both liberal internationalism and military realism, as well as the managerial internationalism, which had informed all aspects of institutional decision-making since the Second World War.[24]

MANAGERIAL INTERNATIONALISM

All the modalities of institutional thought, the countervailing perspectives of liberal and conservative progressive internationalists, the strategic doctrine of the armed forces, and the dispassionate political realism of veteran diplomats had to be mediated within the U.S. foreign policy system. The mediation of diverse perspectives, ideologies, and interests I have termed "managerial" or "technocratic internationalism." The managerial ideology of the modern state integrates the institutional and political interests of the various constituencies of the national government.

In the contemporary American foreign policy system, the interests that bear upon policy come directly from the major political parties, as well as identifiable lobbying groups who have political capital in the White House and in the Congress. In Middle East policy, the so-called "Israel lobby" has been a major factor in presidential decision-making, just as the anti-Castro Cuban lobby, the China lobby of the 1940s and 1950s, and other interest groups attendant to ethnic polities have been important political factors in executive branch processes. In managerial foreign policy ideology, constituencies representing political, economic, and strategic interests are brought together in an intuitive mathematical representation of national interests. During the Vietnam War, John McNaughton, Deputy Secretary of Defense under Robert McNamara, determined that 70 percent of the importance for defending South Vietnam was to protect "American honor." How did McNaughton arrive at the number "70 percent"? Documents from the 1960s decision-making process in the Pentagon offer no scientific methodology for this very precise calculation of national interest. In fact, McNaughton's use of a numerical estimate is descriptive and intuitive. As a very senior foreign policy analyst, he was formulating a practical, management-oriented policy paper for the future direction of the Vietnam conflict.[25]

The managerial ideology, premised on planning and control, played a central role in the formulation and execution of American foreign policy during all the conflicts of the Cold War and current Cold War periods. As a unifying perspective on policy, the ideology integrates the political perspectives dominant in the State Department, with the operational and strategic military perspectives that traditionally have been dominant in the Defense Department. The perspective, which is a necessary one for the development of a coherent policy, integrates information from domestic and international sources. It should incorporate as much information as possible from representative groups, institutions, global, and regional actors, to meet the minimum conditions for a workable foreign policy.[26]

During the first Gulf War, the technocratic ideology of the executive branch mobilized diplomatic, political, and military resources to effect a joint military campaign involving all four branches of the U.S. armed forces in alliance with two dozen allied nations. The war was a textbook example of how a great power should execute a limited international war. Every aspect of the conflict was planned, quantified, and executed with expert managerial coordination by the White House and the National Security Council. In the war's aftermath, years of analysis has quantified the conflict, estimating its political, economic, and military costs. The escalation, operation, and termination of the First Gulf War as a foreign policy process, demonstrated the technocratic managerial ideology of the American state. This ideology was the controlling institutional script for the projection of American power into the Persian Gulf. After the First Gulf War, and through the containment period of the Clinton administration and the Second Gulf War of 2003, the technocratic ideology of American internationalism remained as the dominant doctrinal and operational perspective for the United States.

As of 2008, the results of the Second Gulf War have been more policy failure than success. Nonetheless, the centrality of managerial/technocratic internationalism in the American presidency remains. Following a growth algorithm defined in modern history centuries before, the contemporary post–Cold War period has seen a continued acceleration of technological change. The pinnacle of this change has been the institutional expansion of the U.S. military as a global technocratic organization. Integrating the exponential growth of scientific and technological knowledge with an ever broader definition of national security, the technocratic state has become evermore powerful and global.

SCRIPTS

Managerial internationalism and its ideology have evolved as an integrating perspective on U.S. foreign policy that brings together all the forces that bear upon the state and its leadership. The managerial mode, as with the other political and military ideologies of the contemporary world, is made up of "scripts." Let me explain this mechanism.

Ideologies are very powerful instruments for the shaping of subjective reality and to effect action. I would like to argue that behind all ideological systems, there exist larger and even more potent mechanisms of psychic control, which I have termed scripts. Scripts are powerful unconscious cognitive structures that control human behavior at all levels of human interaction. They exist in the mind, complex products of evolution, and human culture. They also exist within cultural systems as unifying mechanisms for collective behaviors. Throughout history, through mechanisms of verbal and nonverbal communication, scripts have guided the behavior of leaders, followers, and collectivities of all sizes and dimensions. Scripts have informed the actions of small social groups as well as the largest of international institutions. They have been present in the mythologies of national cultures and civilizations, as well as in the particular dynamics of ordinary families and small groups.[27]

In abstract terms, scripts have guided peasants and farmers living quiet lives in isolated villages; they have worked to control the life narratives of kings, despots, presidents, and other leaders. In collective terms, entire cultures, including those of the Middle East, have followed the mechanisms of collective scripts over generations and even centuries. On some occasions, individuals and groups have gained insight about their scripts, but rarely have they learned to control the mechanisms that bear upon their volitions. Scripts, which have been the principal means of connecting individuals with each other and with groups, have determined both success and defeat and various conditions in between. Rarely, however, do the bearers of scripts learn to control them, to surmount the omnipresent powers of unconscious motivations, the true mechanisms of individual and collective narratives.

At the end of the twentieth century, the national actors that converged in the Gulf to fight the First Gulf war carried their collective narratives on their sleeves. Distinct cultural systems, based on tribal, national, and transnational identities collided in the Middle East and the Persian Gulf, a vortex for narratives whose origins were thousands of years in the past.

NATIONAL

National scripts like those of individuals tend to follow distinct patterns rooted within the core identity of the nation itself. The American script, born in the seventeenth century with the founding cultures of the English colonists created a nation-state with expansionist and utopian designs. American national culture, similar to many others, viewed the nation as messianic, destined, according to Protestant eschatology to establish a new Israel or Zion in North America.[28] The particular designs of a radical Protestant commercial nation-state took form in the founding of the United States in the late eighteenth century. As the country developed, expanding, and industrializing with large-scale immigration, the nation's messianic script led it to fashion its own unique form of internationalism. American internationalism combined great ambition with moral certitude and an extraordinary ability to project power and dominance on a world scale. By the middle of the twentieth century, the United States had established itself as the most advanced scientific and industrialized nation on earth, far surpassing the traditional European powers in financial wealth, industrial capacity, and scientific institutions and resources. America's global script combined Christianity with the technocratic ethos of the nuclear age. Opposing the Soviets, who carried their own script grounded in Russian culture and Marxist-Leninist ideology, American power surged through the Cold War. The dimensions for global power were built on an evolving industrial and scientific establishment and the creation of advanced technological systems that led to the global capitalism of the "information age." By the 1980s, American military power, based on the unique information-based scientific and industrial systems of late twentieth-century capitalism, completely surpassed the scientific-industrial systems of the Soviet Union. The political collapse of the Soviet state, and hence the Soviet script, coincided with the intellectual obsolescence of Marxist-Leninism.[29]

With the First Gulf War, the American national script encountered a group of independent national scripts bearing upon a region whose historical and contemporary importance was critical to the international community. The American narrative viewed the Gulf crisis as another test for the United States. Contending groups within American society debated the nature of American action in the context of the national script. At the same time as an internal dialogue began in North America, in the Middle East, powerful domestic scripts went to work in parallel discussions over the emerging U.S. intervention against the determined threat of Saddam Hussein. In the summer of 1990, the diverse Arab nationalisms of the Gulf, Iraq, Kuwait, Saudi Arabia, the smaller emirates of the UAE, Bahrain, and Oman, as well as the non-Arab Kurds, Iranians, and Israelis converged in the struggle for Kuwait and dominance in the Gulf region.

INTERNATIONAL SCRIPTS

Nation-states follow narratives that most often are an interior dialogue. Americans have viewed themselves and their national identity within the context of community narrative, where America has always been the principal actor of importance. The same ethnocentricity defines all nations almost by definition the world must be viewed as revolving around the national narrative of each. Hence, Germans have a world narrative surrounding the path of the German nation through 2000 years of history. The same is true of Russians, French, Italians, Spanish, British, and indeed all the nations and national communities from the contemporary period to the most distant periods of ancient history. Nations, as integrated communities, construct historical narratives particular to their needs and interests, and interact with external actors within the subjective frameworks of their narratives.[30]

In the broadest terms, the interactions of national scripts over time have become what we call international history. The interactions, political, cultural, economic, and strategic, most often having to do with rivalry and war between nations, have become the regional and international narratives of human civilization. The dense and multileveled conflicts between nations as part of a larger region of nations or nation-states, have always involved a working out of collective scripts. I use the term "working out," to mean the unfolding of meaning, the discovery of intentions and the outcomes of critical actions by the actors. Through wars, nation-states learn about their abilities and limitations, and what is most important to their collective interests.

The encounter between the United States and the Gulf region in the late twentieth and early twenty-first centuries was a tragic drama whose actors played on an electronic stage that never seemed to close. World mass media, with the birth of the Internet in the 1990s, exploded in size and diversity of content. Its transmogrification into vast streams of instantaneous information complicated the strategic task of great powers to control or master the mass media. Its new irascible individuation, made the insulation and support of military actions evermore difficult.

ETHNIC NARRATIVES: ARABS, TURKS, KURDS, PERSIANS, JEWS, AMERICANS, EUROPEANS

The Gulf region's political complexity relates directly to the competition between major regional actors whose rivalries were ongoing conflicts over generations, centuries, and in some cases, millennia. Every group within the region had interests and historical relations with other groups that bore upon the balance of power in the Gulf. An ethnocultural map of the area shows a nearly perfect geographic bifurcation between Sunni and Shia religious communities. The Shia region of the Middle East is a largely contiguous region stretching from northern Pakistan, Afghanistan, the entire Republic of Iran, with tributary boundaries flowing through southern and central Iraq, a small coastal region of the emirates, and eastern Turkey. The vast remainder of the region, including most of Northern Iraq, all of Saudi Arabia, Yemen, the Gulf emirates, Syria, Turkey, Jordan, and the Palestinian territories, are nearly all Sunni. In fact, the Sunnis predominate everywhere in the Islamic world with the exception of the Iranian sphere of influence.[31]

Both Sunnis and Shias cherish competing scriptural versions of Islam, a rivalry dating from the founding of the religion in the seventh century. The theological conflict between them, comparable to the schism between Protestant and Roman Catholic Christianity, established a permanent political rivalry in the Gulf region. Even with the introduction of Westernization and secularization into the region in the twentieth century, the intense struggle for political dominance between the two religious sects has preserved a dangerous conflict script that transcends national boundaries. The sectarian script exists parallel with other ethnic and national scripts that complicate an already dense region of rivalries.

During both the first and second Gulf Wars, rivalries between the larger Arab world and the Jewish and Iranian states added to the shifting and contradictory alliances of the region at war. The Iraqi invasion of Kuwait in 1990 triggered not only the war between Kuwait and Iraq, but it also impacted upon a host of bilateral and multilateral relations in the region. In the background remained the Arab-Iranian rivalry dating from the time of King Cyrus in the sixth century BCE and most recently, the Iran-Iraq war of 1980–89. The regional significance of the invasion included the ongoing conflict within the Arab world between the privileged oil-rich Arab sheikdoms and the vast number of the Arab masses who shared in only the most tangential ways in the enormous oil wealth from the Gulf's vast oil reserves. A range of interlocking inter-Arab and inter-Muslim rivalries were packed within the conflict system for the Persian Gulf without even accounting for the Western groups who were present. In addition to the Arabs and the Persians, and the Kurds and the Turkish peoples, there were the hated Jews, Americans, Europeans, and their powerful public and private institutions, who entangled themselves in the already entangled domain of the Gulf.[32]

Very comparable to the complexity of the first and second World Wars, the Gulf Wars ignited dozens of national, ethnic, and tribal narratives who positioned themselves for control of the Gulf region, and its vital and immense assets to the world at large. Since the 1980s, American presidents and their staffs have exposed themselves to the deep and seemingly irreconcilable problems of the Gulf, the Middle East, North Africa, and Central Asia. Self-defined group narratives, based upon vast beliefs in victimization and territorial and political rights, created conflict metanarratives that appeared wholly intractable to both independent observers and participants. It appeared impossible to reconcile Iraqi claims to Kuwait with Kuwaiti claims of national sovereignty. It appeared that ultimate control of the Iraqi state, between Kurds, and Sunni and Shia Arabs, was beyond solution. This appeared true of the Arab-Israeli conflict, which continued into the twenty-first century with only the slimmest hopes of settlement.

For American observers, their own rivalries with European and non-European actors for management of the region, through a dozen or more national scripts into the conflict system, complicating and never simplifying the essential task of establishing peace and stability in the entire quadrant of Southwestern Asia. The international array of actors in the region represented a distinct challenge to the metascript for American civilization, the liberal technocratic order. The technocratic script operating through the nexus of the American state, its executive branch, and its national leader, the president of the United States, hoped to find a path to regional order under American influence. This brings us to the concept of the leader or presidential script.

PRESIDENTIAL SCRIPTS: BUSH, CLINTON, BUSH

The power and importance of scripts in world affairs bears upon the influence delegated to national leaders. No matter how intricate and global the institutions of national power, in almost all modern governmental systems, presidential, or parliamentary, the authority to wage war remains in the hands of an individual. Adolf Hitler started the Second World War with his vision of a general European war that he would win, on the way to a global Germanic empire. Hitler was an agent of history, but his particular life script affected the actions of the German state and the subsequent responses of the other great powers. In other words, Hitler alone, as an individual was a force of history. Through his demonic drive and his executive authority, Hitler became much the father of the Second World War just as Albert Einstein was the conceptual father of the theory of relativity.

When Franklin Roosevelt approved the Manhattan Project in 1941, his signature launched a top secret monumental effort to produce the world's first atomic bomb in less than four years. In response to the atomic bombings of Hiroshima and Nagasaki that were set in motion by one political leader, yet another single individual, Emperor Hirohito of Japan, resolved to end the Pacific War. All of the national leaders of the Second World War, including, Hitler, Stalin, Churchill, Roosevelt, and Hirohito, were individuals, acting with the volition of their respective psyches, shaping the course of world history according to the powerful leadership scripts that dominated their individual consciousnesses.[33]

Stalin's articulation of Soviet expansion into Eastern Europe and Truman's response to that policy launched the Cold War in Europe in the late 1940s. Would another Soviet leader have brought a different course to the division of Europe after 1945? Since this is a counterfactual question, it cannot be answered one way or the other. We do know, however, changes in national leaders have sometimes resulted in dramatic changes in state policies. Chernenko and Andropov, transitional Soviet leaders after Brezhnev, had no measurable impact on the final course of the Cold War; nor is it likely they would have changed their regimes if they had survived longer than the couple of years in the early 1980s that they ruled the Soviet Union. Yet, their successor, Gorbachev, was the leader who ended the Cold War and in fact, Soviet communism in the late 1980s and early 1990s. Gorbachev's life and career narrative, synchronized with the dynamics of the Soviet Union's dying script. In this particular case, the leader's narrative fit with his nation's narrative, bringing down an institutional system that could no longer function viably on the world stage.[34]

Whereas George Washington had an army in the 1790s armed with single shot muskets and artillery systems whose ranges were far less than a mile, George H. Bush in the summer of 1990, commanded an integrated military force of two million, with global capabilities, nuclear, and conventional. While Article 2 of the U.S. Constitution, which established the powers and duties of the executive branch, had hardly changed at all in 200 years, American national power and treaty obligations had grown to a level exponentially greater than had existed in 1790. Washington's republic, no less than Abraham Lincoln's and Theodore Roosevelt's republics, was Lilliputian compared to the enormously powerful technocratic state of George H. Bush, William Jefferson Clinton, and George W. Bush.

All modern U.S. presidents preside over powers and decisions that are many orders of magnitude greater than those of world leaders of the past. Yet, while the technological elements of power, physical, and intellectual were changed radically, the men themselves and the laws governing their powers were largely the same. In the late twentieth century, the leaders of great powers had to make decisions of extraordinary complexity and impact with virtually the same emotional and intellectual skills as their predecessors in early eras.[35]

Three American presidents were involved in the Gulf Wars of 1990 and 2003 and their aftermaths. In their respective approaches to the problem of Iraq, all three men shared distinct agreements. All three of the post–Cold War presidents viewed Saddam Hussein as a serious threat to U.S. national security, and as an actor of supreme evil. The record of his regime was so extreme, including geno-cide, the use of chemical weapons against civilian populations, widespread torture and mass executions, that no American leader could value Hussein other than as a short-term deterrent to Shia fundamentalism in the Persian Gulf. The first president, George H. Bush, spared Hussein's regime in the spring of 1991, pre-cisely because to prevent the disintegration of Iraq was a far greater national inter-est than the physical destruction of Saddam Hussein and his secular dictatorship.

The second president, Bill Clinton, continued the same set of policies vis-à-vis Hussein and his Ba'athist state. Clinton followed the containment strategy that the first President Bush began after the cessation of the ground war in March 1991. Entering office in 1993, he viewed Hussein as a defeated adversary who nonetheless had to be shepherded until Iraqi regime change was possible. Hus-sein's periodic defiance of the United Nations and the United States forced Clin-ton to continue the sanctions imposed on Iraq in 1991. A naval embargo enforced by the United States and its coalition allies strangled the Iraqi economy, limiting oil exports to a fraction of their postwar totals. No fly zones in both southern and northern Iraq protected minority Shia and Kurdish populations from air attacks, and in the north, the United States prevented Hussein from bringing Iraqi Kurdistan under his control. Where Clinton differed from his successor George W. Bush, was in a personal vendetta toward Hussein.

In George W. Bush, Saddam Hussein confronted the son of the first American president who humiliated him in 1991. Hussein had plotted to assassinate the elder Bush upon a visit to Kuwait in 1993, and this act was not forgotten by the younger Bush when he became president in January 2001. In the younger Bush, the script mechanisms appeared to set him on a path of war against his father's enemy. The coterie of the second Bush's advisers included a majority who favored a nationalist perspective on American foreign relations, similar to the ideology of Theodore Roosevelt at the turn of the twentieth century. The younger Bush's for-eign policy group combined a neoconservative ideology, which in fact was a form of conservative progressive internationalism, with the promilitary nationalism that had inspired a generation of American conservatives during the 1980s. In the younger Bush, Clausewitzianism, Christian millennialism, and American nation-alism engendered a hawkish Middle East policy that was consonant with the views of the conservative intellectuals who joined his administration.[36]

The policy group around George W. Bush reinforced his beliefs about Iraq, especially after September 11, when he received the political capital he needed to pursue a very aggressive military strategy in the entire region. The group, whose distinct personalities will become more familiar in later chapters, established a mutually reinforcing circle for the decision-making script for the presidency of the second George Bush. Unlike the first President Bush, whose circle of advisers had a somewhat different orientation toward foreign policy, or President Clinton, who shared the same general view of Saddam Hussein, the second Bush moved directly to war against a very weakened but utterly defiant adversary. The consequences of that group script may appear perilous at the time of this writing, but scripts, whether personal, group, or cultural, work at the level of the unconscious. More often than not, their ultimate paths surprise those who have followed them for years, decades or in the case of nation-states, generations.

CONCLUSIONS

This work will attempt to elaborate on all the elements outlined in this introduction. The Gulf Wars of the last decade of the twentieth and the first decade of the twenty-first centuries were a vortex for the liberal technocratic order. U.S. foreign policy toward Iraq and the Gulf region represented a confluence of major political, strategic, and economic interests articulated by the managerial internationalism of U.S. national security institutions. The vital interests of Persian Gulf oil, WMD (weapons of mass destruction) and after 2001, the global jihad of Osama bin Laden, defined the region for American policy makers. For these individuals, embedded in the culture of national security institutions, the Gulf Wars were launched to achieve specific objectives. These goals, containing and then dismantling the Ba'athist state and projecting American power and influence in the Gulf, represented critical interests for the maintenance and development of the global order envisioned by the policy-makers.

After the successful defeat of Hussein in 2003, the apparent failures of American foreign policy in the Gulf and elsewhere in the Middle East, demonstrated what may be understood as an ingrown flaw in the American script. As in Vietnam, American national power was compromised by native resistance to its means and methods of hegemony. Paradoxically, American power in the Gulf region represented both its dominance and its limitations. The United States demonstrated overwhelming power, extending its military victory through an institutional and cultural presence throughout the Gulf and the Middle East. Yet, as with earlier empires, its suzerainty could not absorb the complex and ancient cultural and political narratives of the region. The powers of the American state and the Western liberal scientific-industrial order could not extinguish the tribal, Islamic, and anti-Western scripts of the indigenous groups that opposed them.

The Persian Gulf and the Late Cold War

The United States also inherited from the Cold War a legacy of strong alliances in Europe and Asia, and with Israel in the Middle East. Those alliances are a bulwark of American power and more important still, they constitute the heart of the liberal democratic civilization the United States seeks to preserve and extend.

William Kristol and Robert Kagan[1]

As I shall be using the term—and I'm not really too interested in terminological adjustments—"imperialism" means the practice, the theory and the attitudes of a dominating metropolitan center that rules a distant territory. "Colonialism," which is almost always a consequence of imperialism, is the implanting of settlements on distant territory. As the historian Michael Doyle puts it, "Empire is a relationship, formal or informal, in which one state controls the effective political sovereignty of another political society. It can be achieved by force, by political collaboration, economic, social, or cultural dependence. Imperialism is simply the process or policy of establishing or maintaining an empire."

Edward Said[2]

STRATEGIC AND ECONOMIC OBJECTIVES

At the very center of postwar political economy was oil. After the Second World War, petroleum had become a vital indispensible progenitor of the international economy. The United States required oil, and in ever vaster quantities as its postwar economy added tens of millions of automobiles, millions of trucks, a global fleet of commercial jetliners, and an ever-growing industrial system that required it for petrochemicals, lubricants, and even for electric power and central heating. The American and world economy expanded decade after decade, with hydrocarbon fuel as its primary industrial stock. So dear and vital was oil to the strategic and economic interests of the United States and its allies in Europe and Japan, the idea any power could or would threaten its supply was an unthinkable and unforgiveable act.[3]

For decades, the Gulf had been an area of primary interest for the United States. Beginning in the 1930s, the Gulf region began producing oil for the rapidly expanding international market. The United States was the world's leading producer of petroleum from the nineteenth century until the 1980s. During the Second World War, the United States accounted for more than half the world's production, and the country was a net exporter until the 1950s. Yet, the region's oil was of considerable interest to the United States at the end of the Second World War and continued to grow in importance as Saudi, Kuwaiti, and Iranian, as well as other Gulf state's production increased. By the 1970s, the United States imported half of its oil and Western Europe and Japan were completely dependent upon Persian Gulf imports for fuel.

By the end of the 1970s, the Cold War policies and fortunes of two U.S. presidents formed the context for direct U.S. military intervention in the Persian Gulf. The geopolitical and geostrategic interests of the country pointed directly to American power moving into the Gulf. This was so, despite the historical enmity of the Arab states toward the West and their opposition to any Western power establishing itself in the heart of the Arab and Islamic world. Soviet power appeared to be ascendant in the Middle East and Southwestern Asia during the presidency of Jimmy Carter. The Vietnam War had damaged the political consensus within the United States to project power outside of the traditional containment spheres of NATO and Northeast Asia. The United States was defeated in Indochina in 1975, and its allies surrendered to Soviet-backed communist regimes. While the United States questioned its ability and moral authority to engage in global containment, Marxist insurgencies challenged the West in Africa, Asia, and Latin America.[4]

Even more worrisome to U.S. national security officials than the Soviets' inroads in the Third World was the apparent strategy of the Soviet Union to achieve strategic nuclear parity with the United States. Not only were Cuban troops supporting new Marxist states in Africa, but the Soviet navy now had full use of the former U.S. Navy base at Da Nang, and communism appeared to be strong around the world, and there was the more dangerous program of Soviet nuclearism. Irrespective of its dialogue with the United States and Western Europe, the Soviet Union continued its massive modernization program for its nuclear capabilities. The drive to achieve nuclear parity with the United States was begun shortly after the 1962 Cuban Missile Crisis. Now, as the nuclear age was in its fourth decade, the Soviet strategy appeared to have achieved success. Soviet strategic strength appeared to match that of the United States. While Soviet-backed armies and guerrilla groups attempted to dominate the Horn of Africa, Southern Africa, North Africa, and

Latin America, the Soviet nuclear establishment was focused entirely on developing an invulnerable transcontinental nuclear force with "first strike" capabilities.[5]

The apparent strategy of the Soviet Union to achieve parity and perhaps military and political dominance vis-à-vis, the United States generated a new post-Vietnam consensus. In Congress and in national security circles around the country, a bipartisan agreement emerged for the need to reverse the country's post-Indochina military decline. There was little dissent at the highest levels of civilian authority in the late 1970s from the views that the United States needed to quickly rebuild its military infrastructure, modernize its weapons systems, and match Soviet power. This ideological unity had clear consequences for international relations. When the Persian Gulf appeared to be threatened by Soviet power, in the wake of the invasion of Afghanistan in December 1979, the Gulf's importance to U.S. national security was suddenly brought into focus. The region's status as a critical interest for U.S. national security strategy was now plain. Any direct threat, as posed by a hypothetical Soviet drive into Iran or Pakistan, required a formidable response. All of this happened quickly, the stage set in the third year of the Carter administration, as two events, the Iranian hostage crisis and the Soviet occupation of Afghanistan dominated the international system.

During the last years of the Carter administration and the first years of the Reagan era, Soviet power and national intentions appeared ominous. The Soviets had sent 50,000 troops to Africa, and supported Cuban ambitions in Central America. Soviet nuclear power had increased exponentially since the 1962 Cuban Missile Crisis and there was little optimism that the Soviets could be persuaded to alter a course of massive nuclear expansion. Although contemporary CIA intelligence suggested that the Soviets themselves faced severe economic challenges to preserve its socialist state, American perceptions of the enemy were laced with the long held beliefs in Soviet duplicity and military strength.

Consequently, the Soviet attempt to stabilize its southern frontier led to an immediate U.S. response by a champion of post–Second World War liberal internationalism, Jimmy Carter. Carter, a devote Southern Baptist, Georgia peanut farmer, and Annapolis trained naval officer, had assumed the presidency in January 1977, inheriting the foreign policy of Gerald Ford and Henry Kissinger. Soviet behavior in Southwestern Asia appeared to be expansionist to Carter and his national security adviser, Zbigniew Brzezinski. The Afghan coup of April 1978 was orchestrated by Soviet agents in an apparent attempt to reinforce Afghanistan as a Soviet client state. In a secret but famous memorandum, Brzezinski urged Carter to initiate support for Afghan insurgents, Islamic mujahideen, to destabilize the newly formed communist regime. He was very explicit in his memo, suggesting to Carter that U.S. covert support could trigger a Soviet invasion which would be in effect a "Soviet Vietnam."[6]

The tactic worked, even though, paradoxically, it ignited an immediate strategic response by the Carter administration. The Soviet invasion of Afghanistan in December 1979 was an expected but ominous event for the Carter administration that coincided with the taking of American hostages in Iran the month before. With the Iranian threat to destabilize the pro-American Gulf Arab states through the export of its Islamic revolution, the Soviet thrust into neighboring Afghanistan magnified the vulnerability of the Persian Gulf to hostile powers. After months of preparation, the Kremlin decided to send a hundred thousand troops into the anarchic regions of its Southern neighbor. It was a country that had barely been scratched by modern history; a diverse multiethnic and tribal land dominated by vast mountain ranges and deserts. It was a land that had bedeviled foreigners for many centuries, including the British who attempted to govern Afghanistan as it did the Indian subcontinent.

Soviet tanks first rolled into the remote mountainous country that had punished foreigners for centuries on Christmas Day 1979. By the first week in January, the designs of a new order of containment were appearing in the analysis of the *New York Times.*[7] The Carter administration recognized the absolute strategic necessity of maintaining access to the Persian Gulf oil reserves. Both Western Europe and Japan were deeply dependent upon Gulf oil. The loss of the region's oil supply through the actions of hostile foreign powers would elicit an immediate crisis in the world's economy and bring NATO to its knees. Since this could not happen, according to U.S. national interests articulated by any president, the White House made certain that the Soviets and other interested parties understood the nature of American commitment to the region. Carter made this plain in his State of the Union address in January 1980, which included an intention to impose an extensive array of economic and political sanctions against the Soviet Union; this at time of considerable strategic tension with the Soviets in Europe and elsewhere.[8]

The enunciation of the "Carter doctrine" by President Carter in January 1980 placed the region under formal U.S. protection. In sending its tank divisions into Afghanistan, Soviet intentions were not to dominate the Persian Gulf. Nonetheless, the presence of a powerful Soviet land army to within several hundred miles of the Indian Ocean reordered U.S. strategic thinking in the context of its global confrontation with the Soviet Union. The Gulf represented most of the oil supply for Western Europe and Japan. In broad strategic terms, U.S. analysts and policy-makers agreed control of the straits of Hormuz and the Gulf region could not be compromised by the Soviet Union. The Soviets had to be deterred from further movement toward Pakistan and Iran and using its ongoing alliance with Iraq to threaten U.S. interests in the Gulf. At the same time, the Iranian revolution had created yet another need for containment. In this case, to prevent not only Soviet but radical Islamic movements that could threaten the Sunni Gulf oil states and other U.S. allies in the Middle East.[9]

In a global context, the last decade of the Cold War was a transformative period for the United States, the Soviet Union, and the world. Over several decades of global rivalry, the Cold War had progressed technologically to the point where its burden on both superpowers and the world itself had come to a climax. By 1980, decades of military confrontation between the Soviets and the Americans had created two very large and powerful military establishments. Enormous resources applied to preparing for World War had created enormous land, air, and sea forces equipped with enough power to destroy world civilization. By the time the nuclear arsenals peaked for both countries in the late 1980s, each had many tens of thousands of operational nuclear weapons. Some were "tactical," some were considered "intermediate or theater" weapons, and many thousands of others were considered "strategic" assets with delivery systems capable of striking quickly and accurately half way around the earth. The missile deployed on U.S. Trident submarines were MIRVs (multiple independently targetable reentry vehicles). One of these nuclear submarines alone carried 24 MIRV missiles, with each missile equipped with up to eight nuclear warheads. The effective power of the Trident's arsenal was 90 megatons of nuclear ordinance for use against 192 separate targets. For their part, U.S. military intelligence estimated the Soviets had 6000 ICBM (intercontinental ballistic missiles) systems deployed by the early 1980s throughout the Soviet Union. The Soviets also had a fleet of 900 intercontinental nuclear capable bombers and support craft and an accelerated modernization program for thousands of submarine-based nuclear weapons. The Soviets also had thousands of scientists and technicians dispersed throughout the Soviet Union dedicated to the development of chemical and biological weapon systems.[10]

The conventional forces of the Soviets included over 40,000 heavy tanks and 160 army divisions. To the Pentagon and to academic and private sector defense intellectuals, Soviet power appeared menacing both in conventional and nuclear terms. Further, Soviet-backed counterinsurgency wars threatened U.S. interests in the Third World including Central America, the Caribbean, and sub-Saharan Africa. Soviet power was present in Northeast Asia, Southeast Asia, and in the Middle East through client states Syria, Iraq, and Libya.

Indeed, the last decade of the Cold War began badly for the United States. A post-Vietnam War and post-Watergate president, James Earl Carter inherited a deteriorating strategic environment. The fall of the Shah of Iran in 1978 left one of the country's most important allies in a state of revolution. The intensely pro-Western Shah Mohammed Reza Pahlavi who had been installed in his throne by the Eisenhower administration in 1953, represented a strategic bulwark to Soviet expansion into the Persian Gulf. The reasoning by the United States was not complicated. As discussed, the strategic value of the Gulf was directly related to the flow of Gulf oil to Japan and Western Europe. The loss of the Shah and his replacement by a strange and hitherto unknown revolutionary Islamic state immediately created a serious problem for the security of the Gulf. Until his fall, the Shah's armed forces, armed impressively with the most modern weapon systems in the U.S. arsenal, represented a powerful deterrent to any Soviet adventurism in the region. As soon as he flew into exile in January 1978, the entire Pahlavi oligarchy and its military establishment disappeared. In its place, a regime of radical Shiite clerics was now in power, who blamed the United States for all the crimes of the Pahlavi monarchy. U.S.-Iranian relations deteriorated throughout the second year of the Carter administration, culminating in the seizing of the U.S. embassy in Tehran and the holding of 62 embassy personnel by "Iranian students."[11]

The Iranian hostage crisis was a deep blow to the Carter administration which did not survive its national humiliation. In 1980, the radical Iranian Islamic regime held one of the world's two superpowers at arm length, ostensibly flaunting international law, and committing an act of war against a country with thousands of operational nuclear weapons. The media spectacle of a major American embassy with its male diplomatic staff held under the gun by its host country mobilized American nationalism for the first time since the early 1960s. A combination of this spectacle and the invasion of Afghanistan by the Soviet Union created a threat environment in the Gulf of deep concern. American power and international prestige was on the line in Iran and Afghanistan while Soviet power appeared to be surging all over the Third World. Further, in the global nuclear arms race, the Soviets appeared to have matched if not exceeded the United States as a nuclear superpower. For some analysts, a new generation of Soviet ICBMs threatened a first strike capability.

By the 1980s, the institutional development of the national security state had progressed for 40 years. Since the beginning of the Second World War and the national mobilization for a global military conflict, the institutional and intellectual domains of American national security had grown into the deepest fabrics of American society. The defense industry employed, directly, or indirectly, millions of U.S. workers. Basic and applied research in science and engineering was heavily oriented toward the needs of the Pentagon for technological innovation. A critical "driver" of U.S. science and technology, especially in the fields of computers, aerospace, and communications, was the Department of Defense. By the 1980s, scores of American space satellites monitored the earth's oceans and land masses, gathering military intelligence on the Soviet Union and other potential threats and rivals. The drive for global security had created a containment system that existed in some form in every region of the world. U.S. aircraft, satellites, aircraft carriers, and nuclear-powered submarines patrolled oceans, the atmosphere, and outer space in an all encompassing need for control and dominance. This technocratic management of the earth began much earlier in the century, formatively with the Pacific and European theaters of the Second World War. By the 1960s, hundreds of military bases supported by 40 bilateral defense treaties had institutionalized a physical American empire designed to defeat international communism and its socialist path to technocratic order.[12]

By 1980, however, in U.S. government documents and in the mass media, there were indications that the Soviet empire was in trouble. Throughout the world, Soviet style industrial and agricultural systems were either stagnating or failing. In the Soviet Union itself, CIA analysts were very aware of the ossification and waste that were a consequence of the authoritarian mechanisms of communist party rule. Nonetheless, the relentless drive for militarizing the Soviet state, even if its ultimate purpose was defensive, presented a global strategic problem that required a parallel response by the United States. In America during the late 1970s and early 1980s, there was a national consensus to expand the size and the capabilities of the global military. The Persian Gulf was a region quintessential to that expansion of national power.

During the decade that ended the Cold War and preceded the First Gulf War, the United States and its national security system, moved deeply into the Persian Gulf, replacing the last remnants of British power. The United States was in the Gulf to preserve the integrity of the energy system that was of such vital strategic and economic interest to the United States and the West. Both Carter and Reagan administrations viewed the Persian Gulf as a vital interest, so important that they were prepared to defend the region with large-scale deployments of ground forces as well as air and naval assets. Western Europe and Japan were completely dependent upon Gulf oil. The loss of access would quickly result in economic disaster not only for critical U.S. allies but for the entire global market economy. Premised on this argument was the assumption made by U.S. analysts and policy-makers, that Soviet control of the Persian Gulf would be a strategic disaster of major proportions for the United States and the entire Western alliance. Hence, the Carter doctrine of 1980 which provided for the creation of a large rapid deployment force to defend the Gulf states came as no surprise to anyone. With the Arab "oil shocks" of the 1970s, the primacy of oil and in particular the vast and accessible petroleum reserves of the Middle East to Western security and political economy became evident to mass as well as elite public opinion all over the world.[13]

The huge price increases during the 1970s had caused both an increase in energy efficiency and the production of new sources of oil and other hydrocarbons. A market surplus reduced significantly the price of oil on world markets. Nonetheless, despite the apparent surfeit of supply, the critical value of Persian Gulf energy remained a permanent concern for U.S. national security. American resolve to defend the Gulf as a strategic asset existed within the larger context of two major regional wars. The Soviet war in Afghanistan, essentially a proxy war between the Islamic Middle East and the United States against the Soviet Union, became a brutal counterinsurgency campaign waged by the Soviets and their Afghan allies against the American financed anticommunist Afghan resistance. The severity of the Soviet intervention, which involved years of search and destroy missions against rural Afghanistan, was matched by the other regional conflict, the Iran-Iraq conflict of 1980–88. This war, which was a more conventional but equally destructive confrontation, had nothing to do with the Soviet-American Cold War, and all to do with the 1000-year rivalry between competing nation-states and Islamic sects.[14]

The secular Sunni Arab Iraq faced its mortal enemy in the Shiite Islamic Republic of Iran. In the first war, America's alignment with the Afghan resistance was clear. In the case of Iraq, long a Soviet client state, U.S. support was para-doxical. Nonetheless, the Reagan administration saw the Iran-Iraq war as an opportunity to serve several critical U.S. objectives in the Middle East. First, Iraq would contain Iran and its fundamentalist Islamic ideology, which was as much a threat to American interests in the Gulf region and the Middle East in general as was the Soviet Union. Second, supporting Saddam Hussein would allow the United States to counter Soviet influence in Iraq and encourage the Ba'athist regime to move toward the West. Finally, the improvement in U.S. relations with Iraq could facilitate Iraqi liberalization of its regime and a future peace settlement with Israel. The combination of all these interests, the security of the Arab Gulf states and their oil resources, the provisioning of Soviet and Iranian contain-ments, Iraqi regime liberalization and Israeli security, all provided viable ration-ales for supporting Iraq. In light of the events of the post–Cold War era in the region, there was a deep irony in American strategy. In both Afghanistan and Iraq, the United States supported groups that would turn against it in the 1990s and on into the next century. Saddam Hussein would fight two wars against the United States. After his final defeat in 2003, his fellow Sunni Arabs would continue the war, bringing apparent disaster to the administration of George W. Bush. Finally, in Afghanistan, the "freedom fighters" armed with American-supplied Stinger missiles and CIA advisors, would form the nucleus of Osama bin Laden's al Qaeda.

THE OIL CRISES

The first oil crisis of the early 1970s, which coincided with the Yom Kippur War and the mobilization of the OPEC (Organization of the Petroleum Export-ing Countries) cartel, changed the dynamics of the entire region. For the United States, the new power of the cartel made oil and energy supply in itself a critical issue related to but also separate from the Cold War. The massive increase in the world price of oil during the decade had a transformational impact on international political economy. Prior to the 1970s, the world oil markets were controlled by the major oil corporations based in the United States and Europe. The widespread nationalizations of oil interests between 1970 and 1980 trans-ferred the economic and political power of oil to OPEC, and principally to the leading oil producers of the Gulf. By the start of the Reagan administration, intellectuals, and strategic analysts had conceptualized oil as a principal national security interest, connected inextricably to the health of the global economy and to the ability of the United States to maintain its defense posture vis-à-vis the oil abundant Soviet Union.

Oil has had an honored and central place in the political economy of the modern world. For the United States, hydrocarbon-based energy systems were the foundation of economic modernization, beginning with coal in the late nineteenth century, and moving to petroleum in the twentieth century. In practical terms, the utilization of oil resources was the pillar of the country's extraordinary industrial expansion and world leadership in the twentieth century. Access to petroleum became a national security interest during the Second World War, when the huge oil requirements of the U.S. military made domestic production temporarily inadequate. The country was the world's leading oil producer at mid-century. Yet, the inexorable expansion of petroleum consumption, a result of an industrial economy designed to expand and consume increasing amounts of cheap hydrocarbon fuels made the United States a net importer of oil by the 1970s. In the 1940s, the United States was producing and consuming approximately six million barrels of oil a day. Between 1950 and 1970, U.S. oil imports rose from negligible to several million barrels per day. By 1978, U.S. oil consumption peaked at nearly 19 million barrels a day, while domestic production met only slightly more than half of the demand.[15] In the space of less than a decade, the cost of oil to the American economy increased more than 1,000 percent in real terms. The second energy crisis of the Carter years produced the deep recession of the early 1980s and contributed to a general belief in both elite and popular opinion that the United States was a civilization in decline.[16]

The economic crisis of the Carter administration, a direct consequence of the economic dependency of the United States on a scarce and increasingly expensive fuel stock, was part of the explanation for the election of Ronald Reagan in 1980. Reagan emerged on the national and international stage in the wake of international economic and political crisis. After two decades of liberal domination in Washington, the Reagan presidency launched a revisionist script for the United States, reorienting public policy to support the profitability of the private sector both domestically and internationally. Aggressive support for world capitalism coincided with equally vigorous action to remonetize the national security state. During the 1980s, the budget for the Department of Defense increased in real terms by 10 percent per year, easily reaching the highest levels of peacetime defense spending in U.S. history.[17]

THE IRAN-IRAQ WAR

If the Afghan War was responsible for the Carter doctrine, the Iran-Iraq war which began in September 1980 was responsible for the economic crisis of Saddam Hussein's Ba'athist regime that in turn led to the invasion of Kuwait in August 1990. As the Soviets began their 10-year war to defeat the Afghan mujahideen, who were supported in a major fashion by the Saudis, Pakistanis, and the United States, the Iraqi strongman saw the opportunity to crush the radical Shiite state as it remained locked in potential war with a nuclear super-power. The Carter administration, bedeviled by its national trauma over the Iranian hostage crisis of 1979–81, could only hope for some measure of Iraqi success. In the ensuing Reagan administration, the Iranian fundamentalist threat to the Arab Gulf added to the centrality of the Gulf to U.S. national security strategy, and improved the status of Saddam Hussein, a dictator of inhuman brutality, who the United States believed was a valuable bulwark against funda-mentalist expansion in the Gulf. However, both the Carter and Reagan adminis-trations feared an Iraqi victory in the war could lead to the dismemberment of Iran and an invitation to Soviet expansion into the fractured state. Nonetheless, the Reagan administration provided direct and covert assistance to Saddam Hussein in part to counter Soviet influence over Iraq. This strategy included a studied silence over the use of chemical weapons by Iraq.[18]

For the United States, the catastrophic war between Iran and Iraq during the last decade of the Cold War was one of two deadly regional conflicts in Southwestern Asia. The war's beginning coincided with the national trauma of the Iranian hostage crisis and the beginning of the Russian war in Afghanistan. The Iran-Iraq war pitted the collective scripts of two very proud nation-states in a brutal conflict for survival and supremacy in the Gulf region. Hussein, champion of the Arab Ba'athist ideology, and wedded deeply to his own extreme narcissism, waged war against the devout Islamic clerics of the Iranian Revolu-tion. Conversely, the Iranian clerics possessed their own theocratic and personal scripts for expansion and glory in the Islamic world. In a real sense, both Hussein and his followers and their nemesis the Shiites were reliving the narratives of early Islam, bringing the seventh and eighth centuries (the first and second centuries according to the Islamic calendar) into the twentieth. For one contemporary observer of Iranian culture, the journalist and author Vali Nasr, the tie to the past in the ideology of the Iranian Islamic Republic was unmistakable. The Ayotollah Khomeini believed he had a sacred mission to change Iran and the world:

> Khomeini argued that God had sent Islam for it to be implemented. No one knew religion better than the ulama, who were trained in its intracies and who carried the Twelfth Imam's mandate to safeguard its interests. God had commanded an Islamic government, and the ulama had to rule if that command was to be executed. Shia ulama had always been the guardians; Khomeini argued that the function could now be properly performed only if they ruled.[19]

If we count the Iran-Iraq war of 1980–89 as a Gulf war, then there were three major conflicts in the region spanning the period of the late twentieth and early twenty-first centuries. A central context for all three wars was the historical conflict between Sunni and Shia Islam and between Arab and Persian civilizations. Since its inception with the British Mandate of 1919, the Iraqi state existed as an amalgam of Sunni and Shia Arab tribes with Kurdish and Christian Arab minorities. Since Ottoman times, the region of modern Iraq has been dominated by the Sunni Arab tribes of which Hussein's tribal group, the Tikriti, were especially influential. Saddam rode to power on the basis of his extended family connections. Although very poor as a child, Hussein quickly rose through the ranks of the Ba'ath Party as a loyal Sunni and member of the Tikriti tribe:

> Saddam, helped by his Tikriti origins, did not have to wait long before being accepted into the Ba'ath Party and beginning his speedy rise through the ranks: already the Tikriti officers group included Herdan al-Tikriti, Mahdi Amash, Adnan Khairallah (Saddam's brother-in-law) and the powerful Ahmad al-Bakr. Bakr, one of the Party's most respected military leaders, soon saw advantage in forming an alliance with Saddam; and it is suggested that a marriage between Bakr's son and Sajida's sisters, and marriages between Bakr's daughters and two of her brothers, further helped to propel Saddam to power. Bakr was by now the Iraqi premier and Mahdi Amash was serving as the defence minister; and when in 1965 Bakr became secretary-general of the Party Saddam continued to cultivate his Tikriti connection. The following year he was made deputy secretary-general of the Party: he had already proved his ruthless dedication to the Ba'athist cause, and he was perceived as an asset in intimidating the enemies of the movement (at Qasr he had experimented with torture methods, sometimes offering victims a list from which they would be forced to select their own torture). Promoted to the Regional Command Council, Saddam had demonstrated his industry and imagination. By the summer of 1963, he was urging the need for a special security body, the Jihaz Haneen, that would be modelled on the Nazi SS. Its main purpose would be to protect the Party against the ambitions of the Army's officer corps, an obvious requirement in circumstances where army-based coups against political leaders were always a possibility.[20]

The Iranian revolution of 1978–79 established the Islamic Republic of Iran, a radical Shiite state dominated by its Persian majority but with half of its population belonging to various Turkic and Indo-Iranian groups.[21] Hussein launched an attack on Iran's ethnically Arab oil region, Khuzestan, that bordered the disputed Shatt Al Arab waterway that provided access to the Persian Gulf for Iraqi shipping. Hussein's motives remain clouded, but undoubtedly his fear of Iranian subversion on his Southern tier worked into this thinking.

SHIA FUNDAMENTALISM VERSUS BA'ATHISM

In American eyes, the first year of the Iran-Iraq war was overshadowed by the ongoing Iranian hostage crisis, which threatened Iran with war against an enraged nuclear superpower. The Iranian Revolution was a crushing strategic blow to the United States. Overnight, the most powerful state in the vital Persian

Gulf had switched from stalwart American ally to permanent enemy. Whereas Shah Mohammed Reza Pahlavi embraced the West and the United States, enthusiastically supporting America's containment policy and the pro-Western policies of the Sunni Arab states in the region, the Shia clerics threatened the abolition of U.S. interests in Iran and an Islamic revolution confronting the remaining American allies in the Gulf. The only mitigation to the disaster was that the clerics, led by the Ayatollah Khomeini, were as deeply anti-Soviet as they were anti-American.[22]

When Saddam Hussein launched the first Gulf conflict, the Iran-Iraq War on September 22 1980, his objectives were plain to foreign observers. His war against Iran was one of opportunity. By taking control of the Shatt al Arab waterway and adjacent islands, Saddam hoped to secure unrestricted Iraqi access to the Persian Gulf. He also hoped to conquer the Arab border province of Khuzestan, seizing its petroleum assets and asserting control of its Shia Arab population who presented a subversive influence on Iraqi Shias while they remained part of Iran.[23]

The deadly war ensued while the Iranian hostage crisis remained unresolved and the 1980 U.S. presidential campaign between Jimmy Carter and Ronald Reagan was at its height. After the election of Reagan and the end of the hostage crisis in January 1980, the Iran-Iraq war went on for eight more years. For the Reagan White House, a stark choice between two ideological evils, Ba'athism and Shia fundamentalism, was easy to decide. The Reagan White House moved quickly to support Saddam Hussein, the fierce Iraqi nationalist and leader of the Iraqi Ba'ath party. Historically, the Ba'athists were pan-Arabists and socialists, with long-standing ties to the Soviet Union and ideological predilections for the modern European totalitarian movements of fascism, Stalinism, and Nazism.

The Ba'athists supported the secularization and modernization of Iraqi society with the intention of building a renewed Mesopotamian civilization, based on the unity of the region's Sunni Arabs. In Iran, the twin enemies of Shi'ite Islam and Persian nationalism threatened the survival of the Iraqi Ba'athist state. The United States was not a natural ally to the Ba'athists who viewed Jews and Zionists as enemies as deeply as they hated Shia's and Persians. Hussein, the adopted son of a proud Iraqi neo-Nazi, and himself an ardent admirer of Joseph Stalin, formed a tacit alliance with the Reagan administration to contain the Iranian Revolution in the Gulf.

SOVIET POWER: THE AFGHAN WAR

The Soviet invasion of Afghanistan precipitated in part by the Carter administration's covert assistance to the Afghani mujahidin inspired fear and anger in the United States. The presence of a large Soviet land force abutting the Hindu Kush mountains placed Soviet control within a few hundred miles of the Indian Ocean. National security analysts argued that this was an attempt by the Soviets to dominate Pakistan and provide the Russians with their historic desire for a warm water port for the Soviet Navy. The strategic consequences of Soviet power drawing so close to the Persian Gulf ignited already deep anxiety for the security of the region. If the Soviets could establish a warm water port near the mouth of the Persian Gulf, the two-mile wide straits of Hormuz, they would have the ability to control the flow of Gulf oil in an international crisis. In lieu of this emerging threat, the Carter doctrine of 1980 authorized the prepositioning of military forces to move into the Gulf to defend America's vital interests in Kuwait, Saudi Arabia, and the UAE.

The Reagan administration continued the Carter doctrine and also began an extensive aid program to the anticommunist forces in Afghanistan. The proxy war between the Soviets and the United States in Afghanistan, which lasted until the end of the 1980s was the seed that led to the rise of the Taliban and al Qaeda in the 1990s. The Soviets had no compunction against using search-and-destroy tactics against the mujahidin. While war had serious domestic consequences for the Soviet leadership, they had no qualms using massive conventional power to pulverize the resistance. However, with the aid and sanctuary of neighboring Pakistan, and the covert assistance of the CIA, Saudi Arabia, and other anti-Soviet forces in the Middle East, the Soviets were forced eventually to give up their occupation.

Both the Afghan War and the Iran-Iraq War made Saddam Hussein a potentially valuable ally to the United States and to the West in general as noted. In the 1980s, there were two major threats to Western interests in the Persian Gulf. The first threat was the Islamic revolution of the Iranian clerics who preached a transnational crusade to defeat secular regimes throughout the Middle East. The second threat was the more traditional one of the Soviets, who saw the Persian Gulf as a strategic prize rivaled only by Europe itself. Clearly, a preponderance of Soviet power in the Gulf would have given them immense leverage against the European NATO countries and Japan in East Asia. For American strategists, the preservation of American power in the Gulf was of inestimable value. To the degree that Saddam Hussein, errant tyrant, could shield the Gulf from Iranian and Soviet expansion, he was potentially a very strong asset for the United States.[24]

THE END OF THE COLD WAR

The end of the Cold War came suddenly and without warning. In a matter of months, during the spring and fall of 1989, the satellite states of Eastern Europe collapsed one by one. In March, the Hungarians decided to hold free elections and tore down the fence that separated Hungary from Austria. In June, the Poles decided to hold elections voting out the communists who had ruled since 1945. The German Democratic Republic fell in the fall. The Berlin Wall, the iconic figure of the Iron Curtain was breached by East Germans on November 14, their celebration of freedom sweeping the entire world. The Bulgarians and Czechs followed the Germans, the Poles, and the Hungarians, ending their respective one party socialist regimes in November and December. Finally, days before Christmas the neo-Stalinist regime that governed Romania fell in a bloody revolt against its dictator. Ceausescu and his wife were executed and his totalitarian state disappeared.

By summer 1990, the United States was negotiating the end of the Cold War with the Soviets, and looking forward to an improbable world, which became more so when the Soviet Union dissolved at the beginning of 1992. In this period of transition to a unipolar international system, American power seemed nearly unlimited. With the end of Soviet control in Eastern Europe and the apparent terminal crisis of the Soviet Union as a nation-state, the United States had the responsibility of forging the "new world order" as the then president, Bush, called the contemporary world.[25]

The end of the Cold War left the American national security system intact and extraordinarily powerful. Its nuclear deterrent alone contained 7000 highly accurate thermonuclear warheads and a fleet of nuclear-capable intercontinental bombers. The U.S. military had highly mobile armored divisions with tanks capable of destroying Soviet-made tanks with new armor-piercing artillery rounds. Attack helicopters armed with laser-guided missiles could destroy tanks, personnel carriers, and supply trucks. The U.S. army had highly accurate artillery systems and computerized command-and-control systems that allowed it to conduct complex joint military operations that combined air, land, and sea forces. No country in the world, could match the mobility, firepower, and global reach of the United States. The United States retained treaty rights to hundreds of bases around the world through its formal military alliances, and counted on the aid of foreign allies on every continent and in every ocean of the world. If that was not enough, the country had a fleet of military satellites that provided an endless stream of electronic and photographic intelligence on adversarial countries, their military installations, and operational forces.[26]

The Bush administration was not sanguine about the threat environment of the post–Cold War era. Government, private sector, and academic observers calculated the range of conflicts around the world, with potential dangers to the United States. The Soviet Union itself, in summer 1990, remained intact, albeit in drastic decline. Yet, even in decline, its massive nuclear arsenal was fully capable of destroying the United States in less than an hour. East Asia, still beset with the military confrontation on the Korean peninsula, as well as potential conflicts involving China, Vietnam, and Taiwan, remained an area of primary concern. South Asia too, presented the potential of war between India and Pakistan. Africa and Latin America also had their own serious problems of war and social and economic crisis.[27]

With the fading of the Cold War, the threat to the Persian Gulf seemed to lessen. The Iranians were exhausted by their devastating war with Iraq. The only problem in the summer of 1990 was Saddam Hussein's threats against his neighbor Kuwait.

THE 'REPUBLIC OF FEAR': BA'ATHIST IRAQ

In summer 1990, the Iraqi state was exhausted and nearly bankrupt from its eight-year war with Iran. A relatively small country had absorbed huge casualties in its long conventional war with its Persian nemesis. The hostility between the Iranians and the Sunni Arabs of Mesopotamia could be traced back to ancient times, when the Babylonians were conquered by Cyrus the Great, the Persian emperor in the late sixth century BCE. Since then, for some 2500 years, successive generations of Arabs and Persians were rivals to each other in the desert lands of the Gulf. The rivalry continued with the arrival of the "universal religion," Islam, and grew more with the division of the monotheistic faith between the respective Sunni and Shia traditions. The Iran-Iraq war had followed the ancient struggle between the two nations as if it was a direct continuation of the Persian conquest from more than a hundred generations into the past. For both societies, the war was a cataclysm comparable in effect to earlier land wars in the twentieth century. The mass attacks of the Iranian forces, desperate because of their lack of advanced weapons, were a tactic that mirrored the suicidal assaults of the first and second world wars in Europe. The end of the war left Saddam Hussein with a self-defined "victory" but a badly traumatized nation.[28]

THE ISLAMIC REPUBLIC OF IRAN

In summer 1990, the IRI (Islamic Republic of Iran) was just recovering from its devastating war with Iraq. The once powerful Iranian armed forces had been reduced from the loss of American arms and technical assistance and an eight-year war of attrition to a shadow of its former self. For eight years, Iran had suffered a nightmarish conflict with hundreds of thousands of fatalities on the battlefield. The Iraqis had used chemical weapons to thwart the human wave attacks of the desperate Iranians whose only advantage over the Iraqis was in the number of soldiers it could sacrifice on the battlefield.

The war took a heavy toll and left behind a damaged Iranian society, with the people attempting to recover from a war that had cost them so dearly. At the same time, the radical Shiite state was burdened in its recovery by poor relations with the West, including an economic embargo by the United States. Internally, its theocratic policies had dramatically weakened the private sector, many of whose most innovative members had emigrated to the West to escape the clerical regime. The IRI was a spent force when Hussein's tanks entered Kuwait City in 1990. Like the Soviet Union which was dying, the IRI was sapped of ideological and material resources to threaten or challenge any external enemy.[29]

The Iranians viewed Hussein as their mortal enemy and the feelings were reciprocal. In fact, the Iran-Iraq War can be viewed as a larger struggle between Sunni Arabs and Shiite Persians for political dominance in the Gulf region. The Iranians had contested control over the Gulf region since Cyrus the Great conquered Babylon in the fifth century BCE. That struggle for dominance continued over millennia as Arabs, Persians, Turks, Mongols, and Europeans asserted their control over the region only to relinquish it. For Arabs, whose tribal memories recalled all of these groups, the Persians were neither Sunni Muslims nor Arabs. They were, in effect, a foreign force threatening the Arab world with the foreign domination which was so present in the history of the peoples of the region. Ostensibly, the Persians threatened Sunni Arab dominion in Iraq, Saudi Arabia, and all the Arab Gulf states and beyond. From the Sunni Arab perspective, the Persians and their Shiite faith were intent upon transforming the Islamic world, converting Sunnis to the apostate faith of Shiite Islam. If the Arab world despised the State of Israel as an intruder in the holy land, they equally feared the Persians who even as fellow Muslims threatened them to an even greater degree.[30]

KUWAIT, SAUDI ARABIA, AND THE OTHER SHEIKDOMS

During the eight years of the Iran-Iraq conflict, the wealthy Sunni Arab Gulf states had spent tens of billions of their collective oil wealth to support their Iraqi Arab brethren in their war against the Iranians. Their loyalty to Saddam Hussein was based entirely on a common fear of the Iranian Shiites who threatened to destabilize every Sunni Arab state from Iraq to Morocco. When Hussein saw the opportunity to seize Kuwait and its vast oil reserves, he wasted no time. Since the first decades of freedom from the defunct Ottoman Empire, the Iraqis had claimed Kuwait as a province of Mesopotamia and a rightful part of Iraq. At several points in the modern history of the Iraqi nation, i.e., after its independence from Great Britain in 1932, the Iraqis had attempted to exercise their historical claim to Kuwait. None of these attempts succeeded because of the protection of Kuwait by Britain. The withdrawal of British power from the Persian Gulf in the 1970s left Kuwait open to the exact threat of a potential invasion by its irredentist and vastly more powerful neighbor. When Hussein ordered his crack Republican Guard divisions to invade the tiny kingdom, he was acting not only as a self-aggrandizing and ultimately self-destructive dictator, he was also projecting the Iraqi nationalist script which saw in its own world narrative, that Kuwait was the "nineteenth province of Iraq." By restoring the land to the Iraqi nation, Hussein satisfied not only his own script, but the collective script of Iraqi Ba'athism, an ideology of dominant force in his life and those of his leadership group.[31]

THE REPUBLIC OF SYRIA

Both Iraq and Syria were secular Arab states ruled by respective branches of the Arab nationalist movement. Despite the very strong ideological affinity between them, both countries were dominated by equally personal and dictatorial regimes that led to an unavoidable rivalry. Hafez Al Assad and his respective familial and Alawite associates ruled the Syrian Baath party and the Republic of Syria with an iron fist, just as Saddam Hussein ruled the Republic of Iraq albeit with far greater brutality. While both were sworn enemies of Zionism and the State of Israel and both accepted extensive military assistance from the Soviet Union, in the last analysis, neither Assad nor Hussein would shed anything but crocodile tears for the other. The invasion of Kuwait did not trigger sympathy or solidarity from Syria. On the contrary, Hussein's radical attempt to dominate the Gulf turned Syria into an American ally albeit for the limited duration of the conflict.

Assad would not tolerate Hussein's annexation of Kuwait, Iraq's southern neighbor, if only because Syria could find itself in a similar position if Hussein was appeased in his blitzkrieg against a much smaller and weaker neighbor.[32]

THE TURKS AND THE KURDS

Both Turks and Kurds feared Hussein as well as each other. The Kurds were a transnational ethnic group who had been deprived of a national state by allies at the end of the First World War. Kurdish tribes existed in Turkey, Syria, Iran, and Iraq, and to some extent Kurdish nationalism was a threat to all four nation-states, three of which were successor states to the Ottoman Empire. The Turks were in the unenviable position of trying to contain their own very sizeable and very rebellious Kurdish population from separating from the Turkish state. At the same time, the mutual hostility of Turks and Arabs, a legacy of more than 600 years of Ottoman Turk rule over Arab populations, prevented any alliance against the Kurds. The Kurds faced hostile groups in all directions, and in the case of Saddam Hussein, a dictator perfectly willing to commit genocide against them, which he did in the late 1980s. The regional dynamics of Kurdish, Arab, and Iranian relations are beyond the scope of this book and my professional competence to elucidate here. Nonetheless, the circle of political forces that surrounded the Turks, the Kurds, and their relations with the Sunni Arab Ba'athist state of Iraq, involved many centuries of enduring conflict. The First Gulf War found both Turks and Kurds as strong allies of the United States against Hussein. For the Turks, fear of Iraqi military expansion and the desire to remain loyal to and protect its long-term strategic and economic interests, in Europe and the United States, made the choice simple. They would align with the United States and the international coalition against Saddam Hussein. For the Kurds, and especially, the Iraqi Kurds, an alliance with a multinational force against Hussein promised the possibility of his overthrow and their liberation from the brutal subjugation they experienced on a daily basis. The Kurds were already in active resistance to the Iraqi army which not only destroyed its villages and gassed Kurdish men, women, and children, but had begun the process of Arabization, whereby the Kurdish homeland in northern Iraq would be systematically purged of Kurds over a period of years.[33]

For the United States, the Kurds and Turks were lynchpins in the regional coalition that would be formed to defeat Iraq. They would be joined by the Saudis, Kuwaitis, and the emirate states of the Gulf, as well as Egypt and Syria and other Arab nations who would make common cause against a ruthless enemy. It was as if Saddam Hussein was an evil diabolical figure straight from central casting in Hollywood. His smile and his resume were enough to mobilize a considerable part of the Arab and non-Arab world against him.

THE STATE OF ISRAEL

An essential element of modern Middle Eastern history is the Arab-Israeli conflict whose origins lie in the nineteenth century but whose impact remained central into the twenty-first century. The Jewish people and the Palestinian Arabs carry their own complex narratives, intricate scripts through modern history that extend far beyond the Gulf Wars.

During both Gulf Wars, the long-standing struggle between the Israelis and Palestinians was a factor, albeit in the background, but a critical one nonetheless. For the Palestinians, Hussein was a major benefactor. He supplied money, arms, and protection to Palestinian resistance organizations, including compensation for the families of suicide bombers and sanctuary to such groups as Abu Nidal.[34] During the First Gulf War, Hussein attempted, albeit with some desperation, to bring Israel into the conflict by launching Scud missiles against the Jewish state. For Palestinians living on the West Bank, Saddam's gambit was a moment of joyous celebration.[35]

For Israel, Iraq remained an enemy from the 1948 war to the conclusion of the Second Gulf War and the destruction of the Ba'thist state. The Jewish national script extended to biblical times. Over several thousand years of diasporas, Jews in disparate communities followed related scripts that enabled survival in the face of seemingly perpetual persecution. When the modern Zionist movement brought dozens of Jewish national communities together in the twentieth century, the commonality among these very disparate groups, separated in some cases by 100 human generations, existed in the Hebrew scriptures transcribed faithfully for millennia, and in the recurring script of the Jews: persecution, survival, and renewal.[36]

In the Jews, whose ancient and sizeable community was expelled from Iraq after the 1948 war and then after the 1967 Six Day War, Hussein faced a permanent enemy. The Israelis and most importantly the powerful Jewish community in the United States viewed him as an illegitimate ruler with an uncompromising hatred of Israel and the Jews. During the First Gulf War, the importance of that mutual antagonism had the greatest relevance because of Israel's strategic alliance and close cultural and political relationship with the United States. Implicitly, Hussein knew that in any confrontation with either the United States or Israel he was at war with both states. For Hussein, the main advantage for having Israel as an adversary was the automatic prestige and solidarity he received from his fellow Arab leaders and the Arab public. In a military confrontation with the United States, his identification as an Arab as well as an Iraqi nationalist was a critical survival mechanism.[37]

THE HASHEMITE KINGDOM AND THE PALESTINIANS

At the time of the First Gulf War, both King Hussein of Jordan and Yasir Arafat, Chairman of the PLO (Palestine Liberation Organization) were allied with Saddam Hussein. The informal alliance was premised on economic, strategic, and political interests. Even after the invasion of Kuwait, the PLO and Jordan remained on the side of Iraq in its confrontation with the other Arab Gulf states, the United States, and Great Britain. In practical terms, Hussein could count on the Jordanians to keep supply lines open to his encircled country. As far as the Palestinians were concerned, their apparent support gave political capital from the so-called "Arab street" for Hussein's defiance of the Western powers. A political theme that Hussein tried to exploit to his advantage before, during and after the First Gulf War was his standing as an anti-Western Arab nationalist who invaded Kuwait to recover the vast oil wealth that accrued to the selfish Kuwaitis. The Kuwaiti patrimony was not shared equally with the rest of the Arab world, most of whose people struggled in deep poverty while the royal family of Kuwait, like the royal families of Saudi Arabia and the UAE, lived in fantastic opulence.[38]

EGYPT AND THE OTHER ARAB STATES

The Egyptians were dismayed with Hussein's invasion of Kuwait. In no shape or form could they countenance the absorption of one Arab state by another. Long allied with the United States and a major aid recipient from both the United States and the Gulf states, the Egyptians were called upon by their benefactors to play a critical role in the Gulf War. The Egyptians supplied the second largest Arab army to the UN coalition. While the United States had to pay Egypt for its participation, a necessity born out of the impoverishment of modern Egypt, it was a negotiated involvement which was of immense benefit to the United States and for Egypt.

The Egyptians could not confront the United States over Iraq. Even though a million Egyptians worked in prewar Iraq, the economic dependence on the United States was far greater. To modernize Egyptian society, a critical need for a desert republic bursting with densely populated slums, the United States and the West were essential. The country could not survive if it did not orient itself toward the West, inviting badly needed trade and economic assistance.

Egypt's vassal like status with respect to the United States and Western Europe compared with the dependent relationships that so many other Arab states had to the developed world. Hussein's challenge to the very heart of the West's economic security, its oil supply in the Persian Gulf, left Egypt with no choice but to align itself against him. There would be no pride in Egypt if the country's economy collapsed in the wake of an Iraqi takeover of the Gulf and the failure of the West and the moderate Arab states to stop him. The enormous resources that Hussein could treat himself to in the Gulf region absent the military power of the West, would have done nothing for Egypt except to increase the impoverishment of an already deeply impoverished society. What could be said for Egypt applied to much of the rest of the Arab Middle East and North Africa, where any largesse from a victorious Hussein would be dwarfed by the economic, political, and strategic disaster of his conquest of Kuwait. Indeed, in the wake of Egypt's cooperation during the First Gulf War, the country's foreign debt burden was cut in half.[39]

THE SUPERPOWERS AND THEIR ALLIES

Long a strategic ally and trading partner of Iraq, the Soviet Union was moving through its death throes in summer 1990. During the long years of the Iran-Iraq war, the Iraqis could count on a steady stream of Soviet-supplied military equipment and advisers. Saddam had a deep admiration for Joseph Stalin and the strong centralized state he built in the 1930s and 1940s. Stalin's totalitarianism was not feared but considered a model for Hussein. Despite its seriously debilitated status as a world power, the Soviet Union was still considered a critical ally by Saddam Hussein in any confrontation he had with the United States and its regional allies. Yet, as Hussein was to learn very quickly, the Soviets would not stand with him after his occupation of Kuwait. The Soviets had far more at stake in seeking Western economic aid and an end to the global Cold War than support for a rogue client state in the Middle East.[40]

While the Soviets strongly disapproved of Hussein's invasion of a neighboring and peaceful Arab state, Gorbachev and the Soviet politburo feared the continued expansion of American power into the Persian Gulf. The invasion placed the Soviets in the unenviable position of protecting its own prestige and interests in the Middle East while making sure that it did nothing to antagonize the United States and its broad coalition Gulf War allies.

GLOBAL, ECONOMIC, AND STRATEGIC INTERESTS

As Hussein mobilized his forces for a lightning strike on the Kingdom of Kuwait, the largest portion of the world's economic and military powers viewed the integrity of the Kuwaiti state as beyond question. The global order, premised on a hydrocarbon-based international economy, poised to expand commensurate with the needs and aspirations of over five billion human beings, would not stand for a strike on the territorial integrity of a member state of the United Nations, a nation of splendiferous monetary and commodity wealth at the very heart of the world's oil supply. Hussein viewed Kuwait through his own eyes and his own script as an Iraqi nationalist and as self-defined redeemer of the larger Arab nation. His view of the world was entirely focused on his image of himself and his perceptions of his entitlements vis-à-vis Kuwait. This view or weltanschauung made his actions logical, at least for him and a segment of Arab public opinion who viewed an Arab strike at the heart of global capitalism as a just response for generations of humiliation at the hands of the West.[41]

In contradistinction, for George H. W. Bush and his advisers, Hussein's decision went far beyond the pale of logic, reason, or sanity. Kuwait's occupation by naked aggression could not be appeased and had to be reversed or undone by armed might. Although he would meet stern domestic opposition to his war plans in fall 1990, Bush was determined to go to war. His understanding of economic and strategic interests, scripted in his vision of presidential leadership, established in him an unalterable resolve to go to restore Kuwait and the integrity of American power in the Persian Gulf. In this way in particular, both George Bush the elder in 1990–91, and his son, the younger in 2002–03, made similar decisions. Each would go to war against Hussein committed to the resolute moral nature of their actions, and the strategic and political necessity for doing so:

> What is at stake is more than one small country; it is a big idea: a new world order, where diverse nations are drawn together in common cause to achieve the universal aspirations of mankind—peace and security, freedom, and the rule of law. Such is a world worthy of our struggle and worthy of our children's future.[42]

3

The First Gulf War

This is an historic moment. We have in this past year made great progress in ending the long era of conflict and cold war. We have before us the opportunity to forge for ourselves and for future generations a new world order—a world where the rule of law, not the law of the jungle, governs the conduct of nations. When we are successful—and we will be—we have a real chance at this new world order, an order in which a credible United Nations can use its peacekeeping role to fulfill the promise and vision of the U.N.'s founders.

George H. Bush[1]

I will speak this time in the context of the sovereignty in Iraq. I want to say that those who do not mean to launch war against Iraq, that this is a form of war against Iraq. If there was more to endure we would tolerate but I believe that all our brothers know the situation and are well informed, hoping, God willing, that the situation will always be good. But I say we have reached a point that we can no longer bear pressure. I believe that we will all gain and the Arab nation will also gain from commitment to OPEC decisions, whether in production or in price and let's rely on God.

Saddam Hussein[2]

THE PROBLEM OF CONTROL

The First Gulf War (in Iraqi history the second) was not unlike any other war by a great power in the history of war. What all world powers have in common is the need to establish control, or order, in the international system. I prefer control because it more accurately describes the modern concept of institutional authority. Institutions create order through control regimes, defined by rules, measured by statistics, and effected by agents who employ institutionally defined and sanctioned means. In this respect, the role of the United States in the Persian Gulf was entirely consistent with what we know of great powers in history. The ancient Chinese empires, while not world powers, required territorial control over the vast provinces of its homeland, building 2,500 miles of fortifications on its northern frontiers to secure it. Chinese imperial controls went from the level of the village and district to the provincial and national levels. Like all empires, the Chinese required efficient control of resources, economic, political, and military. Likewise, the Roman republic and empire maintained physical and organizational systems to secure its boundaries and to enable commerce. "Pax Romana" was for the benefit of Rome, which built roads, buildings, and a multinational army and navy that controlled the Mediterranean, Asia Minor, the Levant, North Africa, and Western Europe for a thousand years. The European powers of early modern Europe established the first state system for the same purposes of earlier great powers, to maintain peace and further economic development. During the nineteenth century, the British navy controlled the world's oceans, building its own transcontinental empire, and ensuring a "Pax Britannica." The Cold War inaugurated the age of "Pax Americana," and like its predecessors in historical times, established a new order. In the American empire juxtaposed to the Soviet, a postcolonial international system took shape. In the new age, scientific and industrial development increased exponentially presaging a period of even greater change.[3]

By the end of the Cold War era, the scientific-industrial civilization of the twentieth century was surging. Global capitalism, fed by expanding international consumer markets, new capital markets, new infrastructure, and continuous technological innovations made the world an ongoing project of modernization. For the United States, the need for control required intricate economic, political, and strategic relationships. The Gulf, the very center of the world's energy systems, required control. Iran had become a threat to that control, or at least that was the perception in the 1980s. The Soviet threat was a presumption from 1945 until the very end of the Cold War. The end of the Iran-Iraq war in 1988 suggested that Iraq was now a threat, albeit an undefined one, to the Gulf. Yet, for U.S. policy-makers, any threat to Western control of the Persian Gulf was intolerable. In his post-Iran territorial disputes with Kuwait, Saddam Hussein appeared to be a threat to that control. In the months prior to his invasion of the country, Western, and Middle Eastern analysts predicted an Iraqi move against Kuwait. Yet, the annexation of Kuwait, easily within the means of the enlarged and experienced Iraqi armed forces, would trigger a formidable crisis not only for Washington but for European, Middle Eastern, and Asian countries dependent upon a secure Gulf. The Iraqis ignored the problem of control in American and Western minds. For Hussein, Kuwait was the richest of prizes and a right of inheritance for his nation. This set the stage for the war, which like all conflicts involves a contestation between national histories and interests. A "battle of scripts," American, European, Middle Eastern, and Iraqi constituted the First Gulf War.

A BATTLE OF SCRIPTS

Paradoxically, while modern wars have been controlled by institutions, mechanized, bureaucratic, impersonal, and machine-like, international wars are usually very dramatic events in human affairs. For diplomats, military leaders, and the world's mass media, a war of any consequence mobilizes energy and focus. All become involved in beehives of activity attempting to make sense of the fog of war. Wars, by their nature, elicit the deepest emotions among the combatants and victims. Combatant and civilian deaths and often horrific war damage place enormous psychic tolls on nations. The compounding effects of loss, dislocation, and destruction make wars primary events in historical consciousness. They routinely mark themselves in collective memory for generations and even centuries. Yet, just as in normal times, international wars are governed by the collective and individual mechanisms of scripts. The unconscious forces at play are very strong, interlaced within powerful multidimensional cultural systems. Connected by networks of individuals and networks of groups, these systems guide human agency at all levels of interaction. An international war is a script or metascript for a complex exchange of information between actors. The narrative may be deadly, even genocidal, but it is a script composed by powerful collective actors who engage in war for reasons embedded in their national histories. In an individual, a script has layers, or dimensions coordinating his or her relationships with groups, larger institutions, and other individual actors. For national leaders, the layers and dimensions of their life script are observed in their public actions. In world history, there have been innumerable examples of charismatic figures rallying nations to war, in their speeches invoking collective memories of national fortitude and greatness. Invariably, such public rituals commemorate historical events that hold powerful emotive qualities as part of a national complex or mythology. For Saddam Hussein, facing the onslaught of the most powerful expeditionary force in history on his southern frontier, he was a representative of multiple archetypes for Arabs and Muslims. He was Saladin, the liberator of Jerusalem; Nebuchadnezzar, the founder of the Babylonian empire; and Al-Musta'sim, the Caliph of Baghdad who defied the Mongols at the gates of the city in 1258, telling the invaders that God would punish them. He was most importantly, the defender of the faith, the liberator of Mecca and Medina from the Western devils and their evil allies, the Saudi monarchy. Never did Hussein nor his inner circle ever doubt his moral superiority to the invaders, the United States led multinational coalition, whose technological superiority in the temporal world did not equate for them with the spiritual claims of the Iraqis defending their nation and land.[4]

Like the Iraqi script, the American historical narrative that came to the Persian Gulf in 1990 was layered through generations of wars and national transformations. The first layer of the narrative included the Pilgrims, the Mayflower

Compact, and the other founding events of the seventeenth century. Other layers added the founding of the American republic and the territorial expansion of the nineteenth century which came under the rubric of "Manifest Destiny." By the last decade of the twentieth century, the script had created an advanced scientific-industrial society with a rapidly expanding base of knowledge and human capital dedicated to the globalization of the American and Western narratives. The national response to the crisis of the Persian Gulf region brought the collective memories of the Cold War, Vietnam, and the Second World War together with the script's earlier layers, its encounters with non-Western peoples of the Americas and the Pacific, the Indian Wars and the Mexican and Spanish Wars, all of these national events were embedded in the collective script of the Americans in their encounter with the Middle East and the Gulf.[5]

On one level, the script viewed the Gulf in terms of political economy and geostrategic interests. As a technocratic civilization at the center of the global technocratic order, American policy-makers viewed the impending war with Iraq as an exercise in managerial internationalism. The Iraqi army, with its First World War tactics and Soviet equipment had to be dislodged from its entrenched formations in the Kuwaiti desert. Kuwait had to be liberated before the society disintegrated under the pressure of the brutal Iraqi occupation. The war was planned carefully over six months coordinating the military assets of more than a dozen countries, mobilizing international public opinion, and the commitments of scores of political allies around the world, to launch a massive air and land campaign against Iraq.

On another level, the American script involved the encounter between George H. Bush, the tall, patrician conservative, a decorated veteran of the Pacific War, stalwart nationalist, and internationalist who viewed the war as a moral challenge to him and to his country. In the contentious prewar debate, the nationalist impulse to strike at an imminent threat to vital national interests was opposed by a vigorous antiwar sentiment in the Congress, the public, and even the military, which saw the moral challenge of the war differently. In the Gulf, two national memories, one of the Second World War and the other of Vietnam, contended for control of public policy. Yet, the deciding factor was the nature of the sitting president whose own personal and leadership narratives revolved around the memories of his youth when he flew combat missions against the empire of Imperial Japan. Bush's autobiographical collection of letters begins with his memory of Pearl Harbor. In the first paragraph of his retrospective commentary, the designs of his future presidential leadership were clear:

> When Japan bombed Pearl Harbor on December 7, 1941, I was a seventeen year-old high school senior at Phillips Academy, Andover. I could hardly wait to get out of school and enlist. Six months later, Secretary of War Henry Stimson delivered our commencement address and advised my class to go to college. He predicted it

would be a long war, and there would be plenty of time for us to serve. Prescott Bush, with whom it was not easy to disagree, hoped I would listen to Secretary Stimson and go on to Yale. After the ceremony, Dad asked me if I had changed my mind. I told him no, I was "joining up." Dad simply nodded his okay. On my eighteenth birthday, June 12, 1942, I enlisted in the Navy's flight training program as a seaman second class.[6]

George W. Bush did go to Yale, but after three years of service as a navy combat pilot where he earned the Distinguished Flying Cross, risking his life in air-to-air combat many thousands of miles from New England and his family's upper class environs.[7]

INTERNATIONAL MOBILIZATION

To fight a war with global implications required the mobilization of the international community, a task for which the Bush White House had exceptional talents. In the space of less than six months, the Iraqi invasion of Kuwait allowed the Bush administration to mobilize a global coalition of regional and global allies to fund, and supply a modern military force to retake the country. In expert fashion, multinational political, economic, and military resources were brought to bear to accomplish the task. The script set in motion with the invasion of Kuwait brought the full organizational skills of the American state into action. War mobilization was not as complicated as administering an occupied territory or negotiating a peace settlement between intractable enemies. Mobilizing military assets, coordinating with allies, and building an effective political strategy to support the war were dependent upon skills that had been established in the course of major wars in the history of the United States. The Pentagon, the State Department, the White House, and supporting agencies and institutions moved in quickly, and adroitly, relying on long-established protocols and institutional memory.

What needed to be mobilized? The logistics for the war were one thing, but the U.S. military had excelled in building huge armies and navies equal to the task. During the U.S. Civil War, a constabulary force of 16,000 men was transformed within a few years into a war machine of over a million men. In relative terms, the achievement was even more dramatic. By 1865, four years after the start of the conflict, 5 percent of the population of the Northern states was enrolled in the Union Armies, a national mobilization equivalent to 12 million in 1990.[8]

The 1990–91 expeditionary force was the most powerful in world history, a result of unprecedented advances in military technology that made one American combat division in the Gulf War, the power equivalent of eight American divisions during the Second World War. Yet, the more critical area of mobilization was political. In this task, international mobilization of public opinion and the support of foreign governments had to be accomplished to make the war winnable. Hussein's invasion was so threatening to the international community, that the rallying of international support was also a quick process. One after another, several allies joined the United States in the coalition to reverse the results of the Iraqi invasion.[9]

REGIONAL ALLIES

The Kuwaiti royal family, the Al Sabahs, had fled the invasion within hours, barely escaping capture by the overwhelmingly superior Iraqi army. Living in hotel rooms in London and Saudi Arabia but with access to over $100 billion in financial reserves, they were of course desperate for U.S. military intervention and the most assiduous of all American allies against Saddam Hussein. Since the 1970s, the Kuwaiti royal family had become fabulously wealthy from the explosion of oil revenues. By 1990, a nation of only a few hundred thousand citizens had been transformed by the international oil industry. Royalty payments and then direct ownership and management of national oil reserves had made the Kuwaitis, per capita, the richest people in the world. The massive opulence of Kuwaiti royalty and wealthiest social strata was in devastating contrast to the way most Arabs lived. Throughout the Arab lands of Southwestern Asia and North Africa, Arab clans still lived in squalid urban slums or impoverished villages, where the necessities of late twentieth century living were a dream. Kuwaiti princes and businessmen lived in large mansions, with foreign servants, air conditioning, fleets of luxury cars, and foreign villas where they could fly to whenever convenient. Their children attended the best American and European universities and no one ever missed a meal. This opulence, which came with indiscrete arrogance toward others of lesser means, contrasted with the vast majority of people in Yemen, Somalia, Egypt, Algeria, Sudan, and other Arab states including Iraq, where clean drinking water, universal education let alone elite foreign universities, cars, telephones, and food beyond the staples of bread and beans, were privileges for many. The Kuwaiti reputation for arrogant narcissism made them a very unsympathetic group and this showed in regional reactions to the Iraqi invasion.[10]

While impoverished groups cheered with the occupation of Kuwait City by the Iraqi Republican Guard, Kuwaiti citizens watched their entire society crushed and destroyed. In total desperation, the Kuwaitis begged the United States and other world powers to save them. In the process of saving them, the Kuwaitis were required to offer substantial financial resources to cover some of the costs of the war. This they did gladly, along with the Saudis, they paid for the expeditionary forces of Egypt, Syria, and Pakistan, including arms, munitions, transportation, fuel, and housing.

In addition to the exiled Kuwaiti government, the most eager and most important regional allies against Saddam Hussein were the Saudis. Despite the enormity of Saudi oil wealth and vast expenditures on the most modern weapons produced by the United States and other Western nations, the monarchy was virtually without an army when the invasion occurred. The Saudis had helped finance Hussein's war against Iran, viewing Iraq as a bulwark against the Iranian revolution. The sudden movement against Kuwait, a fellow Arab state and monarchy, threatened the very existence of the House of Saud. With Hussein on the Kuwaiti border, virtually nothing stood in the way of Hussein's occupation of the Saudi oil fields adjoining the Gulf.[11]

Like the Kuwaitis, in desperate need of protection, the Saudis cooperated fully with the United States as it mobilized an invasion force in fall 1990. When the air war began in January 1991, the Saudis were not only the most important U.S. ally, their cooperation was essential to the war plans to recover Kuwait from Iraq. For the first time in their history, the Saudis allowed Western military forces on Saudi territory. By the time the war was launched, an armada of foreign troops, jets, tanks, and artillery were staged on Saudi territory in an orchestrated assault on another Arab state's occupying army. This was only possible because of the desperation of the Saudis, who like the Kuwaitis faced the collapse of their regime if Hussein was allowed to consolidate his victory.[12]

Other regional allies against Hussein included Egypt, Syria, Turkey, and the UAE. The Egyptians and Syrians provided Arab armies that would be needed if only for propaganda purposes to liberate Kuwait City. Yet, their military and political support were critical to the UN coalition as it massed the most powerful invasion force in the history of warfare.

GLOBAL ALLIES

Hussein's daring gambit, to seize control of a large chunk of the Persian Gulf's oil, triggered an immediate and successful mobilization of major U.S. allies. From the moment that the crisis erupted in August 1990, the Bush administration showed considerable skill in diplomacy. Nonetheless, central to their success was the immediate consensus among major allies that the annexation of Kuwait represented not only a serious breach of international law, but a major threat to the world's economic system. In very short order, James Baker, Secretary of State, was able to establish a formidable military alliance to defeat the invasion of Kuwait. The alliance crystallized along the basic lines of realpolitik as well as the moral outrage of one nation conquering another. Hussein's response to the quick military response to his invasion included the taking of Western hostages, which in the months prior to the war, numbered in the thousands. His duplicity and savagery, long apparent in his treatment of his northern Kurdish population and the ruthless manner the Iraqis had fought their eight-year war with Iran, suggested that Hussein was of such evil character that he had to be defeated and removed from power.[13]

The first nonregional nations that pledged to join the United States included America's closest European allies. Within a week of the invasion, Great Britain and France were brought into the coalition, and each committed significant military resources to the expeditionary forces assembling in the Persian Gulf and in Saudi Arabia. In practical terms, the political support of Western Europe as well as Japan and major Arab states, including Saudi Arabia, Egypt, and Syria, was of greater value to the United States than direct military contributions.

By 1990, the United States was emerging as the world's "sole remaining superpower." In fact, in the world outside the communist bloc, the United States had been the only true world power since the 1950s. Since 1945 in fact, America was the only Western country who could project its power around the world. With the First Gulf War that reality continued and was magnified by the extent to which Western Europe and Japan showed their utter dependence upon the American armed forces to defeat a sociopathic regime which threatened to dominate the Persian Gulf through military coercion.[14]

Western European and Japanese interests in reversing Iraq's annexation of Kuwait were identical to those of the United States. Iraq could not be allowed to dominate the Persian Gulf by absorbing a sovereign nation-state. Kuwait held 10 percent of the world's proven oil reserves, as did Iraq. With 20 percent of the world's oil in his possession, and his armies within striking distance of the oil fields of both Saudi Arabia and the UAE, Hussein could quickly control the entire oil reserves of the Gulf region with the exception of Iran. With such economic power, Hussein's military and political ambitions would threaten not only Israel but the entire world. The mad dictator could if left to his own devices blackmail Europe or East Asia with his control of critical oil supplies.

With the stakes so significant, the Bush administration was able to enlist the material support of all the major NATO powers and Japan. The Japanese were required to pay for a substantial amount of the cost of the war. This was also required of Germany, in addition to Kuwait and Saudi Arabia. The military forces to defeat Hussein's large but obsolete army, came from the United States, with smaller contributions from Great Britain, France, and the Arab nations (Saudi Arabia, Egypt, Syria). In total, more than 40 nations were part of the UN coalition that faced Iraq in the Kuwaiti and southern Iraqi deserts in the winter of 1991.[15]

DOMESTIC POLITICS

While the Arab Gulf states and key NATO allies were eager to contain and if necessary attack the Iraqi occupation of Kuwait, American public opinion was not united at all. The public viewed the confrontation with Iraq largely through the memories of the Vietnam War. Despite the strategic nature of the threat from

Iraq, to world oil supplies and to the spread of WMD throughout the Middle East, key Democratic elected officials opposed the impending war. While the mobilization of troops, materials, and funds began immediately after invasion, the mobilization of U.S. public opinion was never complete right up to the very start of the air war on January 16, 1991. No less an authority on U.S. foreign and defense policy, Senator Sam Nunn of Georgia, then chairman of the Senate Armed Services committee, had grave doubts over the U.S. mission in Iraq. Known for his conservative and promilitary views, Nunn argued in the Senate and in public venues that the "rush to war" was not wise.[16]

The Bush administration tried every diplomatic means to pressure Hussein to withdraw from Kuwait. Intermediation by Iraq's major arms supplier the Soviet Union, as well as by the Arab league, the United Nations and other friendly nations, could never persuade Hussein to back down. In Nunn's eyes, the containment of Iraq through the large military presence on the Kuwaiti border, and the worldwide embargo effectively shutting Iraq off from the rest of the world, were sufficient means to fight the Iraqi dictator. From Nunn's perspective, which was shared largely by the Democratic Party in both houses of Congress, the Bush administration's plan of invading Kuwait to liberate it was a very dangerous and ill-conceived idea. No amount of argument could convince Nunn, nor Senator Joseph Biden or the key House leadership, including Hamilton Fish, head of the House Armed Services Committee, to support a policy of armed liberation of Kuwait through a massive attack on entrenched Iraqi military forces.[17]

While the president saw the Gulf War in the lens of the war of his youth, namely, the Second World War, a larger group of younger Americans understood the confrontation in the Persian Gulf in the fall of 1990 as a return to Vietnam. The lessons of the Second World War, ingrained in George Bush and his generation, that appeasement of an enemy is always wrong, and that a successful war must be a moral one, were lost on most of post–Second World War America, who, if they followed international affairs at all, had a visceral sense of tragedy fighting a land war in a distant land against an enemy we knew little about.

Vietnam had damaged the social and political fabric of the nation, this was a truism that all political observers could acknowledge. Overcoming Vietnam, which was one of George Bush's key motives, resonated with conservatives who at the end the Cold War championed an aggressive internationalist agenda. At the same time, the end of the Cold War was altering the entire necessity of that militarized internationalism in the minds of domestic liberals and even conservatives. The Second World War had transformed American power, reviving the progressive internationalist agenda of Woodrow Wilson. Through decades of war and confrontation, first with the Axis powers and then the communist bloc, the proactive use of U.S. military power to protect the international system was a given. Now, in 1990, with the apparent end of the Cold War, the global mission was open to question and redefinition.

From the point of view of most domestic liberals, the Bush White House was thinking in terms of the 1940s, when it should have been thinking within the framework of the immediate future, the 1990s, the first decade after the end of the Cold War, when military power would no longer be nearly as valuable to protecting the U.S. national interest, as economic, political, and diplomatic tools. George Bush looked at Saddam Hussein and saw a smaller vision of Adolf Hitler, a vicious, cruel tyrant who had to be confronted and ultimately eliminated from the Middle East. From the perspective of antiwar Senators and Congressmen, as well as retired generals and admirals, the Hitler analogy was crude and misrepresented the nature of the crisis. James Reston, editorial writer for the *New York Times* made the argument succinctly:

> It's interesting that even on Veterans Day 1990, when we were supposed to remember the millions killed in this bloody century, little was said about the unpredictability of war or about those two impatient scoundrels, Hitler and Stalin, who fought their way to oblivion. Bush's comparison of Hussein to Hitler, a madman with superior military forces in the center of industrial Europe, is ridiculous, and the growing assumption of inevitable war is at best premature and at worst dangerous.[18]

Moderate antiwar critics said they were not unalterably opposed to war with Hussein they simply imputed the experience of Vietnam into their calculations of benefits versus risks in waging war. Attacking the Iraqi army would not be easy, despite the vast technological superiority of the UN coalition. The United States had the same enormity of superior means, communications, and supply against the enemy during the Indochina conflict, and that war, which had ended just 15 years earlier, was one of total defeat for the United States. The domestic antiwar movement, wanted to wait in the desert, at least until the following September, when the crushing sanctions would have time to erode Hussein's political will.

Bush and his key advisers saw the war very differently. Holding hundreds of thousands of troops in the Saudi desert for almost a year risked the morale and combat effectiveness of those personnel, who would have to endure the severe heat of the region, even through the summer, all the time remaining on edge, ready to go to war when the orders came from Washington. For national security planners, keeping a large chunk of the U.S. armed forces on hold in the Gulf, as diplomatic channels continued to work for months, seemed like a very poor and risky solution. If Hussein were to have a problem with political will, and there was no evidence that the totalitarian Ba'athists were at all susceptible to public opinion, certainly the fragile political will of the international coalition and the notoriously fickle American public, would be in far greater danger of erosion as their forces sat in the desert.[19]

If the war was going to be swift and decisive, as Bush war planners envisioned, the imperfect nature of domestic war mobilization was an acceptable contingency. From Bush's perspective, and that of key aides, including his Secretary of Defense,

Richard Cheney, the stakes in the Persian Gulf were so critical, they trumped the factor of a domestic antiwar movement. The Bush White House viewed the confrontation as a direct challenge to post–Cold War American power, and the war's outcome, would have a foundational effect on the nature of the post–Cold War international system. Understandably, Congressional opposition looked toward several pressing needs of the public. The end of the Cold War promised a "peace dividend," whereby the huge U.S. military budget would be reduced to fund badly needed domestic programs. Liberal constituencies throughout the United States, especially working class and minority areas represented by Democrats in Congress, were afraid of a Gulf war which would become a deadly quagmire that would kill and wound thousands of their young people. They preferred that in the inevitable trade-off between guns and butter, that this time, after the defeat of the Soviet Union, domestic programs to raise the standards of living of poor and working class communities would trump the "Pentagon war machine." In fact, opposition to the First Gulf War was bipartisan and cut across the traditional military-civilian divide:

> On November 28, in hearings before Senate committees, former Joint Chiefs of Staff Heads Admiral William Crowe and General David Jones urged that military action against Iraq be delayed in order to give more time for U.N. sanctions against Iraq to work. They were joined in that advice by former Secretaries of Defense Robert McNamara, Harold Brown, Frank Carlucci, Caspar Weinberger, and Eliot Richardson, along with the other eight out of nine living former Joint Chiefs of Staff Heads. A year and a half later, President Bush's own Joint Chiefs Head, General Colin Powell admitted that he, too, favored delaying military action, although he remained silent at the time. President Bush rejected the advice.[20]

The White House had precious few domestic allies in its war mobilization process. Presidential authority over military action was a legacy of institutional doctrine since the eighteenth century. It was primarily defined by the constitutional authority of the president to wage war. The Congress split almost entirely along partisan lines as did the general public. Saddam Hussein was a monster there was no question of that. Yet, the range of arguments against going to war to evict him from Kuwait, were impressive. The potential costs of the war resonated with almost all who were knowledgeable about the region. Yet, George Bush was not persuaded. The legacy of his youth, waging a global war against a global enemy, cast his view of international morality and U.S. interests for a lifetime. On New Year's Eve 1991, 16 days before the start of air operations, Bush wrote a letter to his grown children on his reasons for going to war:

> . . . We have waited to give sanctions a chance, we have moved a tremendous force so as to reduce the risk to every American soldier if force to is to be used; but the loss of life still lingers and plagues the heart.

My mind goes back to history:

How many lives might have been saved if appeasement had given way to force earlier on in the late 30s or earliest 40s? How many Jews might have been spared the gas chambers, or how many Polish patriots might be alive today? I look as today's crisis as "good" vs. "evil." Yes, it is that clear...

—principle must be adhered to—Saddam cannot profit in any way at all from his aggression and from his brutalizing the people of Kuwait.

—and sometimes in life you have to act as you think best—you can't compromise, you can't give in, even if hour critics are loud and numerous.[21]

DESERT SHIELD

The mobilization of military forces to engage Iraq was a marvel of logistical and political skill. In less than six months, a multinational force of over 500,000 troops were deployed on the northeastern border of Saudi Arabia, primed and ready to launch a joint attack force against an entrenched military force of several hundred thousand men. Operation Desert Shield began the first week in August and climaxed in the middle of January 1991, when it transitioned to offensive operations of Desert Storm. The deployment was a global process organized with expert precision by the global capabilities of the U.S. military establishment.

In effect, the 45 years of the Cold War was ample preparation for the United States. The Pentagon planned a sweeping attack utilizing the doctrines of joint warfare. After a massive wave of air attacks designed to reduce and destroy communications, supply lines, and physical assets, including tanks, artillery, and the power grid and major road systems and bridges, a combined air, land, and sea assault on Iraqi forces was planned, utilizing the vast advantages of speed, maneuver, and battlefield management that the United States possessed over Iraq. Carefully, the assets necessary for the attack were delivered by air and sealift. Several thousand main battle tanks with their crews and support troops were shipped from the United States and Europe. Aircraft carriers were quickly deployed in the Persian Gulf and the Red Sea, their crews and pilots working continuously to perfect their training for the air war. In Saudi Arabia, U.S. Air Force units arrived in August and September, and continued to arrive through the six weeks of the Gulf campaign. U.S. Army and Marine divisions, with their tanks, attack helicopters, and supporting artillery and missile batteries mobilized along the Kuwaiti and Southern Iraqi frontiers.

The more than 40 Iraqi army divisions, although heavily equipped with late model Soviet tanks, artillery, and surface-to-air missiles, were facing a military force that had never existed before in modern warfare. The full might of U.S. armed forces were now brought to bear, not on a global adversary, such as the Soviet Union, the enemy it had been designed to fight for two generations, but a small and relatively backward military force, by world standards, poorly trained, equipped and led. The United States deployed not only better weapons but the supreme advantage of its space age communications systems. In conventional war with conventional armies, an adversary that had a monopoly of satellite intelligence and imagery, one possessing the new "stealth technology" as well, would prove overwhelmingly stronger to the adversary with only steel tubes and large ammunition rounds. The force that could deploy and strike without the knowledge of the other, and who could use its detailed knowledge of the enemy's many vulnerabilities, that force would prove invincible.[22]

THE ALLIES

While Saddam Hussein's military had never been stronger, after a decade of expansion and modernization during and after the war with Iran, the Soviet armed and designed Iraqi war machine would prove no match at all for the international coalition dominated by the U.S. armed forces. Just like the United States, British, French, and Saudi forces had superior Western arms, tactics and training. The deep common interests of the allies in defeating the Iraqi occupation facilitated the expert coordination of the Gulf War coalition. Functioning with the full cooperation of neighboring states and the political imprimatur of the UN Security Council, the United States was able to plan and initiate an intensive air campaign involving around-the-clock air strikes throughout Iraq and the Kuwaiti theater of operation. The United States led the air war, providing more than 80 percent of the combat missions against Iraqi targets. Key allies however, played their part, adding further political legitimacy to the air war that punished an Arab nation in the heartland of the Arab and Islamic world. Central to the success of the operation was the participation of the Arab armies of Syria, Egypt, Kuwait, and Saudi Arabia. While their total military contribution was very modest, the political value of their participation was essential.[23]

Of the few advantages that Hussein could exploit, the political/psychological warfare he employed through propaganda hoped to defeat the allies through the Arab street. In vain, the Ba'athists wanted a mass uprising not only in the Arab nations, but throughout the Islamic world and beyond that would see him as a valiant force against the naked imperialism of the Western powers once again imposing their will on a proud Arab, Muslim and Third World nation.[24]

Yet another area of warfare which the Bush administration excelled at was the political campaign to rally sufficient international and domestic political support for the war effort. Opposition in the United States was quite strong right up to the moment that the war began on January 16, a day after the UN deadline for Iraq's compliance with UN withdrawal resolutions. Yet, the Bush White House had worked diligently to gain just enough support among the Democratic opposition to go to war. It had built just enough support around the world, among many reluctant nation-states, including Japan, Germany, and the Soviet

Union, to execute this short but very decisive military campaign. There was no time to lose. The Iraqi occupation of Kuwait was brutal. Unless this small and battered country that consisted essentially of one urban area could be liberated, the annexation by Iraq would be a fait accompli. The Kuwaitis did not have a year or two years to wait for liberation. In a year or two, Hussein would have had enough to time to complete the absorption of this tiny oil kingdom, deporting or killing its remaining population, and establishing its claim to 100 billion barrels of crude oil.

DESERT STORM

Desert Shield lasted five and a half months, just enough time to mobilize the military and political resources needed to launch the liberation of Kuwait. The entire war lasted less than six weeks. The significance of the war was twofold. In the first instance, the mobilization of several dozen allied nations for a common purpose demonstrated the expert skill of the Bush administration and the prestige and power of the United States at the very end of the Cold War. In the second instance, the technological prowess of the coalition, demonstrated the continued evolution of conventional military power as an instrument of advanced technocratic knowledge and organizational development. What enabled victory for the allies was the ability of the United States to use its satellite intelligence, its advanced battlefield management protocols, and its new and unparalleled force of stealth attack aircraft with GPS (global positioning system)-guided missiles. The enormous expenditures of the defense establishment since the 1940s had produced weapon and delivery systems that were an order of magnitude more lethal than anything in the Iraqi army.

In the first hours and days of the war, which itself, lasted but six weeks, and only four days on the ground, U.S. stealth bombers, invisible to Soviet-designed and operated Iraqi radar systems, inflicted devastating guided missile attacks on key Iraqi assets. Within days, land, air, and sea guided missile systems disabled the Iraqi air defense networks, destroyed the country's electrical grid, its telecommunications and media broadcasting systems, key bridges, and its rail system. With very little loss of life to pilots or ground crews, the U.S.-led assault was an astonishing display of the new systems of modern war. During the entire war, a few thousand tons of guided munitions destroyed the Iraqi military and civilian infrastructure that supported the one million man Iraqi army. Despite enormous firepower on the ground, the Iraqi forces were helpless against the information-based military systems that had been developed by the United States in its 45-year war against the Soviet Union. For their part, the Soviets under Mikhail Gorbachev supported the allied war effort, albeit with great reluctance. The Soviets, themselves an advanced technological society, were humbled by the power and efficiency of the U.S. military. In the Kuwaiti and Southern Iraqi deserts, the Soviets best tanks supplied to Saddam Hussein exploded like giant tin cans. The armor piercing uranium depleted shells of the Abrams tank turned Iraqi armor into massive balls of flames, their extensive steel shells melting and cracking under the force and heat of the explosions.[25]

WAR TERMINATION

A war cannot be considered a success, no matter how well it was fought and how definitive victory on the battlefield, unless it ends with a transformation of the political dynamics that underlay its origins. The lack of a true political settlement bedeviled the end of the First World War and countless others in modern times. In the First Gulf War, the problem with the war settlement process was precisely the fact that there was no definitive end, the issues that ignited the war were not resolved but held in abeyance. Hussein did order the withdrawal of his shattered armies from Kuwait but he had not signed documents of surrender, nor had he accepted responsibility for the invasion and annexation of a sovereign nation. Hussein waxed poetic in his defiance:

> O you valiant men, you have fought the armies of 30 states and the capabilities of an even greater number of states which supplied them with the means of aggression and support. Faith, belief, hope, and determination continue to fill your chests, souls, and hearts. They have even become deeper, stronger, brighter, and more deeply rooted. God is great, God is great, may the lowly be defeated. Victory is sweet with the help of God.[26]

Hussein's defiance resonated with Sunni Arabs throughout the Middle East. The wealthy citizens of the Gulf states recognized him as a demonic force, a threat to their existence, but for others, he was a champion of the Arab nation, against foreign imperialists. For Iraqi and Arab nationalists, the destruction of half of the Iraqi military and the invasion albeit temporary of the country by Western armies was a deep humiliation. Arab historical memory was embodied in the consciousness of clans and tribes reaching back to the prophet Mohammed and to antiquity. Under no circumstances would Saddam Hussein or any of his allies within Iraq and outside of it, accept a determination of boundaries by the United States, Great Britain, and the other members of the coalition.

The unbending pride of Hussein was matched by the ruthlessness of his Republican Guard divisions that saved the republic in the face of widespread rebellions in the north and south by Shiite and Kurdish populations. Just as soon as Norman Schwarzkopf, CENTCOM commander negotiated an armistice in the Kuwaiti desert, Hussein swiftly reconstituted his surviving Republican Guard divisions. Within weeks, the rebellions, motivated in part by the words of President Bush were crushed. The end of the war left Iraq and the Ba'athist state whole and this was according to plan. The Bush administration understood the complex structure of Iraq and the fragile balance of power in the Gulf region between Sunnis, Shiites, and Kurds. Hussein was to be contained, his forces reduced and his occupation reversed, these were the operational and strategic goals of the Bush administration and of the key Gulf allies, the governments of Kuwait, Saudi Arabia, and the UAE. Despite furious criticism in later years, Bush had no intention of destroying the Iraqi army, the pillar of the modern Iraqi state. Nor did he ever entertain the idea of occupying Iraq for the purposes of liberation:

> Trying to eliminate Saddam, extending the ground war into an occupation of Iraq, would have violated our guideline about not changing objectives in midstream, engaging in "mission creep," and would have incurred incalculable human and political costs. Apprehending him was probably impossible. We had been unable to find Noriega in Panama, which we knew intimately. We would have been forced to occupy Baghdad and in effect, rule Iraq. The coalition would instantly have collapsed, the Arabs deserting it in anger and other allies pulling out as well. Under those circumstances, there was no viable "exit strategy" we could see violating another of our principles. Furthermore, we had been self-consciously trying to set a pattern for handling aggression in the post–Cold War world. Going in and occupying Iraq, thus unilaterally exceeding the United Nations' mandate, would have destroyed the precedent of international response to aggression that we hoped to establish. Had we gone the invasion route the United States could conceivably still be an occupying power in a bitterly hostile land. It would have been a dramatically different-and perhaps barren-outcome.[27]

To effect a workable armistice that preserved the Iraqi state but contained the dangerous ambitions of Hussein's regime, the United Nations under the aegis of U.S. military power imposed strict terms. To protect Kurdish and Shiite populations from genocidal attacks, no-fly zones were imposed on the Iraqi air force in both the north and south of the country. In the north, Kurdish provinces above Kirkuk were physically separated from Iraqi state authority, in the south, more limited protections were given to the Shiites whose marshlands were systematically destroyed over the ensuing decade.[28]

The terms imposed on Iraq by the United Nations and the major world powers required strict inspections of Iraqi military facilities and the destruction of all WMD. Iraq was denied both import and export markets until in response to the humanitarian crisis, the "oil for food" program was begun in 1995—a program deeply corrupted by Hussein who used it to siphon off funds for his own bank accounts and to reward political collaborators throughout the world.

The most important terms of the war settlement process were the imposition of the inspection regime of the IAEA (International Atomic Energy Agency). The CPA (coalition provisional authority) along with the IAEA, dismantled all of Iraq's known chemical, biological, and nuclear programs, most of which were unknown to the international community until after the end of the First Gulf War. In doing so, postwar Iraq was now a defiant but disarmed force in the region. Under the determined watch of the United States and the UN CPA, Hussein ruled his totalitarian state, but was effectively contained. While he continued to defy the United Nations and the major Western powers for more than a decade, he was no longer an eminent threat to Kuwait, Saudi Arabia, or any of his other neighbors. By this broad measure, the war settlement process of the First Gulf War was a success. It was incomplete, the issues surrounding the conflicts of the region remained, but by restoring United States control and in effect the control of the international community on the Gulf region, the war had concluded successfully.[29]

Yet, the success was not viewed that way by contemporary observers. Hussein's continued hold onto power was considered a failure by many in the United States. Critics saw Iraq as a permanent threat to the international community as long as the Ba'athist regime remained. The whole region continued under the cloud not only of Hussein's survival, but the unresolved issues of the twentieth century. The regional antagonisms between the ethnic and sectarian groups were deep, visceral, and seemingly insoluble. The Gulf war had protected the world's oil supply and defeated a serious threat of nuclear proliferation but in the end, the conflict did nothing to resolve the collective scripts that perpetuated war and instability throughout the region.

Regardless of the triumph of the coalition forces, Arabs remained in historical conflict with the Persians, Sunnis remained opposed to the expansion of Shiite power and influence, and the Kurds remained in conflict with both Arabs and Turks over their national autonomy. In the larger Middle East, Muslims remained in opposition to the Jewish state, and more immediately, millions of Palestinians, Syrians, and Lebanese Shiites were dedicated to the destruction of Israel. The occupation of the holy land by the Jews mobilized impassioned Muslims throughout the Islamic world against not only Israel but the entire Western world which appeared to be collectively intent on the humiliation and destruction of Islam.[30]

For a brief time, the disastrous defeat of Saddam Hussein offered a window of opportunity for the Arab-Israeli conflict. The PLO was driven to bankruptcy after its support of Hussein resulted in the loss of virtually all its financial support from the Gulf states. Destitute, Yasir Arafat was forced to negotiate with the Israelis, which resulted in the ill-fated Oslo Accords. But immediate benefits that accrued to the United States, including its newfound status as the world's sole remaining superpower, faded quickly in a world undergoing dramatic social, political, and economic change. Despite winning the Gulf War in a spectacular show of military might, the United States could not impose itself on the region, anymore than other great powers in history were able to impose themselves completely on regions brought into their orbit.

_____

The Interregnum: Clinton and the Gulf

. . .we must be prepared to use force again if Saddam takes threatening actions, such as trying to reconstitute his weapons of mass destruction or their delivery systems, threatening his neighbors, challenging allied aircraft over Iraq or moving against his own Kurdish citizens. The credible threat to use force, and when necessary, the actual use of force, is the surest way to contain Saddam's weapons of mass destruction program, curtail his aggression and prevent another Gulf War.

Bill Clinton[1]

In the path from the First to the Second Gulf War, 1990–2003, three presidential administrations were engaged in managing the international system. The first president George H. Bush encountered the crisis of the Iraqi invasion of Kuwait by organizing a carefully designed multinational coalition. His administration quickly mobilized the assets of the national security state, an institutional system long designed to project military forces on a global scale and executed a strategy based on long established military and political principles. His successor, the topic of this chapter, took his legacy and continued the same framework for the management of Iraq and the Persian Gulf. William Jefferson Clinton was distinct from his predecessor. His predilections for leadership were focused on domestic policy, rather than global management, the career forte of the first Bush. The political literatures on the three presidencies, still emerging as recent history, represent distinct personalities managing international affairs according to the idiosyncratic designs of their own personalities and the state of the times in which they governed.[2] What the political narratives have tended to miss in their usual focus on events and personalities have been the underlying forces that moved the United States and the world from the First Gulf War to the Second.

As I have emphasized throughout this book, individuals and groups operate through scripts. Those scripts control the texts and the subtexts of events, crises, and processes, driving history in directions that may or may not be in the conscious intentions of the actors involved.

To be clear, Clinton was a different personality, a different leader than his predecessor, George H. Bush. His center-left politics and affiliation with the Democratic Party inclined him more to emphasize different policies especially in domestic politics. However, differences in foreign policy were overshadowed by deeper continuities. The Clinton administration's doctrines in foreign policy reflected ideological continuity with prior administrations as far back as the nineteenth century. In basic beliefs, on the importance of free trade, human rights and democracy, and the military responsibilities of the United States, Clinton and Bush were virtually identical. The broad designs of American internationalism, if only window dressing to critics on the left supported a liberal international order where American power was dominant but beneficent.[3]

While enamored of the same script for national power and greatness, Bush and Clinton most differed in what they brought to the designated role of president and world leader. In his narrative about the Clinton years, David Halberstam suggested that Bill Clinton came to the presidency with little interest or knowledge about foreign policy. In an early speech to the country, Halberstam noted the former governor of Arkansas devoted just 141 words to foreign policy out of more than 4000 he enunciated. In fact, in his first public policy speech as president, his address to a joint session of Congress, only one paragraph out of a 7000-word text was devoted to foreign policy.[4] His predecessor had been director of the CIA, ambassador to the United Nations and to the Peoples Republic of China, in addition to eight years as Ronald Reagan's vice-president. Clinton assumed office with no substantive experience in statecraft. Yet, as with all presidents, he immediately assumed constitutional authority over the entire executive branch and with it the entire portfolio of U.S. obligations and relations with more than 100 nation-states. By the end of his presidency, at the turn of the new century, the official statement of the White House suggested he had become a world leader, involved in dozens of international concerns:

America has done much over the past seven years to build a better world: aiding the remarkable transitions to free-market democracy in Eastern Europe; adapting and enlarging NATO to strengthen Europe's security; ending ethnic war in Bosnia and Kosovo; working with Russia to deactivate thousands of nuclear weapons from the former Soviet Union; ratifying START II and the Chemical Weapons Convention; negotiating the CTBT, and the Adaptation Agreement on the Conventional Armed Forces in Europe (CFE) Treaty; securing a freeze in North Korean fissile material production; facilitating milestone agreements in the Middle East peace process; standing up to the threat posed by Saddam Hussein; reducing Africa's debt through the Cologne Initiative and the Heavily Indebted Poor Countries Initiative (HIPC);

helping to broker peace accords from Northern Ireland to Sierra Leone to the Peru-Ecuador border; fostering unprecedented unity, democracy and progress in the Western Hemisphere; benefiting our economy by reaching over 270 free trade agreements, including the landmark accord to bring China into the World Trade Organization; and exercising global leadership to help save Mexico from economic disaster and to reverse the Asian financial crisis.[5]

Despite the conclusion of the Cold War, the international system abounded with crises. The world was full of local and regional conflicts and formidable problems relating to global poverty, underdevelopment, ecology, and nuclear proliferation; these issues had been evident for decades. Paradoxically, despite a series of wars including the Rawandan genocide, the Yugoslav civil wars, and the rise of al Qaeda, Clinton's presidency appeared to have been a shaky interregnum, not only in the Persian Gulf but in the international system as a whole. George H. Bush and his cohorts had ended the Cold War with Mikhail Gorbachev carefully managing to end a worldwide military confrontation involving over 100,000 nuclear weapons. Soviet power, an extraordinary force in world affairs since 1945 melted away in the four years of the Bush administration. The Red Army, long feared for scores of heavy tank divisions aimed at Western Europe, withdrew from East Germany and then Poland, its huge inventory rusting from lack of maintenance. The same was true of the Soviet navy which was forced to dismantle and decommission much of its fleet after the final dissolution of the USSR.[6]

The Soviet Union's collapse in late 1991 left the world in a unipolar system, where American military power appeared invincible and omnipresent. The global dissolution of Soviet power left all of the world's oceans under the protection of the U.S. navy. In East Asia, the carrier battle groups and submarines of the Pacific Command controlled the international waters from the Sea of Japan to the Straits of Malacca. In the Atlantic, there was no rival to the U.S. navy and its NATO allies from the Falkland islands and Antarctica all the way to the top of the northern hemisphere where Greenland, Iceland, and the Canadian Arctic were also under control of NATO and its dominant partner, the United States. Finally, in the Indian Ocean, the Mediterranean, and the Persian Gulf, there was no opposing naval force of any significance.

In air power, with the drastic decline in Russian air power attendant with the dissolution of the USSR, there was now no serious rival to the United States in either the air or outer space. While the post-Soviet nuclear arsenal deteriorated and was reduced, the U.S. nuclear forces, even with reductions in modernization programs, gained a predominant position against not only the new Russian Republic but the still socialist Peoples Republic of China. U.S. air power included a whole new generation of fighters, bombers, and missile systems with precision guided and stealth technologies that were a generation ahead of other armed forces. Even in land power, the relatively small U.S. Army and Marines were capable of defeating any army in the world without any difficulty. The whole global structure of U.S. military power, air, naval, and land forces, strategic weapons, and electronic intelligence, made the country a truly global power capable of projecting its military might over the entire surface of the world. While this enormous strength was not complete or permanent, as numerous counterinsurgency wars showed, the United States in the last decade of the twentieth and into the first decade of the twenty-first, was a primal force on the planet. The 1995 Annual Defense Review described the scope of U.S. military power in a global context. The missions required for U.S. forces were as follows:

> American leadership in the world has never been more important than it is today. Exerting leadership abroad can make America safer and more prosperous—by deterring aggression, fostering the peaceful resolution of dangerous conflicts, underpinning stable foreign markets, encouraging democracy, and working with others to create a safer world and to resolve global problems. Without active U.S. leadership and engagement abroad, threats will worsen and opportunities will narrow. Without the necessary commitment, the United States will lose influence over events abroad that affect its security and well-being at home. If America chooses not to lead in the post–Cold War world, it will become less secure.

> The imperative for American leadership arises from the nature of international relations on the eve of the 21st century, the unique position of the United States, and the rapid pace of global change. The world today is more complex and integrated than at any time in history. The number of active participants—nation states and, increasingly, nonstarter actors—pursuing their interests and vying for influence continues to increase. In some cases, this competition is proceeding with fewer international constraints than in the bipolar world of the Cold War era. At the same time, the world is becoming increasingly interdependent. International borders are no longer the barriers they once were. While interdependence has many positive features, such as greater prosperity, it also means that events in other parts of the world are increasingly able to affect the United States.

> American security is now increasingly tied to the security and stability of other regions. Imagine, for example, the impact on the U.S. economy of any major disruption in trade as a result of instability in Asia or Europe. One quarter of the U.S. gross domestic product is now tied to either exporting or importing. Potential events that would not have been at the center of America's security concerns in the past—the spread of ethnic conflict in Europe, the breakdown of law and order in the Caribbean, the disruption of trade—could pose real threats to the security and well-being of Americans.[7]

The global primacy of the United States was a given for the Clinton administration, even while it was committed to the reduction of the size of U.S. forces and level of defense spending. Yet, from the point of the mid-1990s, there simply were no rivals or alliance partners of equal stature to the country. The United States was expected to lead, and to structure the post–Cold War world to achieve regional and global goals. Despite the nature of American power, the seeming invincibility of the United States as an economic, military, and political empire, the country still did not have the ability nor did it have the inclination to control the world as either a formal or informal hegemony. The country's influence was immense but so was the world.

Assuming the enormity and complexity of that world community, the idea of empire in the classical sense did not seem possible. There were over six billion human beings, populating six continents over 150 million square kilometers of land surface and oceans that were three times that size. In think tanks and policy institutes and university social science departments, the ideas of global planning were a subject of both academic and policy interest. Nonetheless, with the ongoing expansion of human knowledge and capabilities, there was a commensurate understanding that political control of the world was permanently elusive. American power and global control had to be concerned with the broad structures of the international system. Even so, globalism in the form of Clinton's innovative trade policies and international agreements on a host of strategic, economic, and political issues, were always a product of intense negotiations and often fragile compromises. American power was enormous, but understood, implicitly to be tenuous.[8]

The country's vision for world affairs remained messianic, but it was a divine mission that was tempered by material interests. Doctrinally, the United States remained committed to a just Wilsonian world, but the national culture was more in tune with consumerism and commercial popular culture, than with the achievement of long-term international goals. There were limits to all areas of U.S. power if only because of the structure of the American state. William Jefferson Clinton was not a dictator nor was he a Roman emperor. As with all presidents before and since, his executive powers were limited by the legislative and judicial branches of government and by the general forces of civil society. Despite apparent global dominance, the Clinton presidency approached international crises more reactively than proactively. Clinton dealt with crises, Somalia and Rwanda in Africa, Haiti in the Caribbean, Israel-Palestine and Iraq in the Middle East, India-Pakistan in South Asia, and Bosnia and Kosovo in Southeastern Europe. He showed skill in most of them, but his solutions came late, or were ineffectual or never implemented. For Clinton, there were too many crises, and too few resources to devote to them. Clinton, followed a presidential script that made him a skillful negotiator in both international and domestic politics, but it was a narrative that allowed for very little greatness or uniqueness. His moment was not that of Woodrow Wilson or Franklin Roosevelt, or Harry Truman who shaped the structure of the twentieth century. Rather, Clinton's role was to balance himself and the American state, as the world continued on its path of very rapid economic and political modernization.[9]

For the two Gulf Wars, the Clinton presidency was a period of containment and waiting, as the asymmetric force known as al Qaeda grew around the world, a cancer nearly undetected as far as great power politics was concerned. Clinton inherited what appeared to be an amorphous international system, plagued with many problems but without the framework of the Cold War's bipolar system, it appeared to be a threat environment without substance. His reputation was one of personal brilliance and deep political skills, but he had no foreign policy experience at all. This was not unusual; many presidents, including esteemed predecessors Woodrow Wilson and Harry Truman lacked genuine experience in foreign relations. In fact, very few presidents in modern American history had prior experience for managing the extraordinary complexity of U.S. foreign relations. Perhaps the George H. Bush, the man Clinton defeated was an exception. He had built a nearly perfect coalition to fight the First Gulf War, and with his able cabinet and advisers had orchestrated both a stunning victory and a successful termination of the conflict.

To be successful in foreign policy, a president must have an extraordinary set of skills. He must be able to hire and rely on advice of a highly skilled cabinet and executive staff that in turn is responsible for three interrelated systems: (1) a massive bureaucratic apparatus of the U.S. government including all three branches of government; (2) a domestic political system with all its attendant relationships with the federal state; and (3) an international system as it relates to the interlocking institutional systems of the U.S. government and society. Within and between these three systems or spheres, there are thousands of actors who are important and need to be managed, visualized, and accommodated in a president's cognitive roadmap of the world.

Clinton inherited George Bush's post–Cold War world, where global conflict between major powers appeared to have receded to the point of disappearance, but where regional conflicts abounded. With the apparent decline and near disappearance of global warfare, the young president who was most familiar with Arkansas government, assumed the machinery of the post–Cold War national security state. It was an institutional system of enormous assets and strategic responsibilities, which now required careful restructuring and downsizing, for whatever Clinton was compelled to do, as were all his predecessors since Woodrow Wilson. His mandate of office, was to maintain the international system, to support the health of the world's economy, preserve world peace and shape global society and culture toward the Wilsonian ideal of a global community of democratic nation-states. To do that he needed to lead the international system attempting to restructure itself in the wake of the death of the Soviet Union and the internecine conflicts in Africa, Asia, the Americas, and southeastern Europe. Nonetheless, for the most part, Clinton's contemporaries in the foreign policy community viewed his humanitarian interventions as ineffectual, and his negotiations with adversarial powers as timid and equally ineffective.[10]

In fact, he was more assertive than his contemporary critics suggested. Clinton was aggressive in his containment of Iraq, which included a near war over Hussein's noncompliance with UN mandated weapons inspections. His policies in the Balkans included the Kosovo war which threatened a military crisis with Russia. By the end of his presidency, his foreign policy was more coherent and muscular if not virile enough for the neoconservative wing of the Republican Party. In the end, if only by his penchant for indecision, Clinton avoided large-scale foreign interventions and before he left the world stage, he received a standing ovation from the United Nations.[11]

In addition to a complex international system that seemed to be bleeding with internecine conflicts, Clinton's presidency also involved a rapid transformation in military doctrines and technologies that would critically reflect on future military conflicts. By the end of his presidency in January 2001, the country had undergone a less noticed but seminal transformation in its military affairs. A peacetime military establishment, adjusting to the apparent end of great power conflict and the nuclear confrontation with the Soviet Union, came of age in the new information age of transformational warfare and global terrorism. The enormous speed of technological change, framed by the revolution in the speed of information processing and distribution, was creating a new reality for military affairs and international relations.[12]

STRATEGIC ISSUES AND PLANNING

For decades, since the 1940s and Second World War, the institutional script for American national security had responded to transformative events and processes. The 1990s were no different from earlier decades when political, economic, social, and technological processes forced structural changes in national security policy. In broad terms, the end of the bipolar system and the rapid rise of transnational terrorism left the United States in a strategic environment that was self-perceived as quite vulnerable. A range of international crises faced the Clinton administration, forcing an erstwhile domestic president to focus on an inherently unstable international system.

European issues, including the reconstruction of post-Soviet Eastern Europe and the vast realm of the former Soviet Union itself, required Clinton's attention. In the Balkans, the Yugoslav civil war, which involved several small but very dangerous conflicts involving Yugoslav Muslims, Catholics, and Orthodox Christians threatened a post–Cold War conflict between the Russians and the West. Other conflicts, in Africa, South Asia, and East Asia as well as the Middle East threatened regional wars, with some potentially becoming nuclear. Looking around the world the early and mid-1990s, one observes that, besides the containment of Iraq in the Persian Gulf, a huge array of problems, political, economic, and strategic, threatened the stability of the international system.

In global terms, the Clinton White House had to consider the critical questions of world development, the sustainability of the world's economy and ecology and the evolution of political systems in 200 nation-states that would support the survival of six billion human beings.

From the perspectives of their neoconservative critics, the Clintonians were negligent if not incompetent in world affairs. They reduced the force structure of the armed forces to save money for domestic programs just as the world was becoming more not less dangerous. The Republican government in exile, which included a range of former Bush and Reagan administration officials including Richard Perle, Paul Wolfowitz, Dick Cheney, and many others, saw nothing but chaos in Clinton's foreign and military policy. The decline of the U.S. army forces in force readiness, modernization, and total number of combat troops, ships, and planes was a disaster. The country under the leadership of Bill Clinton and his small group of dovish and mediocre advisers were ignoring the responsibilities of a great power, in fact, the "sole remaining superpower" on earth.[13]

This analysis, which informed several contemporary book length critiques of Clinton's foreign policy, was partially correct. Clinton's interventions in Haiti and Somalia were ultimately ineffectual. Both countries remained failed states despite the interdiction of American arms. In Rwanda, the United States responded far too late to prevent one of the worst cases of genocide since the Second World War. In the Balkans, U.S. intervention was successful in Bosnia, but only after Serb nationalists had committed years of atrocities on Bosnian Muslims and Croatians. China, North Korea, the former Soviet Union, and Iraq all tested the strategic and diplomatic skills of the Clinton administration, and the government in exile at the American Enterprise Institute, the Hoover Institution, and the Heritage Foundation found deep flaws in doctrine and execution. Finally, in response to the emergent threat of terrorism, neoconservatives and traditional conservatives were appalled at Clinton's ineptitude. Faced with bin Laden's naked act of terrorism against U.S. embassies in Kenya and Tanzania, he did nothing but launch ineffective surgical strikes on his base camps in Afghanistan and a suspected chemical arms factory in the Sudan.[14]

IRAQI CONTAINMENT AND LIBERATION

Clinton and his advisers perceived Iraq no different from any other administration. Hussein was seen as a serious danger to the international community fully capable of subverting UN controls on his stalled WMD programs. His obstinacy in the face of the will of the international community, and his horrific human rights violations, which ranged from medieval torture of suspected dissidents to the recent genocides against Kurdish and Shiite populations, left Clinton and his administration with a singular view of his evil. In eight years, they enforced a strict sanctions regime against Iraq, including a UN embargo,

mandatory weapons inspections, and military exclusion zones that directly compromised Iraqi sovereignty. The scope of these programs humiliated and impoverished the Iraqi regime, which remained defiant in the face of international and
U.S. controls. On two occasions, Clinton used air power to punish Hussein,
once for the attempted assassination of George H. Bush when visiting Kuwait,
and a second time in the face of Hussein's rejection of UN weapons inspections.
For the entire length of his presidency, Clinton continued in essence the Iraq policy of his predecessor. Like George H. Bush, he strictly enforced containment
while supporting covertly and then openly the "liberation" of Iraq through the
encouragement and financing of opposition forces both inside and outside the
country. These policies, containment and liberation were supported widely by
public and private parties in the United States. Opposition in the domestic
sphere came from neoconservatives, who urged liberation over containment.
The neoconservatives, or "neocons," were a strident voice in the wilderness in
the 1990s. They supported a revival of interventionist internationalism characteristic of U.S. foreign policy in the first decades of the Cold War and America's
pre–First World War role in Latin America. "America was endangered," or so
leading conservative intellectuals argued as the Clinton presidency came to a
close. Saddam Hussein, from their perspective had to be removed through war
if necessary. Richard Perle, a leading conservative voice on the issue of Iraq stated
the movement's position succinctly:

> If we do not develop a strategy for removing Saddam now, we may be unable to do
> so later. Once he is in possession of sophisticated weapons of mass destruction, our
> options will have narrowed considerably. It is clear that the dangers his regime poses
> cannot be eliminated as long as our objective is simply "containment" and the
> means of achieving it are limited to sanctions and exhortations.[15]

Despite the aggressive push of national security conservatives with Clausewitzian
perspectives on the international system, Clinton remained wedded to the more
moderate strategy he inherited from the first Bush administration. The global
and domestic contexts of Clinton's presidency left him with a dual strategy to
deal with Saddam Hussein. Bush had defeated Hussein with a massive expeditionary force and an air assault that was unmatched in its intensity since the Second World War. After the victory, Bush's policy had remained strictly a policy of
containment, with the hope that over time the Iraqis would rid themselves of the
Ba'athist regime. While it is true that Clinton signed the "Iraq Liberation Act" of
1998, the substantive effect of that legislation was minor. Clearly, the United
States hoped to help Iraqi dissidents both inside and outside the country to challenge and overthrow the Ba'athist regime, but the amount of aid that the Clinton
administration provided could hardly have achieved regime change even if it had
been continued for many years. While he feared Hussein as a genuine threat to

international security, Clinton had no new ideas or initiatives for Hussein, other than to continue to the containment policy that had established no-fly zones in the southernmost region of Iraq inhabited by the Shiites, and the northernmost region of the Iraqi Kurds. Clinton enforced the zones, as well as the UN embargo and nuclear inspections regime. Bill Clinton was not the same person as his predecessor, but his policy predilections vis-à-vis Iraq, and indeed for most of the world, were hardly different. Both Clinton and the elder President Bush subscribed to the mixture of political realism and Wilsonian idealism that had characterized U.S. foreign relations since the First World War.

UN SANCTIONS

To punish Hussein for his invasion of Kuwait and its attendant destruction and to force his compliance with UN disarmament treaty specifications for Iraq, the United Nations imposed heavy economic penalties on Iraq. Despite his oil wealth, the Iraqi leader could only sell a small fraction of his prewar production capacity and only to purchase food and medicine for his suffering population. The sanctions pauperized Iraq, although Hussein and his leadership were not prone to suffer. Siphoning off whatever they could from the Oil-for-food program, or with money made from smuggling oil through Iran, the Ba'athist elite continued to live in luxury. Despite the sanctions, Hussein continued his defiance of the United States and its allies. UN inspections, designed to ensure that Iraq remained free of WMD and free of the capability to produce them were also subjected to Hussein's disdain and obfuscation.[16]

THE INSPECTIONS REGIME

The UN inspections regime was firmly in place when Clinton took office in January 1993. For the next eight years, UN inspectors tasked with the very complex job of accounting for and supervising the destruction of Iraq's arsenals of prohibited weapons and delivery systems were subject to various levels of deception, noncompliance, and intimidation by Iraq. The size of Iraq's pre–1991 arsenals of chemical and biological weapons, and materials were daunting. Its nuclear program was also very advanced toward the building a small arsenal of fission-type weapons, and involved scores of sites and thousands of scientists and engineers. Hussein and his Ba'athist leadership found the stipulations of the UN inspections regime to be a deep humiliation and affront to Iraq as a nation. They cooperated, only because the full might of the U.S. armed forces imposed the regime upon them.

The cooperation by Iraq with the United Nations was forced but in the end effective. A Congressional research report issued in September 1998 reported that UNSCOM had destroyed almost 40,000 chemical weapons, 690 tons (i.e., 480,000 liters) of chemical warfare agents, and 3,000 tons, or 1,800,000 liters, of chemical precursor agents. Since 1991, and the beginning of the inspections regime, the inspectors had also documented and destroyed 819 Russian-made SCUD missiles, and a small number of missile launchers and chemical warfare warheads. With respect to biological warfare, Iraq had acknowledged production prior to 1991 of nearly 4 tons of nerve gas, 19,000 liters of botulinum toxin, 8,400 liters of anthrax and 2,200 liters aflatoxin.[17] The lethality of anthrax in particular was deeply worrying to UN inspectors and to the international community. The Office of Technology Assessment had determined in a 1993 study that 200 kilograms of anthrax spores dispersed over a large metropolitan city by an air burst ballistic missile would result in fatalities in the range of 130,000 to 3,000,000 depending upon atmospheric conditions.[18] Clearly, if Iraq had the delivery systems, they had the capability of producing enough anthrax to duplicate the fatalities produced by an equivalent number of nuclear missiles in an attack on large cities.

REGIONAL DYNAMICS

The Clinton era observed a post–Gulf War Middle East, North Africa, and Southwest Asia that had changed little from the late Cold War. The Islamic world remained a simmering cauldron of sectarian and ethnic violence, with internal and international warfare either going on or very close to the surface. From the Maghreb and the brutal civil war in Algeria to the militant dictatorship of Mummar Kaddafi in Libya, the authoritarian regime of Hosni Mubarak in Egypt, the ugly Arab versus Christian civil war in Sudan, and all the sundry dictatorships of the Arabian peninsula—all of these intermixed with terrorist organizations and liberation movements. Arabs fought Israelis, Arabs fought Arabs, Arabs fought Americans, Arabs confronted Persians, Kurds fought Arabs and Turks, Turks confronted Arabs, Persians confronted Israelis, Arabs, Americans and British, Sunnis fought Shiites, liberals fought Islamists, and despotic regimes fought their peoples and each other. In this dense world of confrontation and war, the Clinton administration had several distinct goals.

KURDS AND SHIITES

Within the complex tribal and ethnocultural matrix of the Iraqi state, the Kurds and Shiites required protection from Saddam Hussein. Both had rebelled violently against Hussein, the Kurds repeatedly in the 1970s and 1980s, and the Shiites along with the Kurds in the post–Gulf War uprising of March 1991. In all cases, the Ba'athist republic maintained control through overwhelming and indiscriminate force against civilian populations. Hussein's loyal subordinates carried out acts of genocide against both Iraqi Kurds and Shiites. In the aftermath of the Gulf War, only the determined use of force prevented Hussein from continued atrocities.

The Clinton administration accepted its mandate from the first Bush administration and the international community to protect the northern and southern zones of Iraq, where Hussein was prohibited from using his air force to destroy his domestic enemies. In the Kurdish north, the protected enclave established by Bush remained in place. The Iraqi armed forces in their entirety were excluded, forced to cede autonomy to the Kurds, allowing them to establish a U.S.-protected de facto state in the small enclave that straddled Turkey, Syria, and Iran. Clinton had to protect these groups and wanted to, compelled by domestic and world opinion and his own conscience. Nonetheless, his administration could do little to manage the internecine violence that continued in the transnational region of Kurdistan, where various factions waged war against national authorities in Turkey, Syria, Iran, as well as Iraq. [19]

The existence of widespread and determined Shia and Kurdish opposition together, three-fourths of Iraq's population, suggested the fragility of the Ba'athist dictatorship. Only the most ruthless and militarized regime could maintain power with most of its territory and population militantly opposed to its existence. In the 1990s, Hussein could count his enemies all around him. He had Sunni Arabs in his own country and in the Gulf states who wished his destruction, along with Kurds and Arab Shiites and the Iranians who had fought against him for 10 years. The Israelis, the Americans, the British, and many others in the world community supported his removal, although not by the use of foreign armies.

ISRAEL AND PALESTINE

The lodestone of Middle East policy was the Israeli-Palestinian conflict. With Iraq contained under the UN sanctions regime and no fly zones, the focus of Clinton's policy in the region had to do with solving the interminable war between Israelis and their Arab neighbors. During the 1990s, efforts to end the conflict had appeared to have made significant progress during Clinton's first term, with the signing of the Oslo Accords and the desire of the Israeli Prime Minister, Yitzhak Rabin to move toward a resolution of the conflict. Yet, as happened before and since, the appearance of progress was an illusion. No matter the intensity of Clinton's commitment to a diplomatic solution, the conflict system that tied the Israelis to the Palestinians and to the larger Arab and Muslim world remained in place. The currents in both Israeli and Arab societies were very powerful, very complex, and ultimately immune from the international consensus that demanded an end to the war.

Iraq's relation to the Israeli-Palestinian issue was secondary. Hussein was an active supporter of Palestinian groups who fought the Israeli occupation. His antipathy toward Israel, rooted in a lifetime of hatred toward Jews and Zionism, was made reciprocal by Israel and the worldwide Jewish community who viewed him as a demonic threat to Israel's existence. For its part, Israel maintained limited covert assistance to Kurdish groups in the north, themselves survivors of Hussein's genocidal campaigns in the 1980s.

Strategically, the Israelis were a military threat to Iraq both before and after the First Gulf War. On a global level, the threat was magnified by the influence of American Jews on U.S. foreign policy, whose animosity toward Hussein's anti-Semitism resulted in a long-term campaign by American Jewish intellectuals, most often referred to as "neoconservatives." For Jews who strongly identified with Israel and Zionism, Hussein's overt and covert support for Palestinian factions intent on committing terrorist acts against Israeli civilians, and his perennial threat to develop a nuclear weapon to confront Israel with, made him their mortal enemy. In time, this collective narrative involving Jews and Ba'athists would come to an end after September 11. Then a confluence of anti-Ba'athist forces, including Israelis, American Jews, Kurds, and other Iraqi opposition groups would converge on a Washington establishment ready to finish the war that had begun in August 1990.[20]

IRAN

Clinton's policy toward Iran was little changed from his predecessors. The Islamic Republic of Iran was openly hostile and suspicious toward the Clinton administration as it was toward all previous governments since the 1979 revolution. Essentially, Clinton's strategy was also containment, in effect, creating a dual containment for two perceived threats, the Ba'athist regime in Iraq and the Shiite state in Iran. Like Iraq, Iran's national government was a unique form of autocracy. The Iranians were absolute in their rejection of the West, seeing the secular cultures outside of the Middle East as inherently threatening to the reconstitution of an Islamic society in Iran. From the perspective of the ruling clerics, the United States remained the "Great Satan," the source of secular and Zionist inspired subversion. At the same time, they were also viewed the Arab Gulf states including Iraq as their enemies. Indeed, the Clinton presidency was just five years after the end of the Iran-Iraq conflict, a devastating war for Iran that was fought by Iraq but bankrolled by Iraq's Sunni Arab allies, Saudi Arabia, Kuwait, and the UAE.

For Clinton, Iran remained a black hole in the treacherous landscape of the Middle East and Southwestern Asia. The country bordered Iraq, but could not be enlisted as an ally against their mutual enemy. Iran also had boundaries with Afghanistan, Pakistan, and to the north the newly independent and strategically important republics of Central Asia. There was much opportunity and danger in the territorial nexus surrounding Iran, but for the Clinton administration, there were twin problems of limited resources and divergent problems and conflicts all over the world to devote too much energy to a hostile but ultimately weak and impoverished nation that Iran was in the 1990s.[21]

THE ARAB GULF

If Iraq were to be contained and if possible liberated, and Iran also contained as its revolution stewed with discontent, the Arab Gulf states were of diametric status. The Gulf War had been fought for them. The United States rescued Kuwait and Saudi Arabia and the former Trucial States because of their quintessential importance to the world's economy. A threat to the flow of the oil from the Gulf, as discussed in earlier chapters, meant a danger to the entire economic system of the world, the potential collapse of major industrial economies, and the political stability of the international system. The centrality of this interest to the United States and to virtually all U.S. allies made the continued military presence of the country's combat forces a given, not just for Clinton but for any occupant of the White House.

Toward this end, relations with all the Gulf states were close and very important. The issue that continued to divide the rich and conservative Arab Gulf from the United States was not Iraq, which all agreed had to be contained. Rather, the source of tension in the relationship related to the Israel-Palestine conflict, a policy space that consumed more of Clinton's time and energy than any other in the Middle East. Quite sensibly, Clinton understood the critical necessity for solving the conflict once and for all. Without a settlement of the long-standing war between Palestinians and Israelis, U.S. vital interests everywhere in the region, including the Persian Gulf, were to be compromised.

With Iran on the one hand, a contained but inherent threat toward the Arab Gulf, and Iraq on the other hand, a smoldering enemy albeit trapped by international sanctions, the Saudis, Kuwaitis, and smaller emirates could count on the stable and firm policies of the Clinton White House against these threats. The other threat, however, metastasized during the 1990s. It was created and spread through the decade, a transnational terror movement that would have an historic impact in the first years of Clinton's successor, George W. Bush, Jr.

RISE OF AL QAEDA

Perhaps the most significant political event of the Clinton years went largely unnoticed until the late 1990s. In the aftermath of the Gulf War, Osama bin Laden began to organize his jihad against the West and the Saudi monarchy. He had cut his teeth in the Afghan War, learning the elements of insurgent warfare with the help of the Pakistani intelligence service (ISI) and its sponsor the CIA. Bin Laden's emergence as a major terrorist threat became apparent with his attacks on the U.S. embassies in Kenya and Tanzania and the daring attack by a suicide bomber against the U.S. navy combat ship the USS *Cole*. The cumulative effect of large scale terrorist attacks on U.S. interests, beginning with the bombing of the World Trade Center in 1993, raised public discourse on the threat of terrorism to national security and led directly to the establishment of a national commission to evaluate the nature of U.S. national security in the "information age."

Bin Laden declared war on the West during the Clinton administration issuing a fatwa against the Jews, the United States, and the "Crusaders" of Western Europe, all enemies of the Islamic world. In the eyes of bin Laden and his movement of Islamic fundamentalists, these groups individually and collectively were responsible for the corruption and degeneracy visited upon Islam. They were responsible for the destruction of the last Caliphate, a religious ruler for all of Middle East, which occurred with the dissolution of the Ottoman Empire and imposition of League of Nation mandates throughout the Arabian Peninsula, the holy land of the faith. The Western powers had imposed Israel upon them, resulting in the loss of Jerusalem and the humiliation of the Palestinians, Arabs, and Muslims throughout the world. The destruction of Iraq during the First Gulf War and the introduction of Western forces into Gulf on a permanent basis continued the assault on Islam and the Muslim "ulama." Al Qaeda's leadership came from the professional classes of the Middle East, backgrounds consistent with those of all modern revolutionary movements. Their ideological and strategic objectives centered on the destabilization and overthrow of the Muslim regimes that had compromised with the West and had brought Western values and culture into the center of the Islamic world. For bin Laden, the Saudi royal family was as deserving of destruction as the Jews who had occupied Palestine. The overthrow of the Saudi monarchy and its replacement with a regime loyal to the extremist ideology of al Qaeda was a central objective for the group. The eviction of the U.S. military presence from the Gulf was central to the long-term plan to transform the region and ultimately the entire ulama from Morocco to India and beyond. To accomplish this, they were willing to commit the most ruthless and destructive acts of terrorism.

By the mid-1990s, al Qaeda under bin Laden and his close lieutenants were at war against the enemies of Islam. A global network of terror cells were organized, thousands of supporters coalesced around the clandestine objectives of waging war against the West, Zionism and the pro-Western monarchies and secular regimes of the Islamic world. Yet, most of this activity was only known to government intelligence services. The political discourse on foreign affairs in the United States mentioned terrorism only tangentially. In the memoirs of leading Clinton administration cabinet officials, respective Secretaries of State Warren Christopher and Madeline Albright, the threat of global terrorism was only briefly mentioned. To these leading actors in U.S. foreign policy, the challenges of reorganizing the international system and preserving the mainly peaceful transition of post-Soviet Europe were of more importance than transnational terrorism. The containment of Iraq, Iran, North Korea, and the former Yugoslavia took precedence over containing al Qaeda.[22]

HART RUDMAN REPORT ON HOMELAND SECURITY

A major intellectual achievement of the Clinton administration was a nine-volume study of the country's national security system. The U.S. Commission on National Security for the twenty-first century was an effort inspired by the emergence of international terrorism as a major threat in the 1990s. Congressional hearings in 1997 led to a bipartisan consensus that a commission needed to be appointed to review every aspect of U.S. national security policy as a first step in the modernization of the post–Cold War executive and legislative branches of government. The commission held its first meeting in October 1998 and issued its third and most comprehensive report to Congress in April 2001, just five months before the fateful attacks of September 11.[23]

After the September 11 disaster, the commission, also known as the Hart-Rudman Commission, was viewed as prophetic in its assessment of the sorry state of U.S. domestic security and the central threat that Middle Eastern terrorism presented to American society. A careful reading of the commission's documents illustrate not only the "institutional decay" that the group found in U.S. foreign policy institutions, but also the cognitive map that the writers had of the American state, its architecture, its strengths and weaknesses and transformations that were occurring in a world driven by accelerating technological innovation.

Dramatic and revolutionary technological change characterized the post–Cold War world, according to the commission's reports. The integration of scientific discovery with technological innovation was generating geometric progress in the fields of information technology, nanotechnology, biotechnology, and related disciplines. The commission noted that in the 18 months between the issuing of the initial "phase one" report and the final "phase three" monograph, critical breakthroughs had been achieved. In just that space of time, the Human Genome Project was completed, and a prototype of a quantum computer chip was developed. Scientific and technological revolution appeared to be an omnipresent and vital element of global society as it entered the twenty-first century. This transmogrification had enormous promise for humankind, but it also presented the dangers of misuse and a technological dystopia for the world if the huge forces of change were not managed effectively.[24]

In the context of radical global technological change, the commission reports conceived of the post–Cold War world as an "American moment." This meant that for the present and perhaps the next two decades, the international system would be characterized as unipolar, with the United States as the predominant power in all aspects of international relations. In this one power world, the exponential change propelled by the information technology of the end of the twentieth century suggested that all assumptions regarding the use of force, global change, and development and the future of the international system were indeterminate.

THE CALM BEFORE THE STORM

The Clinton era was indeed, as neoconservative critics have long pointed out, focused more on the domestic issues confronting the country, including the seamier in hindsight deeply irrelevant issues of the Monica Lewinsky scandal. The state of world affairs were not ignored, but they were simply understood from a different ideological perspective than that of political opposition. Clinton addressed all the issues in foreign policy but primarily as a neo-Wilsonian. His principal advisers understood the nature of the international system as a post–Cold War liberal international order. The objectives of the Democrats were toward the creation of a stable, peaceful global order that promoted free trade, sustainable economic development, and the adjudication of international conflicts. They hoped to continue the successful transition of the Russian Republic toward a normal postcommunist nation-state that would no longer be a strategic threat to the United States or to Europe. In China, the same structural processes of trade and cultural diffusion it was hoped, would continue, bringing the world's most populous nation to the same state of progressive liberalization as the world's largest country, Russia. In the Americas, free trade and democracy, it was hoped would continue the same processes of modernization that were supporting positive change in Russia and China. In other parts of the Third World, the same hope existed for globalization and democratic liberalization fostered by the world community. In postcommunist Europe, the hope was that an expanding and modernizing NATO and European Union would contain the dangerous conflict in the Balkans with the assistance of the United States as a NATO power and UN Security Council member.[25]

In the Middle East, the Palestinian-Israeli conflict and the containment of Iraq loomed large, as did the containment of Iranian and Sunni extremists determined on destabilizing the region. In this regard, Clinton was hardly different from either his immediate predecessor or successor. All three presidents were intent upon using U.S. military power to stabilize the Persian Gulf, as well as to deploy U.S. political assets to attempt the resolution of pressing national and sectarian conflicts within the region.[26]

Clinton's presidency ended in January 2001, some seven months before September 11 and some 26 months before the invasion of Iraq. As a foreign policy leader, his predilections were always neo-Wilsonian. His ideological affinity for the liberal wing of the Democratic Party oriented his administration's emphasis on diplomatic actions. Over eight years, he proved a definite proclivity for an incremental approach to the use of force. He was reluctant to use force in the Balkans, in Somalia, in the Arabian peninsula, and finally, in reprisals against the emergent threat to the United States, Osama bin Laden's base of operations in Afghanistan. When his successor entered office, George W. Bush was more hawkish on the use of force, especially vis-à-vis Iraq, but on most other issues, his administration demonstrated as much continuity as change in America's role in the world.

The Third Act: George W. Bush and the Gulf

We are not imperialists. We do not want any more territory. We do not want to conquer any people, or to dominate them. The Russian propaganda says that we are imperialists and want to conquer the world. That just isn't true. We know the Soviet Government is a menace to us and to all the free world. That is why we are building up our strength, not to march against them but to discourage them from marching against us and the free world.

We want to help the people in other countries to help themselves, because that makes for prosperity for us all. I want you young people to understand that if we accomplish the purpose which we propose to accomplish, it means the greatest age in the history of the world—you will live in the grandest and most peaceful time that the world has ever seen.

Harry Truman[1]

A QUESTION OF TIME

In historical analysis, the concept of agency has always been open to interpretation and often vigorous debate. Most often this has been true in recent political history, where the issues of cause and effect and moral responsibility have a weight that skews any form of dispassionate analysis. It is hard, indeed impossible, to view the actions of Adolf Hitler or Pol Pot with dispassion or an analytical skepticism when the moral claims against these actors were and are so great. No historian of the last half century or of the present can write of the Holocaust or the Cambodian genocide without taking sides—condemning these events as they were. While these are extreme examples, the same may be true in evaluating any historical actor whose actions elicited very powerful emotions among contemporary observers. To a large degree, evaluating an American president and his administration remains a distinctly political act. This is most common when the feel of events forces historians and political scientists to view the present or very recent past through the distinct moral lenses of a political ideology.[2]

Despite this observational burden, one area of science offers some insight into dilemmas that historians deal with in discussing very contemporary events. Consider the following line of argument. Recent thinking in theoretical physics has proposed traveling through space-time to the past may be possible given the technical means. Extremely powerful propulsion systems may allow future astronauts to leave the present and to physically transport to an earlier point in space-time where they would not only be able to observe the past but they actually would be there. While a future time traveler might transport himself to the actual space-time of the Middle Ages, the laws of physics suggest that even by being there the course of history could not be changed. Although it sounds counterintuitive, the laws of quantum physics cannot allow the past to alter future events. Past events, from the birth and death of individuals to the fate of wars and the discovery of knowledge, are all unalterable because they have already occurred and will not occur again. Only the future, a product of the infinite actions of near-infinite agencies, is subject to forms of agency. In some sense, the indeterminacy of the future provides areas of autonomy or at least indeterminacy in human events involving contemporary actors.[3]

From an historian's perspective, the past indeed must be determined. Napoleon lost the Battle of Waterloo, and no manner of historical interpretation can change the material facts of his loss and the implications it had for the future of the European state system. Likewise, the invention of the telegraph, typewriter, and Bessemer steel process, the discovery of oil in the Middle East, and other seminal events and processes cannot be changed in any historical narrative. As far as the future is concerned, the only future condition in history is the anticipation of future events by historical actors. If actors in the present have free will, this would be because the future has not occurred and can in some ways be determined through their agency. Global warming, an issue of present urgency, may be responsive to or determinable by actors, individuals, groups, or institutions, active in the early twenty-first century, which move to alter the future of global climate change through proactive methods in the present age.

Yet, the agency of contemporary actors says nothing about the agency of historical actors. In fact, no historical actor has agency, whether the actor's time and place is last year, last month, or even last week, or a hundred years ago or thousand or many thousands of years in the past. The same rules of historical determinacy apply to Julius Caesar, to Genghis Khan, James Madison, Abraham Lincoln, Sigmund Freud, Albert Einstein, Enrico Fermi, and indeed modern U.S. presidents, including George W. Bush, Jr. No matter the immediacy of historical time, the actors observed through documents, audiovisual recordings, and other primary sources of information were not in control of their actions or destinies.

As historical actors, their destinies in historical time were and will always be determined.[4]

Contemporary political history has not been kind to George W. Bush. At the end of his presidency, the two wars that his administration initiated continued and one of them, the Second Gulf or the "Iraq War" looked to have been the worst foreign policy decision since the War of 1812. The second war against the regime of Saddam Hussein has been viewed as a military response that arose out of the particular circumstances of the Bush presidency as it entered office in January 2001. With September 11 as a catalyst, and the Gulf War as its foundation, the Iraq War of 2003 has been attributed to the personality and leadership circle of George W. Bush. According to critical contemporary narratives, it was George Bush and his coterie of experienced Washington advisers, including one group that earned the metaphoric name "Vulcans," who were directly responsible for the war whose aftermath had engulfed Bush's presidency and inflamed passions around the world.[5] The mechanics for launching the war and the intellectual foundation for it were indeed a central part of George W. Bush's presidency. It was his decision and his alone to launch the "Iraq War," just as it was his father's to execute the first war against Saddam Hussein in 1991. Vietnam was also Johnson's war, and Harry Truman was responsible for the Korean conflict and its attendant consequences for the future of U.S. national security policy. The office of the President of the United States has formidable power to shape the direction of the United States and the course of world affairs.[6] Having said this, I need to argue, just as I have throughout this monograph that George Bush Jr. and his White House staff were not autonomous agents with respect to the Iraq War nor were any of the actors involved autonomous as understood by historians. With autonomy comes responsibility and free will. As much as Westerners desire to believe in personal responsibility and the inherent right of free will, it is not at all clear to me that individuals were or are free and autonomous actors at any level of human interaction.

The Bush administration went to war in Iraq because Saddam Hussein had defied three presidential administrations. Despite his decisive defeat in the First Gulf War against the United States and the coalition organized under the United Nations, Hussein refused to cooperate fully with the victors. To do so, no doubt, would be to act in a manner befitting a vassal state. His deliberate lack of cooperation on UN weapons inspections and his continued refusal to stop the genocidal repression of Kurdish tribesmen in his northern provinces and Shiite Arab populations in Southern Iraq made him a perceived threat to the entire Gulf region and hence a menace to the security of the world's oil supply and the stability of all of Southwestern Asia. This broad ideological perspective was understood by the "neocons" who pushed for a new war to remove Hussein as early as the first years of the Clinton administration. There is no doubt the neoconservative group that surrounded the oval office during the first term of the Bush administration was a critical factor in bringing the Second Gulf War into being. However, neoconservative ideology was not the only factor in the invasion. There was a wider consensus of opinion among many conservative strategic thinkers and public officials in the United States and elsewhere that Hussein's horrific regime constituted an intolerable threat to the international system.[7]

The event that catalyzed the neoconservative script, bringing it to brief doctrinal supremacy in the United States, was the enormity of September 11. In world historical terms, it appeared that two powerful and irreconcilable ideologies, the passionate conservative internationalism of the neoconservative group in the United States and the intense collective script of the radical Islamists under Osama bin Laden, collided with each other. This was a huge collision premised on the larger metascripts that defined Western and Middle Eastern civilizations. The two forces, each carrying the narrative imperatives of messianic doctrines encountered each other in the second week of September in the first year of the new millennium. The Islamists had planned the attack long before George Bush and his neoconservative round table had won the presidency. If not for a chance failure in the arcane presidential election process, a ballot failure in one county of one state, another man with another set of advisers would have sat in the presidency on September 11. But for a small accident, Al Gore would have been president on the fateful day that triggered both the Afghan and the Iraq wars. And because of that accident, it will remain unknown if Gore would have gone to war against Hussein in 2003, or at any time, or rather continued the containment doctrine of his would-be predecessor Bill Clinton. Perhaps, the Iraq War like so many other critical historical events was merely an accident; a random event, just as the Kennedy assassination was probably random albeit seminal in the path of modern U.S. history. Perhaps, all political history, while under the ostensible control of very powerful scripts, remains a random process subject to the influence of very small but critical chance events.[8]

The historical collision of radical Islamists and the impetuous "redeemer nation" was not by chance. It was an inevitable cataclysm comparable to massive ocean storms moving toward each other, controlled by atmospheric winds, and ocean currents statistically determined to force their encounter. Just like the Russo-German and the Pacific Wars were inevitable products of the Second World War once the powerful scripts for that conflict were set in motion, so too was the encounter between the United States and radical Islam in the post–Cold War era. Richard Perle and Paul Wolfowitz and Scooter Libby denizens of the neoconservative camp, set the path with their skilled political campaign to create a new Bush foreign policy, centered on the Middle East, and the resurgence of American nationalism in the international system, but the context for the war was also set by Saddam Hussein and his clique of loyal Tikriti Ba'athists, who defied the United States, challenging American power in the Persian Gulf and the Middle East.[9] Finally, the context was also set by al Qaeda, which had already declared war on the United States and the West, determined to inflict extraordinary damage in a messianic quest to restore the ancient glory of Islam and the Arab nation.

The metascript for September 11, in the first years of the Bush administration, after the al Qaeda attacks, worked like a giant magnet, pulling together the United States and its allies into the Middle East. It brought all the actors within the conflict system together. The Iranian clerics contributed their own narrative, as they continued their encounter with both their Sunni and Arab antagonists in the Gulf region and with Israel, its Zionist enemy in the holy land. The Saudis and Kuwaitis and the sheiks of the UAE continued their generational narratives, extracting enormous wealth, and perpetuating the privileged hegemony of their royal families while deep resentments seethed in the backgrounds of their societies and in the larger Arab world. The same resentments and antipathies that had fueled support for Hussein in the first Gulf War remained in the age of al Qaeda. The same families who lived the most lavish lives, protected by the armed might of the United States breathed life into the extremist ideology that produced bin Laden and his followers. In the view of the Arab and Muslim world the same dynamics, that left Israel in control of Jerusalem, and thriving, at the expense of Palestinians, created al Qaeda's script. As the Bush White House established its presence, al Qaeda had already planned its extraordinary terror plot. The Middle East crisscrossed with sectarian and ethnocultural divides had already positioned itself vis-à-vis the United States and the world. Even if the September 11 plot was the bizarre working of a score of security failures, where the chance of weather, a cloudy day, would have altered its outcome, the ideological forces were in play. The encounter between the United States and the West and the Islamic world was set. There was going to be a war of sorts in an encounter that, bin Laden would remind the international media had begun a thousand years before.

Journalists, like soldiers, work at the street level. Looking at events from day-to-day or at most over the course of a year produces a very myopic sense of reality. This is the conundrum of contemporary observers who have vast riches of information around them, a present sense of perceptions held by other participants, but at the same time they must be two-dimensional. At street level, the events of the first years of the twenty-first century look too chaotic to describe. The Bush White House lost in its tragic-comedic role of incompetence, mishandling military, political, and diplomatic strategies with stunning results; destroying the public image of the United States, their actions were feckless in every respect.[10]

Yet, the larger encounter was far above the street. Historical forces were at work driving world history with the rapid change generated by the age of technology and global integration. As the Bush White House carried on its plot, a conflicted story that evoked many past encounters in the world outside of Europe, the global economy expanded at a rate and an order of magnitude faster than in previous centuries. Technology itself continued its exponential trajectory, transforming military power, international communications, and the scientific and technological innovations characteristic of the age. The economic and technological explosion was also connected to new concerns about potential threats from the catastrophic effects of global warming to the equally dire possibilities of international terrorism exploiting the weak points of postmodern societies, using new deadly biological, chemical, or radiation weapons to inflict tremendous damage on major world capitals.[11]

Was the new war a revisiting of the first or second World Wars, as the prominent neoconservative Norman Podhoretz suggested, or was the new encounter which sent the United States and Western forces in to South Asia a return of the nine-teenth century Indian wars in the American narrative, or alternatively, the colonial insurrections in British national memory? In the larger scheme of historical agency, the Bush presidency, like all others, followed a script woven into the larger narra-tive of the nation that it represented. The Bush White House was not an anomaly, an intrusion by an elite cabal. On the contrary, as I have argued throughout this work, its collective behavior was a response to external and internal events was established according to the larger narrative of the United States as a dynamic his-torical actor, a country of enormous power and size that no one group or individ-ual could dominate sui generis. American society in turn found itself embedded in the larger mechanisms that shaped the global narrative in the early twenty-first century. A number of related forces acted upon Bush and his group as they moved toward war in the second year of his administration. The forces in question coa-lesced, pushing Bush's actions toward war, just as Saddam Hussein and his familial-based leadership responded to the United States as an enemy. Hussein's defiance and resistance planned to carry over into the occupation of his country was a cultural response to a familiar kind of adversary. His Quixotic stance against a superpower was constructed by his unique historical and cultural roots as an Iraqi, as a Sunni Arab nationalist, and self-aggrandizing dictator resolute in his beliefs in personal glory. Hussein's place in history is a question of cultural perspec-tive. For the Arab world, as one of his Arab biographers has noted, Hussein was an authentic nationalist irrespective of his savage rule:

> Saddam' role and reputation must be weighed along with the unfulfilled desires of the Iraqi people, and their justified historical belief that they have been denied the right to realize the potential of their land and earn it a place among modern nations. In other words, Saddam as an individual may be unique, even demonic, but he is also a true son of Iraq. Even his use of violence to achieve his aims is not strictly a personal characteristic, but rather an unattractive trait of the Iraqi people reinforced by their history.[12]

For the United States in the Gulf, the first act in the drama was the First Gulf War, where a masterfully built international coalition supported the largest and most powerful air and land invasion since the Second World War. The second act involved the containment regime of William Jefferson Clinton, where a deeply embittered and recalcitrant Hussein was subjected to an intensive array of sanctions and a covert strategy of regime change. The third act in the drama ushered in a second Bush presidency, one that would result in a massive escalation of U.S. involvement in the Gulf region as well as the war that would end the rule of the Ba'athist party in Iraq and ultimately the lives of Saddam Hussein and his sons.

George W. Bush came to the presidency in January 2001, eight years after his father's defeat and ostensibly a restoration of the White House to the Republican party of George H. Bush. Yet, as I have discussed throughout this book, in foreign policy the new administration had turned the corner not only from the Clinton administration but from the Republican White House whose conservative political realism had continuity with the earlier Republican regimes of Ronald Reagan, Gerald Ford, and Richard Nixon. As noted, the distinguishing factor in the new Republican White House was the new neoconservative ideology that came to dominate Republican foreign policy thinking in the 1990s. The neocons brought a new script, a new ideology for U.S. foreign relations that combined an enduring belief in military power with the neo-Wilsonian passion for democratization. The ideas of a strong military establishment and the spread of democracy were not new ideas at all in new American foreign policy discourse. What was unique about the neoconservative synthesis was its use of nationalism and Wilsonian internationalism as twin agents of the foreign policy system. The neoconservative vision for the world prior to 2001 and afterwards required a concept of a powerful and aggressive nation-state projecting its influence including its ever-expanding and improving military resources into the Middle East and indeed all over the world.[13]

In the new Bush foreign policy, Iraq would be confronted and if necessary challenged militarily in ways that Bill Clinton's administration did not have the means or the political will to do so. American power would be enhanced, even transformed through the technological revolutions of the early twenty-first century under the managerial expertise of Donald Rumsfeld, a Secretary of Defense committed to the modernization of the Pentagon into a vastly more responsive and adept military organization. Rumsfeld's expansive concept of American military power was parallel to Vice President Cheney's views. Both of these men, by far the most important of Bush's foreign policy advisers, exemplified the conservative and neoconservative doctrine of the primacy of military deterrence and the projection of military power to protect U.S. interests in the international system. They equally shared the idea of an "imperial presidency," to use Arthur Schlesinger's term from the 1970s. With the extension of U.S. military power came the attendant view of the superiority of the executive branch over the Congress in conducting international affairs.[14]

Irrespective of the rise of neoconservative doctrine, the military orientation toward foreign affairs, a legacy as old as the country was a singular element in the world view of George W. Bush. The nationalist military realist orientation of this conservative White House was entirely consistent with promilitary allegiances and predilections of all Republican administrations. What was new however was the Wilsonian idealism that younger neocons brought to Bush's foreign policy. Many of the neocons who shaped the Bush foreign policy were former liberal democrats. These converts, most often Jewish intellectuals, were younger or at least outside of the most inner circle of the Bush White House. They came to the Republican Party especially during the halcyon days of the Reagan administration, when in the post-Vietnam era promilitary views had been largely expunged from the Democratic Party. Richard Perle and Paul Wolfowitz fit this description as did many others. Wolfowitz illustrated his philosophical roots in a year 2000 essay on American foreign relations. In the body of the essay, he tempered his neo-Wilsonian ideas with the other source of his thinking, pragmatic realism he had acquired as a student and practitioner of national defense policy:

> Thus, while core of American foreign policy is in some sense the universalization of American principles, this is not a Kantian notion which ultimately only the purity of one's intentions counts. Rather, policies must be effective in the world...no U.S. president can justify a policy that fails to achieve its intended results by pointing to the purity and rectitude of his intentions.[15]

The idealism of the Bush White House, its determined faith in universal democratization, was not new or exceptional in American foreign relations. In fact, these beliefs were quintessential to American culture and public diplomacy since the eighteenth century. The ineffectual nature of the policy was also entirely consistent with American history. From Woodrow Wilson to Franklin Roosevelt and John F. Kennedy, American presidents had championed democracy while simultaneously supporting dictators. In still earlier times, Americans and their presidents had celebrated the creation of the Latin American Republics under Simon Bolivar, Greek Independence from the Ottoman Empire in the 1820s, the defeat of Santa Ana at the Battle of San Jacinto in 1836, and the liberation of Cuba from Spain from 1865 to the Spanish-American War of 1898. Traditional American ideology espoused universal liberty and democracy while not always living up to those principles either at home or abroad. So it was with the administration of George W. Bush, who understood that democratization was a long-term moral and strategic interest of the United States, but who, despite intense efforts, had profound failures.[16]

From the day George W. Bush entered the presidency a second war against Saddam Hussein seemed to have been almost predestined. The mandate from the Clinton administration was to contain Iraq through the continuation of the no-fly zones, the extension of the military and economic embargo on Iraq, and the continuation of the weapons inspection regime which was under constant assault from Hussein. The mandate also included the stated aim of regime change established by the passage of the "Iraq Liberation Act" by Congress in December 1998. For several years prior to G. W. Bush, the CIA and the State Department had been authorized to assist Iraqi exile groups in their activities to foment internal dissent against the regime. The intent, in retrospect naïve, was to see if Hussein could be overthrown through domestic insurrection.[17]

Despite the building consensus among not only neoconservatives but traditional conservatives and moderates in Congress and in the wider Washington establishment of foreign policy institutes and academic departments, there remained considerable opposition to a larger land invasion to overthrow the Ba'athists. The facts against Hussein, this merciless dictator, made a policy for his overthrow quite palatable. That Hussein had used chemical weapons against civilian populations, both Iraqi and Iranian, and was guilty in all likelihood of genocide against Iraqi Kurds and Shiites, and was an active threat to the security of Israel, were established and corroborated in great and odious detail.[18]

The Bush policy to eliminate Saddam Hussein and his demonstrably sociopathic regime perpetuated the existing policies of the Clinton administration. However, what differentiated George W. Bush from his father and his immediate predecessor was the policy that eventually led to the invasion and occupation of Iraq by the United States. Such a policy went far beyond Clinton's policy of strategic containment and regime destabilization. When Bush assumed office, he and his advisers did not have the political means to pursue war against Hussein. The catalyst that made all of these things possible was the national trauma of the attacks of September 11, 2001. That event provided the necessary context for a "preventive war" against Hussein. Without the spectacular terrorist attacks that destroyed the World Trade Center towers in lower Manhattan and damaged the Pentagon building in Arlington, Virginia, the war to destroy Saddam Hussein's Iraq would have lost a major catalyst. Perhaps the war would have happened anyway, driven by the neoconservative ideology to "transform" the Middle East. That transformation involved reasserting American power and influence into the Persian Gulf as a bulwark against the anti-American and anti-Western forces that appeared to threaten this most vital region for the world's economy.

2001: PRE–SEPTEMBER 11 STRATEGIC POSTURE

The essential characteristics of the Bush administration's foreign policy have been represented by the concepts of neoconservative foreign policy, whose acolytes were drawn from specific intellectual origins in conservative national security policy circles. In fact, much of what is understood as neoconservative or "neocon" ideology pertains to fundamental principles of liberal technocratic thought in the United States in the late twentieth century. The Hart Rudman report, discussed in the previous chapter, was a product of the last years of the Clinton administration. Its extensive recommendations and worldview were inherited by the Bush administration and because of its recommendations for a Department of Homeland Security it became one of the doctrinal lodestones for early twenty-first century U.S. foreign policy.[19]

Hart Rudman concluded, after several years of intensive staff research and analysis, that U.S. national security in the new century had to be premised on 14 basic assumptions. These were as follows:

a. America will become increasingly vulnerable to hostile attack on our homeland and our military superiority will not entirely protect us;

b. Rapid advances in information and biotechnology will create new vulnerabilities;

c. New technologies will divide the world as well as draw it together;

d. The national security of all advanced states will be increasingly affected by the vulnerabilities of the evolving global economic infrastructure;

e. Energy will continue to have a major strategic significance;

f. All borders will be more porous and some will bend and some will break;

g. The sovereignty of states will come under pressure, but will endure;

h. Fragmentation or failure of states will occur, with destabilizing effects on neighboring states;

i. Foreign crises will be replete with atrocities and the deliberate terrorizing of civilian populations;

j. Space will become a critical and competitive military environment;

k. The essence of war will not change;

l. U.S. intelligence will face more challenging adversaries, and even excellent intelligence will not prevent all surprises;

m. The United States will be called upon frequently to intervene militarily in a time of uncertain alliances and with the prospect of fewer forward deployed forces; and

n. The emerging security environment in the next quarter century will require different military and other national capabilities.[20]

These conclusions, discussed in detail over several thousand pages of analysis and recommendations crystallized the worldview and the strategic thinking of the United States national security establishment as it approached the world transforming events of September 11 and embarked upon the Afghan and Gulf wars that have marked the beginning of the new century. These central conclusions represented the strategic framework for U.S. national security as understood by the bipartisan commission. In effect, their collective representation of the country's threat environment was the operational view of the Bush administration as it came into office in January 2001. The world was according to point (a) an increasingly hostile environment where "military superiority" could not guarantee security. In fact, the bold emergence of al Qaeda in the late 1990s had made U.S. defense analysts very aware of the serious dangers posed by terrorism and "asymmetric warfare." The problem for the United States was that decades of military innovation and institution building in national security affairs had still left the country deeply unprepared for the spectacular and potentially devastating attacks of radical transnational terrorists who had virtually unlimited opportunities to strike modern societies at their most vulnerable points.[21]

Indeed, despite a rapidly growing literature in the late 1990s that promulgated the primacy of U.S. power, which continued after September 11, the Hart Rudman report, a 25-year planning document for the U.S. government, assumed that such primacy was fleeting. In fact, the report assumed the rise of intense competition from East Asia through the year 2025 and beyond as a rival to both North America and Europe as a global center of power, political, economic, and eventually military. Dramatic forces were at work in the world, which made the United States still by far the world's greatest power, vulnerable to both the dangerous asymmetric threats of the underdeveloped world as well as the inevitable relative decline that global modernization promised vis-à-vis the rising powers of Asia and Europe.[22]

There was a strong paradox in the full report, which weighted the enormity of U.S. power against the compendium of threats to it, including such things as America's deficient primary and secondary education systems which threatened the long-term decline of the country as a scientific-technological leader. Technological change, highlighted by a research group that weighed future studies as an important field of public policy research, recognized that the country was part of an historic acceleration in the pace of modernization with profound implications for both the United States and the world. Information technology, which had produced a second industrial revolution of the "information age," was also responsible for a revolution in military technology that was changing the nature of warfare on land, air, sea, and space. Near-earth space itself was now considered a vital area of military concern, just as vital as the new area of international terrorism and asymmetric warfare.

In broad terms, the agenda facing U.S. national security at the start of the new century was as daunting as at anytime in the nation's history. In addition to the terrorist threat, which seemed to be spreading like a virus immune to existing national security protocols, there were a host of threats that needed to be addressed on an urgent basis. WMD, long a deep concern, remained an even greater threat given the uncontrolled proliferation of chemical, biological, and nuclear technology among both state and nonstate actors. The weaponization of biological agents, suspected or presumed to be operational in Iraq despite the inspections regime, was considered a very dangerous threat to U.S. national security prior to September 11, 2001 and prior to the inauguration of George W. Bush.[23]

In addition to the proliferation of WMD and terrorism, the threats of conventional wars remained. The traditional role of a great power, to maintain the balance of forces between other states, continued to be of concern even in a world that seemed in a state of rapid cultural and economic integration. Although the Internet and international trade were booming, international war remained a possibility in most areas of the world. In South Asia, the confrontation between India and Pakistan was sustained and made far more dangerous by the introduction of nuclear arsenals in both countries. The enmity between them grew not only from centuries of sectarian rivalry between Hindus and Muslims, but also by the societal stresses of a grossly overpopulated subcontinent. Extreme poverty and political conflicts combined with nuclear and conventional forces made South Asia deeply worrying. The same was true for East Asia and in Europe, Russia, and the Balkans remained flashpoints for potential international wars.

In such a dangerous world, with emerging and uncontrollable forces bearing upon the security of the nation, the programmatic concerns for U.S. security were sweeping.

> We believe that American strategy must compose a balance between two key aims. The first is to reap the benefits of a more integrated world in order to expand freedom, security, and prosperity for Americans and for others. But second, American strategy must also strive to dampen the forces of global instability so that those benefits can endure and spread.
>
> On the positive side, this means that the United States should pursue, within the limits of what is prudent and realistic, the worldwide expansion of material abundance and the eradication of poverty. It should also promote political pluralism, freedom of thought and speech, and individual liberty. Not only do such aims inhere in American principles, they are practical goals, as well. There are no guarantees against violence and evil in the world. We believe, nonetheless, that the expansion of human rights and basic material well-being constitutes a sturdy bulwark against them. On the negative side, these goals require concerted protection against four related dangers: the proliferation of weapons of mass destruction; international terrorism; major interstate aggression; and the collapse of states into internal violence, with the associated regional destabilization that often accompanies it.[24]

The gist of this statement is purely neo-Wilsonian. It was a statement of purpose that Franklin Roosevelt, John F. Kennedy, Lyndon Johnson, and Jimmy Carter would have felt most comfortable with. However, even the more conservative and nationalist foreign policy ideology of Republican presidents since the beginning of the twentieth century, would have felt comfortable with the traditional redeeming qualities of this statement of major foreign policy principles. What was most unusual about this statement was the Hart Rudman emphasis on international terrorism as one of the major dangers to world peace. In fact, while terrorism was an emerging concern in foreign affairs in countries around the world, its identification as a pillar of global disorder and a global threat was unique. The importance of terrorism in this report was in fact greater than perceived by the outgoing Clinton or viewed in prospect by the incoming Bush administrations. In fact, prior to September 11 neither Republican nor Democratic officials, or public policy analysts considered international terrorism of nearly equal importance as the threats posed by other world powers and rogue nations possessing WMD. All of this changed in a matter of hours.

SEPTEMBER 11 AND AFTERMATH

The day of September 11, 2001, resonates in American and world history as a day of disaster as well as a day of clarity. As a day of disaster (or among the radical Islamists a day of celebration), the spectacular destruction of New York's World Trade Center by high-speed collisions with hijacked commercial airliners was worthy of a major Hollywood release designed to shock a worldwide audience. The critical difference was that the massive explosions, fire, and thunderous collapse of a million tons of concrete and steel were entirely real. The *New York Times* observed that watching the events unfolded on CNN was other worldly. The pictures sent electronically across the world were so horrific and surreal it was impossible to ascertain if the action was part of a Hollywood disaster film or something else, a terrifying assault by an invisible and very dangerous enemy.[25]

This moment in time, a few hours when the world's "sole remaining super-power" fell into a state of aphasia, panic, and trauma, was destined to become a moment of world-historical significance. The clarity of the event came later in the day when the worldwide media had distributed the knowledge that was all too apparent to the national security establishment when the planes first hit at 9 a.m. that morning. Beyond the spectacular destruction of the morning hours of that day, the event crystallized the new security regime first conceptualized by the Hart Rudman Commission from 1997 to 2001.

"Nine Eleven" established a political foundation for the expansion of the national security state both in the United States and around the world. The vulnerabilities discovered by Hart Rudman and laid bare by Nine Eleven were frightening to a nation that had long considered itself invulnerable to attack. During the Cold War, the prospect of nuclear annihilation hung over the country for nearly two generations. Yet, the nuclear terror was something predictable, quantifiable, and ultimately under control of the two superpowers. With the asymmetric threats of international terrorism, the physical survival of the country was of less concern than the country's penetration by terrorists who could inflict catastrophic damage without warning. Not only could planes be turned into giant missiles loaded with jet fuel, but the targets available to determined Jihadists were vast and global in number.[26]

Once the assumption was made that al Qaeda and its affiliates were at war with the United States, assessments of national and local vulnerabilities produced a staggering array of possibilities. Silent and anonymous terrorist cells, having penetrated the United States, could inflict mass death and catastrophic damage on cities, blowing up power plants, bridges, tunnels, nuclear sites, chemical and natural gas plants, and other critical infrastructure targets. Determined terrorists who had subverted U.S. international and domestic security systems could, in theory, detonate nuclear dirty bombs in major U.S. cities, causing panic and the contamination of profoundly important central city locations. They could attack transportation systems, as they did subsequently in Madrid and London, or attempted to do in other major European cities. The enemy may not have been technologically advanced, but in order to inflict serious damage, al Qaeda terrorists did not have to be.

With the events of September 11, U.S. national security was reorganized. The country's boundaries were its line of defense against penetration from al Qaeda, a force whose capabilities were both exaggerated and underestimated. Their abilities were vastly overstated in the sense that the movement had no real operational capability in the United States, nor was it ever particularly popular in the Middle East. Al Qaeda could not muster a millionth of the total military power the United States could project on a daily basis. Nonetheless, the Sunni Islamic movement, while considered deadly was underestimated until the moment the planes hit the towers. It was not clear to the American public most of whom were complacent about the global "threat" environment, that terrorism was a critical factor in national security in the year 2001. In a defense conference held the week before September 11, international terrorism and al Qaeda were not on the agenda.[27] More telling was the indifference of the Secretary of Defense, Donald Rumsfeld who strongly implied in a 2002 Defense Budget hearing that the $11 billion spent on terrorism-related issues by the government was taking money away from far more important issues, such as national missile defense:

> Money is money, and, you know, $100 is a lot of money. But the reality is that we're spending something like 11-plus billion dollars on terrorism issues for the United States government, and we're spending a much smaller amount on missile defense. So it is difficult to say what's too much or what's too little, but the loss of a major city or the loss of—or an attack on one of our allies or deployed forces—you keep using the phrase "attack on U.S. territory." We have interests besides the continental limits of the United States. We have deployed forces overseas, we have allies in NATO, we have allies in Asia; and the ability to threaten them affects us quite directly.[28]

In the entire transcript of the hearing before the House Armed Services Committee, the word terrorism appeared only once. Terrorism, which would transform American foreign policy, was referred to only once and in passing by the

Secretary of Defense in a committee transcript of 20,000 words. For one of the most important intellectual architects of Bush's foreign policy, Paul Wolfowitz, Donald Rumseld's Deputy Secretary of Defense, terrorism was part of a long list of potential threats against the United States. In questions prepared in advance for his confirmation hearing before the U.S. Senate Armed Services Committee in February 2001, Wolfowitz was asked to describe "the principle threats to U.S. national security interests." His response was very concise, once again using the word terrorism just once in the entire hearing:

> The centrifugal forces in world politics have created a more diverse and less predict-able set of potential adversaries, whose aspirations of regional influence and whose willingness to use military force will produce challenges to important U.S. interests and to those of our friends and allies. Modern technology and its proliferation also confront us with an expansion of unconventional threats, including nuclear, biologi-cal, and chemical (NBC) weapons, missiles, terrorism, and the newer threats against space assets and information systems. At the same time, we have traditional respon-sibilities to existing allies in key strategic theaters that remain in our vital interests.[29]

Neither Wolfowitz, in his answers, nor the Senate Armed Services committee, in its prepared questions, discussed terrorism as a major national security threat. Far more important were the issues of the global balance of power in the post–Cold War era, the ability of the United States to respond to simultaneous conventional warfare in different areas of the world, and finally the issues related to "NBC" weapons carried by rogue states. International terrorism was a new threat, along with the proliferation of nuclear, chemical, and biological weapons with Third-World despots, and the threat to the nation's space communications and national information infrastructure. Yet, all of these threats were still conceived as tied to the nation-state. The idea that a lone terrorist organization could inflict cata-strophic damage on the United States appeared to be at the lower end of Wolfo-witz' and the Armed Services' list of national security threats.

In the first seven and half months of the Bush administration, indeed up until the morning of September 11, the guiding presidential directive for counterter-rorism was the Clinton administration's PSDD (Presidential Security Decision Directive) 39, issued in June 1995. The primary responsibility for international terrorism was placed on the State Department, the CIA, the Justice Department, and the FBI. The threat of international terrorism as a principal asymmetric threat to the United States was not trivialized. Indeed, the possible catastrophic effects of a WMD terrorist attack were included in national security doctrine. Yet, while neither Rumsfeld nor Wolfowitz as leaders of the Bush Defense Department, nor Colin Powell as Secretary of State, focused on terrorism as the predominate threat to the United States, the intellectual foundation for its post–September 11th enshrinement was well established. In addition to the Hart

Rudman Report, the Quadrennial Defense Report working group at the National Defense University discussed the concept of terrorism and asymmetric threats to the "homeland" in detail.[30] The risk of "catastrophic terrorism" was deemed an emergent threat to the homeland, but nonetheless, just one of a menu of asymmetric and symmetric threats that had to be defended against. The link between September 11 and the fear of Saddam Hussein was directly related to the doctrinal framework for the new category of asymmetric warfare. The working group report referenced a particular scenario that would become of enhanced priority during the First Bush term and beyond:

> The consensus is that the U.S. homeland will become more vulnerable to new threats, particularly chemical and biological weapons in the hands of rogue states and terrorist groups. The ability to transport such weapons in small packages that can easily be smuggled is often cited as a contributing factor. In addition, rogue regimes such as in North Korea are attempting to develop ballistic missiles capable of reaching the continental United States. States that do not possess fissile material could opt for chemical or biological warheads.[31]

On September 12, 2001, just like December 8, 1941, the day after Pearl Harbor, the United States and its global institutional system began to mobilize for war, aided by willing allies in Europe, the Middle East, and around the world. The threat of asymmetric attacks, emergent in analytical monographs since the mid-1990s, was now an established fact for the "homeland," a new term in itself to describe American society and nationhood in the twenty-first century. Its use was paradoxical, being such an old-fashioned concept of nationalism, more commonly used by small nations to describe their historical attachments to a territorial ethnocultural legacy. Now, with the al Qaeda assault, the United States was not just a civil society but a "homeland" with, in due course, a Department of Homeland Security. It would be the fear of terrorism and asymmetric warfare against the homeland that would form a major psychological pillar for the Second Gulf War. In the interim, war was directed at the source of the September 11 attacks, the Islamic Republic of Afghanistan.

AFGHAN WAR

As soon as the images of destruction on September 11 swept across America through the vast and immediate mass media, the Bush administration was ready to move against the perpetrators. It was no secret at all; in fact, the moment the towers were hit senior administration officials, including George Tenet, the Director of Central Intelligence and many others, knew who was behind the worst act of terrorism ever committed in the United States. If Afghanistan was barely known to the American public, its vital role in Islamic terrorism was a long-established fact to national security analysts in Washington and elsewhere.

The intimate, perhaps symbiotic, relationship between al Qaeda and the Taliban government in Kabul made war with Afghanistan a foregone conclusion. The only question was how the war was going to be launched and conducted. Days after the World Trade Center and Pentagon, the European allies of the United States pledged their entire support, moral, political, economic, and military to invade Afghanistan.[32] Within four weeks, the United States began its air war against the Taliban, flying jets, and launching cruise missiles from the Persian Gulf. The war was brief and quite successful, forcing the surrender of the Taliban's army and the exile of its surviving leadership. For Osama bin Laden, the losses were nearly catastrophic for his organization. All his training camps and a large number of officers were lost. Bin Laden and several of his key lieutenants fled into the tribal lands of Pakistan, becoming a buried icon for resistance to the United States and the West.

The Afghan War, like its successor, the Second Gulf War, was short and successful for the United States and its coalition allies. Nonetheless, the Afghan conflict, like the Iraqi, was never "won." As of this writing, intense resistance to the American-supported Hamid Karzai government continues unabated. In many ways, both the Afghan and Iraq wars were sisters. In both cases, a great superpower, akin to the great powers, or empires that had occupied both these countries through the ages, descended upon them. In Afghanistan, among the most technologically backward societies on earth, the short war of the winter 2001 pitted the most deadly conventional weapon systems in the U.S. arsenal and some of its best troops, the special forces of the various service branches, against an army of Third-World peasants, armed with older Soviet era weapons. The United States brought to bear all its assets against the Taliban regime, which hoped, forlornly, that they could lure the Americans into a protracted and unwinnable ground war.[33]

Unlike in Vietnam, however, the Americans came with few troops other than the elite special force units that aided rebel Afghan armies to attack and defeat the Taliban and its allies, al Qaeda. The war was quick and decisive precisely because the United States did not deploy major ground forces, but relied on its twenty-first-century air power and its very highly trained and expert special force units that assisted Afghan resistance groups to defeat the Taliban, forcing the remnants of that movement into the mountains and tribal areas of Pakistan. American power was decisive in Afghanistan, although, as it later turned out, the Taliban were not quite defeated in 2001. After a brief period of dormancy, their insurgency revived after the withdrawal of Western forces from remote areas of the country and continues in the present. What the war did accomplish was to give the new Bush administration a resounding victory in the short term; a victory that they could luxuriate in for at least some time in the feeling of accomplishment in Afghanistan. They had destroyed a tyrannical regime that enslaved women and had served as the major training ground and safe area for the most dangerous terrorist organization of modern times. They had also nearly given a severe blow to that terrorist group, whose leader and the remnants of his command survived in the mountains of the tribal areas of Pakistan.[34]

ASYMMETRIC THREATS

September 11 brought the whole concept of "asymmetric threats" to the center of public awareness. In national security doctrine, asymmetric appeared as a new scientific term for military threats that could not be quantified or established as specific to a nation-state. The old Soviet Union was a "symmetric" threat to the extent it could be measured and understood according to basic principles of realist foreign policy. Forty Soviet divisions deployed in forward positions in the German Democratic Republic was a symmetric threat, as were the fixed deployments of Soviet air and naval forces and nuclear missiles that targeted the U.S. mainland and Western Europe. The whole idea of symmetry was reassuring to an intellectual community populated by engineers and managers who were trained to understand military threats as predictable and statistically reliable.[35]

In a genuine sense, asymmetry was a challenge to the whole concept of technocratic strategic thought. Al Qaeda did not follow the same rules as nation-states with standing armed forces, official doctrines, and historical patterns of behavior in war and peace. The followers of bin Laden and Zawahiri were an undetermined number. They had no high technology or advanced communications or strict territorial interests. As an international terrorist group with a central dogma, but not a great deal else, al Qaeda was nothing like a massive land army, like the German Wehrmacht or the Red Army. It challenged the West through its diffuse presence among Sunni Islamic extremists, determined to damage Middle Eastern and Western societies through the workings of clandestine and anarchic attacks. Divided into hundreds of very small clandestine cells, the "asymmetric threat" was very real and very serious to West Point army planners, who founded an institute dedicated to its study.[36]

TRANSFORMATIONAL WARFARE

At the turn of the twenty-first century, the intellectual lodestone of U.S. military policy was the new doctrine of "transformational warfare." In every branch of the armed services and in all the civilian branches of the Defense Department and in every military institute scores of studies and papers worked on the ideas of modern war undergoing a profound transformation requiring a totally new conceptualization. Beginning in the first years of the Clinton administration, there was an extraordinary awareness of the "information warfare" and its attendant advances in battlefield communications. By the late 1990s, the term information warfare transitioned to "net-centric warfare." These were very powerful terms that described the impact of the technological transformations of advanced communications and information processing systems on the battlefield and theater of operations.[37]

The extraordinary advances in the ability to manage the battlefield through this new dimension of war provided a growing confidence in the superiority of the United States against less technologically advanced adversaries. Conventional foreign armies and air forces could not compete with the extraordinary speed and precision targeting U.S. military forces could deploy with their emerging capability of thousands of delivery systems acting in concert. At the same time, however, this technological supremacy also came with a new awareness of the dangers of the military revolution. Advanced weapons systems would eventually be developed by foreign powers. Information warfare or terrorism that targeted America's information infrastructure was a vulnerability of enormous strategic and economic significance.

Transformational warfare was the mandate that Donald Rumsfeld brought to the Department of Defense in the first months of 2001. His approach to both the Afghan War and the Iraq War was premised on the essential concepts of the modernization vision for the U.S. armed forces. The primacy of American technological superiority, in particular the revolutionary implications of advanced information-based weapons systems and military operations (i.e., net-centric warfare) informed every planning and guidance document, produced by civilians and military personnel in the Department of Defense. Rumsfeld's mandate was explicit in his 23-page June 2001 QDR (Quadrennial Defense Report) Guidance document. Among the critical worldwide objectives of the U.S. Department of Defense just months before September 11 were to:

> Select, develop and sustain a portfolio of key military capabilities to prevail over current challenges and to hedge against and dissuade future threats, focusing particularly on information operations, countering anti-access strategies, and defending against threats to U.S. and allied territory and assets. Maximize the effectiveness of the men and women in the U.S. Armed Forces by leveraging superior technology.

> Exploit U.S. advantages in superior technological innovation; its unmatched space and intelligence capabilities; its sophisticated military training; and its ability to integrate highly complex military systems in synergistic combinations for distributed and networked military operations.[38]

Also in June 2001, an advanced information warfare workshop titled "Continuing the Revolution in Military Affairs (RMA)," was held at the Marine base at Quantico, Virginia. The state-of-the-art conference on future military strategies and technologies was sponsored by the Office of Naval Research and the "CADRC (Collaborative Agent Design Research Center)" at Cal Poly State University.[39] The published proceedings of the three-day workshop illustrated the focus of the

U.S. military just prior to the September 11 attacks. U.S. military power in June 2001 was considered formidable but not dominant worldwide. In fact, the future presented a range of threats both from other hostile large nation-states and from the gray area of asymmetric threats which transcended the normal categories of military-diplomatic thinking. At the conference, the cutting edge in military technology included various papers on net-centric or information-centric warfare, which was and remains the core vision for the U.S. military through the twenty-first century.

The battlefield technologies of the 1991 Gulf War were spectacular. For the first time, an international audience were spectators to GPS missile systems that inflicted deadly accurate hits on Iraqi targets. Yet, this was the very beginning in the information revolution. By 2001, the rudimentary information technology deployed 10 years earlier was being replaced rapidly by a technological revolution that was transforming not only military science and technology, but the very nature of world civilization. In a fragmented and often anarchic international system, the U.S. military saw its mission as inherently transformative. They believed they could dominate any battlefield, including a global one with the unique information technologies that were quickly being developed.

War in the twenty-first century was understood as a very capital-intensive and intellectually demanding profession. The military battlefield was now a very structured and controlled environment. Using the most recent and advanced technologies, with which the planners believed they could engage any number of countries, including Iraq, U.S. planners assumed the deployment of elite military units, whose movements and targeting and delivery systems would be commanded in real time by senior officers. Future wars would be planned according to the new technologies of information-based warfare. Indeed, the conference papers discussed a plethora of revolutionary concepts for conducting war. Neural networks, fuzzy, and complex systems, decision-support systems, and architectures were some of the concepts that were now being established in the navy's new concept of war. One new concept and major battlefield program was the "Integrated Cooperative Decision Model (ICDM Architecture)," a new and revolutionary information-based command and control system. ICDM was a software system designed by the navy to facilitate a number of support tasks for conducting naval operations, including ship repairs and ordinance tracking.[40] The gist of this new technology relates to the ideas of transformational warfare and the revolution in military affairs. The extension of U.S. military power into the Persian Gulf which began before the 1991 Gulf War continued with the new Bush administration. The technocratic organization of global society in the early twenty-first century promised forms of military power that incorporated the epistemological revolution of the new era. In another conference paper, a senior computer scientist explained in very technical language some of the theory behind the new type of information-based warfare:

If the key to symbolic reasoning is representation then it certainly follows that the foundation of expert-system-based, decision-support systems is the rich manner in which the entities, concepts, and notions relevant to the domain space(s) are represented...

Interoperability between disparate decision-support systems is crucial to the operational effectiveness of information-centric, decision-support systems. As the emergence of such systems increases the need to support inter-system collaboration at the information level becomes increasingly critical. By constraining valuable, perspective-based biases to local, system-specific filter ontologies coupled with the use of core, relatively unbiased ontologies, interoperability between disparate information-centric decision-support systems becomes both feasible and effective.[41]

For the military or civilian laymen, the terminology and concepts used by this information scientist were daunting and perhaps unintelligible. "Expert systems" did not exist prior to the 1990s, or at least not in national security discourse. "Ontologies" is a concept that was most often encountered in philosophy and biology but not in relation to the management of the battlefield. The language and complex conceptual frameworks discussed at the June 2001 conference were representative of the new age, where military theory, planning, and operations and national security doctrine were part of the dramatic transformations of exponential technological change. None of this however, had any impact on al Qaeda. Using the most elementary of tactics, their attack was entirely low tech, freed from decision-support systems, and net-centric warfare. Well known, they accomplished their devastating attack with box cutters and pocket knives, subverting the liberal international order not with technology, but with stealth, cunning, and determination.

CENTERING: THE POST–SEPTEMBER 11 STRATEGIC VIEW

After September 11, the strategic view of the world changed almost overnight. Prior to that date, asymmetric warfare was not viewed as a critical focus for U.S. national security doctrine. The center of Bush administration thought was directed at rogue states and nuclear proliferation and ongoing concerns with the future of Russian and Chinese power politics. A state centered approach to security was premised on the idea that only nation-states were capable of threatening the United States and its interests in international peace and security.

Post–September 11, the prevailing strategic doctrine was transformed. Al Qaeda's dramatic success vaulted it to the very center of American foreign policy. Not only was this subterranean group deemed a threat but an essential one to the future of the United States as a liberal democratic society. The new strategic view placed al Qaeda and its allies, real or imagined, at the center of a new reality;

it was a new time and a new war, termed "World War IV" by the famous neocon Norman Podhoretz, and the GWOT in official U.S. documents. Within five years of the emergence of this new war, the United States had undergone external and internal organizational changes, designed with the intent of creating a new security regime to counter the new dimensions of global asymmetric war.[42]

AL QAEDA

Al Qaeda appeared to have emerged like a cancer in the heart of the Islamic world, metastasizing from a handful of individuals in the 1980s into an extraordinarily dangerous and global movement. Well known to U.S. intelligence in the 1990s, its evil mystique became well earned in a long series of violent and indiscriminate attacks against civilian populations. The Bush administration believed that the war had badly damaged or nearly destroyed al Qaeda by January of 2002. Most of the leadership was believed dead or captured in Afghanistan and Pakistan. Its charismatic leader, an outsized wealthy Saudi, was now hiding somewhere in the Hindu Kush.

Despite this success, the scope of al Qaeda was believed to be global. There were cells of fervent Islamic terrorists inspired by or under the command of bin Laden and his core group of advisers and managers hidden in the fundamentalist heartland of Afghanistan and Pakistan. The group's power was understood to derive from its international ideology of Sunni Islamic jihad and the rejection of the West. The problem with this was not the numbers of bin Laden's followers nor their access to weapons. By being committed to a fanatical objective to rain death and catastrophe on Western societies and especially those allied with the State of Israel, al Qaeda promised a threat of unlimited scope and potential stretching as far out into the future as any analyst or public official could contemplate. With more than a billion Muslims in the world, settled in scores of countries on every continent, the presumed threat of massive sabotage and destruction by al Qaeda-linked terrorists appeared incalculable.[43]

THE "AXIS OF EVIL"

In addition to al Qaeda, the asymmetric threat was compounded by the "Axis of Evil," a phrase that was derided by the Bush administration's critics, who were growing nationally and internationally after the war with Afghanistan. Bush used the term to describe an implied collusion between states assumed to be opposed to the United States and its interests worldwide. The most dangerous aspect of these states, according to U.S. intelligence represented the desires of all three to obtain nuclear weapons. Nuclear weapons were the ultimate guarantee for these anti-Western states. Going nuclear would enable them to deter invasion and give them leverage in any military confrontation with the United States. The logic was impeccable. All three countries, had desired nuclear status, and in the offing, North Korea would become a declared nuclear state.[44]

The assumption guiding Bush's foreign policy was the rogue nature of these states and their ambitions to upset the liberal global order, to deprive the United States of international order on its own terms, a de facto unipolar system centered in Washington. There were links in the axis, specifically, North Korea's trade relationship with Iran, that transferred missile and possibly nuclear technology to the Islamic Republic. As for Iraq, it certainly was not an ally of Iran, but the presumption of the Bush administration, unduly influenced by Iraqi exiles, was that Saddam Hussein had a strategic relationship with al Qaeda, and his pursuit of nuclear weapons remained very active more than a decade after the Gulf War.

THE IRANIAN THREAT

In the Zeitgeist of the Bush administration, the Iranian regime was essentially equivalent to Iraq as a providential adversary of the United States. This too was largely a continuation of U.S. policy toward the Islamic Republic of Iran that existed under three earlier presidencies. The Iranians, as noted earlier, were considered a subversive threat to the stability of the conservative Sunni regimes that had long-preserved United States and Western interests in the Gulf. The new script brought to the White House by the neoconservatives had the same action-oriented ideology toward Iran as they had toward Iraq and the other factions and groups that opposed American and Western power in the Middle East. While Iran clearly shared Iraq and al Qaeda as enemies with the United States, cooperation with the regime by the Bush administration would only be superficial. The underlying argument against Hussein, the Iranian clerics and other anti-Western forces was precisely the fact that they were such. Iran's radical Shiite religious ideology was perceived as an immediate and a long-term threat to Israel, the Sunni Arab states of the Gulf and the standing of the West in the entire region. Iranian goals were clear, if not attainable. Primary objectives included the liberation of Palestine from Jewish control and the removal of the Western powers from the Middle East. In these regards, they shared the very same objectives as Sunni Muslim movements throughout the Islamic world and beyond. What made the Iranian ideology unique was its confessional claims to Shiite Islam, to Sunnis, a form of the religion which violated the most basic tenets of their religious beliefs and culture.[45]

The Bush administration had the same concerns about Iran as they had about Iraq, that both were potential strategic threats by virtue of their efforts past, present, and future to acquire nuclear and other WMD weapon systems. The Iranians were not only a threat because of those weapons, but because the regimes clandestine institutions, in particular its Al Quds force, was believed to have established an international terror network linked to devastating attacks in

Argentina against Israeli and Jewish targets, as well as direct funding for Shiite Arabs in Lebanon and Palestinian terrorist groups on the West Bank and Gaza.[46] Viewed in broad geostrategic terms, the doctrinal problem presented by Iraq and Iran and other Muslim nations was underdevelopment. The only way to eliminate the severe threats posed by these regimes and others in the Muslim world was to create conditions that would foster rapid democratic change throughout the region. This transformation, it was surmised by many thinkers especially after September 11, saw the problems of the Iranian regime primarily with respect to the country's failure to modernize, to create a liberal democratic society predisposed to the interests and needs of the Western and now global liberal order.[47]

NORTH KOREA

In the Bush Weltanschauung, North Korea was the antipodean threat. Iraq and Iran threatened the Persian Gulf, Israel, and the West. The North Koreans or PRK (Peoples Republic of Korea) threatened South Korea, Japan, and the integrity of East Asia. The mutual animosity of the PRK and the United States predated Ba'athist Iraq and Islamic Iran by decades. At the same time that Bush inherited Clinton's containment and "liberation" policy for Iraq, he was also given a similar policy of containment for the PRK, an unpredictable and increasingly vulnerable radical socialist state in perfect opposition to the United States and its principles for international development and democratization. With respect to the Second Gulf War, North Korea or the PRK was a contingency threat. Any military action taken against Hussein had to be viewed within the global context of rogue regimes. The PRK took advantage of Bush's deep military focus on Iraq, using the Bush administration's distraction over postwar Iraq to become an undeclared nuclear power.

IRAQ

Having come into office with a determination to rid the world of Saddam Hussein's regime, various elements of planning for regime change in Iraq began before the destruction of the towers and the attack on the Pentagon. The Afghan War was quick with overwhelming support from the American public and the international community. Even, Iran, ostensibly a committed adversary, gave covert support to the war to eliminate its nemesis, the Taliban. By January 2002, the Afghan war had ended, with military and political success albeit short lived. Bin Laden was driven into the mountains and beyond his organization virtually destroyed by the invasion and occupation of his bases and organizational headquarters. With the terrorist assault on the United States revenged, and al Qaeda now underground in the tribal areas of Pakistan, the agenda for the newly termed GWOT soon turned to Iraq. The Second Gulf War appeared to have been seeded, first by September 11 and then by the Afghan War which brought U.S. forces into the region in greater numbers and with more firepower than at any time since the First Gulf War in the early 1990s. The expanded presence of the U.S. armed forces in the Gulf and the ordained agenda to rid the world of "Islamic fascism" provided the necessary grounds for the neoconservative drive, then a decade old, to finish the destruction of Saddam Hussein.

The Second Gulf War

There is no easy or risk-free course of action. Some have argued we should wait—and that's an option. In my view, it's the riskiest of all options, because the longer we wait, the stronger and bolder Saddam Hussein will become. We could wait and hope that Saddam does not give weapons to terrorists, or develop a nuclear weapon to blackmail the world. But I'm convinced that is a hope against all evidence. As Americans, we want peace—we work and sacrifice for peace. But there can be no peace if our security depends on the will and whims of a ruthless and aggressive dictator. I'm not willing to stake one American life on trusting Saddam Hussein.

George W. Bush[1]

CAUSALITY

From the point of view of most historians, it is far too early to write a history of the Second Gulf War or "Iraq War." The subject is far too close to the present, and not enough information is available from archival sources to produce a professional diplomatic history of the conflict. Nonetheless, the purpose of this book has not been a definitive or comprehensive study of either the First or Second Gulf Wars as international history or within the history of U.S. foreign relations. Rather, my objective has been to provide a contemporary analytical narrative of the United States in the Gulf region that defines the distinct characteristics of American power and international history in the late twentieth and early twenty-first centuries. I have wanted my readers to discern a broad understanding of how this period fits into both American and international history and how the actors involved were connected to the larger forces of history.

Typically, the causes of any war are complex.[2] The First Gulf War, as we have seen, grew out of changes in the Gulf region and in the international system.

Relieved of the pressures of the war with Iran and the bipolar confrontation between the superpowers, Hussein had the opportunity to move against his much smaller and very wealthy neighbor. The financial pressures of the eight-year conflict with the Iranians, combined with the impulsive drive of Hussein to exert his power rationally or irrationally, set the script for the First Gulf War. The trigger for the West and for the United States was easy enough, the invasion of Kuwait, and a presumed threat to the Saudis and the UAE. Bush Sr. had only to be told of the invasion. As soon as the fall of Kuwait was a fait accompli, his administration mobilized the institutional mechanisms of the national security state. In six months, a carefully constituted international coalition launched their war against Hussein, whose respective tribal, Iraqi and pan-Arab identities left him no choice but to face the Western coalition and to fight, using his large, powerful but woefully inadequate military.

American power and the American script responded reflexively to Hussein in 1990. The debate in Congress suggested a reluctance to go to war premised on the legacy of Vietnam. That conflict, just a decade and half in the past was a vivid historical memory in the minds of law-makers just as it was for high-ranking military officers and executive branch policy-makers. Yet, the compelling interest of the Gulf and the other historical memory of twentieth-century America, of Munich in 1938, established the script for war. Saddam Hussein's aggression triggered a cascade of defensive reactions by several dozen countries all of whom had national interests in preventing Iraq's consolidation of its conquest. The war in 1990 brought the modern Western script for global order against the singular historical narrative of Saddam Hussein, an agent of anti-Western, Sunni Arab nationalism, who in effect challenged the Western system that had dominated the Persian Gulf since the end of the First World War. In the global mass media, newspapers, magazines, television, and radio, American nationalism and internationalism pitted itself against the Ba'athist ideology of the Iraqi state and won the propaganda war. The Iraqis claimed Kuwait as part of historical Mesopotamia, "the nineteenth province of Iraq."[3] In contrast, the United States and its allies referenced international law and the inviolability of internationally recognized boundaries. In systemic terms, the United States viewed Iraq as a threat to the entire Gulf region and to the political, strategic, and economic interests of the nation. The international order that was constituted upon the liberal scientific political economy of the West could not tolerate the tribal warfare of the Ba'athists and the sociopathic designs of their leader.

THE NEW GULF WAR CRISIS

The Second Gulf War was grounded in the script processes of the First Gulf War and the containment regime of the Clinton administration. This war was not driven by the geostrategic imperatives for protecting the Persian Gulf.

In point of fact, the basis for the war had little to do with protecting Kuwait, Saudi Arabia, and the UAE because they were already protected. The trigger for war had built into the American script every day since the cease-fire of 1991. Hussein's continued defiance of the United States and the United Nations and its weapons inspectors, and his ongoing savage persecution of Kurds, Shias, and other non-Arab Sunni minorities stewed in the minds of U.S. public officials who viewed Hussein's survival as a misfortune, an error of judgment, and a moral shame. Hussein's perpetual challenges to U.S. power and his ostensible social pathology were a magnet to neoconservative intellectuals such as Richard Perle and Paul Wolfowitz who saw him as an incarnate evil.[4] The ongoing revelations not only about his genocidal actions against Kurdish and Shiite populations, but of even greater concern, his legacy of WMD, the huge programs he had sponsored with Stalinist intensity in the 1980s, made him a deadly threat. It had to be assumed, unless proved by strong evidence to the contrary, that Hussein was in possession of some forms of WMDs and had ongoing programs to expand his deterrent and possible offensive capabilities.

The second war was a continuation of the first one. Yet, its trigger was a threat based upon supposition and nuance that was ultimately proved wrong. Its most vociferous proponents, the "neoconservatives," assumed a dark view of the Middle East and its antagonists. Indeed, the new conservatives, who acquired values and practices from across the American ideological spectrum, practiced their craft of internal and public diplomacy for more than a decade in and out of government. As noted, figures such as Daniel Pipes, Norman Podhoretz, Richard Perle, and Douglas Feith pushed their very dark views of an Islamic or Islamofascist threat to the American homeland. In the wake of September 11, they tied two disparate Middle Eastern groups together into an image of pure evil, with a key September 11 operative meeting with Hussein's agents in Prague prior to the hijackings against New York and Washington. For a brief time, the neoconservatives gained some traction tying Hussein to al Qaeda. Yet, no immediate threat to the Gulf existed in spring 2003. The war grew in the suspicions of the policy makers and the public, a fire kindled by the self-designed misperceptions of political elites.[5]

The new Gulf crisis that began in the fall of 2002 was directly related to the deep trauma inflicted by September 11. An enemy that was to be contained quickly became one to be eliminated to a large degree; the second Gulf crisis that led directly to the Second Gulf War was manufactured by paranoia and ideology. It may be argued that the Bush administration's war policy was a logical continuation of its predecessor's; that in fact, regime change was always deferred pending the time and conditions that would allow the United States to finish its confrontation with Saddam Hussein. The existing evidence supports the conclusion that the decision to go to war to overthrow the Ba'athist state was made prior to the beginning of the administration of George W. Bush and that September 11 provided the political capital to effect that long established goal. The core beliefs of the conservative national security intellectuals around the new president had long decided that keeping Hussein in office was keeping a major threat in place.

As we have seen the script for the national security state under George Bush was laid in the context of ideological constructs that informed the so-called "neoconservative" school in U.S. foreign policy. However, while the neocons dominated the intellectual life of the Bush presidency's internationalism, a range of foreign policy thinkers also supported the view that Hussein had to be removed as a strategic threat to the United States. At the time the crisis emerged, the summer and fall of 2002, a year after the fateful day of September 11, an array of elite public opinion that transcended the neoconservative label believed the crisis was genuine and supported the removal of Saddam Hussein.[6] In October 2002, two days after the president's speech to the nation on Iraq, a distinguished panel contemplated war at the Middle East Policy Council.[7] For Anthony Cordesman, perhaps the most learned of military analysts on the Gulf region, the presumed evidence of Iraq's pursuit of WMD was too compelling to decide against war:

> Perhaps the most important question is still do we need to fight this war, and that is an answer, which I think has to be given very tentatively. The arguments for and against are actually relatively well balanced. I would say that personally and with great reluctance I would say that we probably do have to fight this war. I have simply watched what has gone on in Iraq too long and I think that what has been uncovered, provided in the British white paper and to a lesser degree the new CIA white paper documents far more of an active process of proliferation than people seem to realize.[8]

Many questions were raised by Cordesman and the other members of the panel about the readiness for war, and the formidable consequences, most of which, they understood, the Bush administration had yet to account for, but the argument for war was made predominantly by the immediacy of Iraq's threat of WMD proliferation.

Arguably, the crisis involving the Iraqi state became internationalized in summer 1990 and remained so through 2003 and on. The desires to defeat and overthrow the Iraqi regime were premised on the well-deserved reputation of Saddam Hussein for duplicity, aggression, and voracious ambition for power. Hussein was just as defiant of the world community in 2002–03 as he was in 1990. His human rights record was better only because of military constraints placed upon him. He could not use nerve gas against Kurdish villages in his northern provinces, as he did in the 1980s, killing over a 100,000 Kurdish civilians. The Ba'athist slaughter of Shiites in Southern Iraq was similarly constrained throughout the interwar period of the 1990s and early 2000s by the southern no-fly zone.

Yet, despite his resume, Hussein did not initiate the Second Gulf War. The script for the war came from inside America, in the minds of American nationalists, military strategists, pro-Israeli politicians and neoconservative intellectuals, all coalescing in the institutional system of the George W. Bush administration. Catalyzed by September 11, the Bush White House was desirous of the regime change that its predecessors, the earlier Bush and Clinton administrations had both wanted. To effect military action to end the Iraqi regime, Bush's domestic and foreign policy teams followed a carefully designed strategy to mobilize domestic and international public opinion to launch an invasion of Iraq.[9]

Domestic public opinion was an easy task, given the antipathy of more than a decade to Hussein and his despotic methods of torture, genocide, and terror and his apparent love of WMD. The hard part of war mobilization even in lieu of September 11 was the orchestration of international support. Unlike the First Gulf War, the Second Gulf War proposed the invasion of a sovereign state with no obvious legal justification under international law. The Sunni Arab states of the Middle East, while having no sympathy for Hussein, rejected war against a fellow Arab nation. The loss of life and national humiliation that would result inevitably with an American invasion made the public support for war impossible for key Arab states.

At the same time, the lack of an imminent threat from Iraq, straitjacketed by no-fly zones and strictly enforced UN sanctions made the dangerous and costly idea of armed invasion unpalatable for many NATO allies. The escalation to war that began in earnest in the fall of 2002 and culminated in the March 2003 invasion of Iraq was driven by the fears of American president and his cabinet that somehow, Saddam Hussein's Ba'athist state had formed a holy alliance with al Qaeda and was pursuing a coordinated campaign of global terror. The famous "Axis of Evil" speech which George Bush delivered to a largely believing audience, the Congress of the United States, asserted that there was collusion, an evil synchrony between anti-Western regimes and groups to damage and destroy the liberal democracy in the United States, and its allies around the globe. For its part, the *New York Times* editorial board approved Bush's attribution and his leadership:

> The president's speech, delivered with plain-spoken eloquence, sought to rally Americans behind three "great goals": the war on terrorism, the ensuring of domestic security and the revival of the economy. The public was probably most eager to hear what Mr. Bush plans for the next step in the battle against terrorism overseas, and in this area he was appropriately forceful. He named Iraq, Iran and North Korea as part of "an axis of evil" that threatens America, and he put those countries on notice that the United States will not stand by and let them develop biological, chemical and nuclear weapons.[10]

PREWAR INTELLIGENCE

Massive intelligence assessments in the years prior to the war concluded that Iraq was actively pursuing WMD and possessed operational chemical and biological weapon systems that could and would be used against Iraq's array of regional enemies. The degree to which prewar intelligence was wrong on Iraq's WMD potential and existing arsenal would be the subject of profound anger and disbelief among members of the Washington establishment, the American public and observers around the world. It seemed ludicrous that an intelligence establishment that was so lavishly funded and focused on the task, could have been so utterly mistaken about Saddam Hussein's phantom WMD arsenal. Yet, as the Senate Intelligence Committee report on prewar intelligence so aptly summarized, the intelligence failure was first and foremost a product of an ordinary psychosocial process that has been termed "group think."[11] Simply put, since Hussein had a huge arsenal of WMDs in the recent past, and nothing seemed to preclude Hussein's destruction of them, U.S. intelligence analysts assumed the arsenal existed. To their defense, the same flawed psychological denial was present in the intelligence services of all major U.S. allies, all of whom made the same essential error. The Germans in particular, were critical in supplying unwittingly bogus intelligence that formed part of the bedrock of Colin Powell's argument before the United Nations in February 2003.[12]

PUBLIC DIPLOMACY

"The Coalition of the Willing"

Flush from the successful campaign in Afghanistan, the Bush administration was riding a wave of public support in the United States and throughout much of the world. This uniformity of support especially among key allies appeared to vanish in the summer of 2002 as the White House began to indicate its intentions to confront Iraq militarily. Faced with open opposition to war against Saddam Hussein, notably by France and Russia, and to a lesser extent Germany, the Bush foreign policy team reacted with a public display of anger. Confronted with European opposition to a second Iraq war, Rumsfeld said famously that the opponents of American policy were the voices of "old Europe." The new countries of the European Union, those of the former Eastern Bloc, were the "new Europe" and they supported the Bush administration.[13]

The strangeness of Rumsfeld's remarks carried throughout the world. The diplomatic mastery of George Bush's father's presidency mobilizing international support in 1990 was a far cry from the blunt and apparently inept strategy of the son's White House. In truth, the methods were not wholly inept. By the start of the war in March 2003, a "coalition of the willing" did in fact include a significant number of U.S. allies who accepted the strategic and moral argument of the United States to eliminate Saddam Hussein. The American desire to overthrow the Ba'athist Iraqi state coincided with the motivations of virtually all of Iraq's neighbors. Hussein had destroyed and plundered Kuwait during the First Gulf War. He set fire to Kuwaiti oilfields and flooded the Gulf with oil. Both actions had caused huge economic and environmental damage. The massive destruction was accompanied by the stripping of Kuwait City of cars, luxury items, whatever could be transported back to Iraq by Iraqi soldiers. Since Kuwait's national existence had hung by a bare thread in 1990, his threat to them and to Bahrain, the UAE and Saudi Arabia was self-evident in the region. In 2003, Saddam Hussein was viewed in the region as a terrifying figure capable of anything. It was Hussein, after all, who had used chemical weapons against his own Kurdish population and against the Iranians during their eight-year war of attrition in the 1980s. He had murdered and tortured hundreds of thousands if not millions of men, women, and children. The dictator was oblivious to world opinion and indeed any elite's opinions that did not have a serious military and economic leverage on him. His invasion of Iran in 1980 was just as bold as his attack on Kuwait in 1990. Iranians had suffered incalculable damage from their "Gulf War" against a Sunni Arab nationalist who despised them for both their religion and their ethnicity. For Kuwaitis, who were plundered, and for Kurds and Iranians who were subjected to chemical warfare, and for the Shiite Arabs of Iraq and the Sunni Arabs of the wealthy Gulf states all shared the common view of Saddam Hussein as a menace to their existence. As a mortal albeit contained threat to the Persian Gulf, Hussein was just as detested in 2003 as he was some 13 years earlier when he annexed a fellow Arab state and brought the full weight of the international community against him.[14]

Despite the weakened status of the Ba'athist state in 2003, the Israelis continued to view Iraq as a serious strategic threat. Israeli concerns were represented in Washington by its formidable lobbying group led by AIPAC whose allies included the Christian coalition and major figures in public and private life. Israel did not have the ability to initiate an American attack or the invasion as it was planned in 2002–03. However, the broader alliance of Israel and the United Sates in the Middle East was premised on a deep interconnection between the two nations that resonated throughout American society but most particularly among evangelical Christians.[15]

The "coalition of the willing" in February 2003 included the overt and covert support of groups that were threatened and damaged by Hussein's continued control of Iraq. The Gulf Arab states provided the grounds and facilities for the invasion of Iraq, a critical need that was met by Kuwait, Bahrain, Qatar, and Oman.[16] The Kurdish forces in Northern Iraq were always part of the military plan to overthrow the regime in Baghdad. They fought bravely and in the aftermath of the war, the Kurds considered themselves the most advantaged of the peoples liberated. It is not clear if Iran and Israel had any role in the 2003 war, but clearly, they were major beneficiaries of the elimination of Saddam Hussein and his Ba'athist state.

The advertised version of the coalition of countries who allied themselves with the United States and Great Britain included long-term NATO allies Italy, Spain,

Portugal, Denmark, Iceland, and the Netherlands, as well as other recent additions to NATO, Ukraine, Poland, Czech Republic, Hungary, Bulgaria, and Romania. From East Asia, Japan, the Philippines, and South Korea, from East Asia, as well as Australia, enlisted in the invasion of Iraq. All told, 49 countries with a total population of over 1.2 billion people were formally committed to the military invasion and occupation of the Republic of Iraq. The only formal Arab member was Kuwait. While seemingly impressive, notably absent were key American allies France and Germany. Canada refused to participate as did India, China, and Russia. Over 150 countries with more than five billion people did not endorse the multinational coalition. Further, despite the formal support, 93 percent of the troops for the attack were supplied by the United States.[17] Nonetheless, the United States had enough support at the international level to launch the invasion, even with the opposition of the Secretary General of the United Nations, Kofi Annan, who viewed the coalition's actions as illegal.[18]

THE QUINTESSENTIAL TASK: MOBILIZING THE PUBLIC

With a thin but effective amount of international support for the war plan, the Bush administration had the task of mobilizing sufficient Congressional and popular consent. For the political establishment in a representative democracy, no task is greater than gaining the consent of the public to launch a war. Without clear consent, evidenced in public opinion polls and the support or at least acquiescence of the legislative branch, a major war, involving significant casualties, financial costs, and the international prestige of the nation, cannot be executed. The administration was convinced that Saddam Hussein was actively engaged in the concealment, procurement, and development of advanced WMD and delivery systems. The evidence from the recent past, which the Clinton administration found compelling, was the same for the Bush administration.[19] There was no greater advocate of war against Hussein than Vice President Richard Cheney. Cheney had been a principal architect of the first Gulf War as Secretary of Defense under George H. Bush. Now in the aftermath of September 11, and 12 years of undeclared war between Hussein and the United States, Cheney was explicit about the administration's views of him. His speech before a sympathetic audience of war veterans at the end of August 2002 was illustrative of his view of Hussein six months prior to the war:

> Saddam also devised an elaborate program to conceal his active efforts to build chemical and biological weapons. And one must keep in mind the history of U.N. inspection teams in Iraq. Even as they were conducting the most intrusive system of arms control in history, the inspectors missed a great deal. Before being barred from the country, the inspectors found and destroyed thousands of chemical weapons, and hundreds of tons of mustard gas and other nerve agents.

> Yet Saddam Hussein had sought to frustrate and deceive them at every turn, and was often successful in doing so. I'll cite one instance. During the spring of 1995, the inspectors were actually on the verge of declaring that Saddam's programs to develop chemical weapons and longer-range ballistic missiles had been fully accounted for and shut down. Then Saddam's son-in-law suddenly defected and began sharing information. Within days the inspectors were led to an Iraqi chicken farm. Hidden there were boxes of documents and lots of evidence regarding Iraq's most secret weapons programs. That should serve as a reminder to all that we often learned more as the result of defections than we learned from the inspection regime itself.[20]

The intensity of Cheney's beliefs may have had an effect on his audience, but in a news analysis of the speech some days later, the *New York Times* reported that the vice president's convictions were dramatically different from those of all major Arab allies and European governments. Even, a former NATO commander, Wesley Clark expressed deep frustration with his views:

> . . .critics of the Cheney campaign about Iraq argue that, at least based on what is known publicly, the equation hasn't changed much. "Where is the sense of urgency coming from?" Gen. Wesley Clark, one of several former military officials who have urged the administration to take a deep breath, asked on television. "He's had weapons of mass destruction for 20 years. He doesn't have nuclear material, and we'd likely have some notice of the breakdown of the containment regime."[21]

Neither Cheney nor any of the other neoconservative public policy intellectuals in Washington had the moral authority to persuade a skeptical Congress and world community of the necessity of war against Iraq. Saddam Hussein's evilness aside, the costs of such a war in the months before its launch were considered far in excess of any benefit from an invasion and occupation of Iraq. The task for mobilizing the American and international public for war was given to Colin Powell. It was his well-deserved stature as a statesman and soldier and superb public speaking skills that were needed and mustered by the Bush administration. Just two weeks before the start of the war, the Secretary of State gave his huge domestic and international prestige to the war aims of the administration.

COLIN POWELL AT THE UNITED NATIONS

Colin Powell was in February 2003, among the most trusted public figures in the United States. Without question, a critical event in the mobilization of domestic support for the war involved the historic presentation of evidence to the UN Security Council by Secretary of State Colin Powell. His stature as former general, now a statesman known for his integrity in both the United States and internationally, was impressive and renowned. He was the first African American Secretary of State, as well as the first black Chairman of the Joint Chiefs of Staff and national security adviser. His formidable resume, experience, and accomplishments in high public office were legendary. A tall, powerfully built man, Powell had been viewed by the public as a potential president. At the height of his fame, he was the most trusted public figure in the United States.

Speaking before the United Nations as the representative of the United States, his demeanor projected both authority and sincerity. Listening to his measured but forceful presentation most American observers believed they were given a clear and absolutely forthright and honest representation of the threat posed by the Iraqi state. Powell's presentation was chilling. The Iraqi dictator, according to the best U.S. intelligence had used stealth and subterfuge to hide active chemical and biological warfare factories from UN inspectors. There was eyewitness proof, according to the Secretary of State, that Iraq had mobile biological weapons laboratories where undoubtedly his scientists and engineers were perfecting deadly agents for use against the United States and other foreign enemies. It was clear, according to the most authoritative spokesman in the nation, that Hussein was determined to build an arsenal of prohibited and dangerous WMD to reestablish his power in the region and give him the capability to inflict extraordinary harm on his enemies. Hussein's ruthlessness was equal to that of the Nazis and to the Japanese fascists during the Second World War. He had performed biological warfare experiments on prisoners, which were observed by an "eyewitness" and were similar to Nazi and Japanese atrocities. Secretary Powell was explicit:

> We also have sources who tell us that, since the 1980s, Saddam's regime has been experimenting on human beings to perfect its biological or chemical weapons.

> A source said that 1,600 death row prisoners were transferred in 1995 to a special unit for such experiments. An eye witness saw prisoners tied down to beds, experiments conducted on them, blood oozing around the victim's mouths and autopsies performed to confirm the effects on the prisoners. Saddam Hussein's humanity–inhumanity has no limits.[22]

Powell's speech came but four weeks before the start of the Second Gulf War. It was a brilliant piece of public diplomacy and war propaganda that played to an international as well as a domestic audience. In the years following the speech, its evidentiary foundations were torn to shreds, revealing a mixture of governmental deceit, incompetence, and large-scale misperception or "group think." Postwar, it would have serious consequences for the Bush administration's standing in the world, but as political theater and ideological mobilization, Colin Powell fulfilled his mission to the highest degree. To the end, as the country's highest ranking diplomat, he remained a "good soldier."[23]

With Powell's imprimatur, the Bush administration was to proceed with its plan for imminent war. In a matter of weeks, an expertly devised invasion swept across the Iraqi desert, capturing Baghdad and every major Iraqi city and town. Hussein's regime came to end. No WMD were found, although Hussein's tyranny was evident in mass graves and torture chambers, and in the testimony of thousands of victims. Yet, neither prewar nor postwar propaganda by public officials and sympathetic journalists would protect the Bush administration from its intelligence failures and its disastrous occupation of Iraq.

STRATEGIC AND OPERATIONAL PLANNING

"The Future of Iraq"

The neo-Wilsonian objectives of the Bush administration in the Third World were no different from those of previous administrations over the last century. The idea of turning post-Saddam Iraq into a liberal democracy was an explicit and sincere objective of the Bush administration. Numerous models of Wilsonian transformation or attempted development exist in the records of U.S. foreign policy. The fact that the impetus for democratization in U.S. foreign policy existed side by side with antidemocratic policies is paradoxical but consistent with the complexity of foreign policy as an instrument of national power. The prevailing analogy for the creation of a post-Saddam Iraqi society was modeled on the successful transformation of Germany and Japan during their occupation by the allies in the years immediately following the Second World War. The rhetoric and the internal planning within the administration revealed optimism and commitment to what had earlier been derided as "nation building." The White House had commissioned a multivolume study for the postwar reconstruction of Iraq aptly titled, "The Future of Iraq." The postwar planning for Iraq began in the State Department in October 2001, with various working groups of Iraqi exiles and U.S. policy experts convening over a year and a half before the war, to envision a detailed architecture for the new Iraq, where the all of the horrible abuses of Saddamist rule would be obviated. The analysis detailed how the new Iraqi state would be built and would function according to the aspirations of the people for a new and humane civil society. The design of course was a Western democratic institutional model where a rational and fully functional central government created a modern liberal society based upon procedural and substantive forms of liberty and democratic governance. The report was explicit in its aspirations: "It is important for Iraqis to start thinking and imaging their country without Saddam Hussain and to set in motion the seeds for a robust, independent and free civil society."[24]

The civil society working group envisioned an Iraq with a free press, free labor unions, and voluntary organizations of every stripe both religious and secular.

In effect a civil society that North Americans, Europeans, and other democratic societies took for granted in the twenty-first century but had not existed in Iraq for half a century. The logic was impeccable:

> The intention of building a civil society is to shift power away from the central government to the people through empowering their private establishments. Iraq's future constitution needs to make provision for an Iraqi bill of rights guaranteeing the basic rights of its citizens, including freedom of speech, freedom of congregation, freedom of religion, freedom of press among many other bills. These rights ought to be exercised to be meaningful as a new culture based on the tenets spelled out in the bill of rights as established...the presence of a free, independent and vibrant civil society is key to protecting and maintaining Iraq's anticipated established freedom, liberty and democracy for generations to come.[25]

The State Department's planning was extensive, with volumes dedicated to transitional justice, democratic governance, economic development, oil, and energy production, and a new Iraqi military—in effect, a new and robust nation that would become a model for the creation of secular democratic nation-states throughout the Middle East. What the reports lack was any grounding in an effective implementation of its vision. The Iraqi and American working groups labored intensively on the details of the birth of a new society after the fall of Ba'athist rule. The fate of refugees as well as war criminals was taken into account, in addition to the practical needs of supplying basic government services to a burgeoning of population of 25 million largely impoverished people. Yet, the plans were two-dimensional. They did not reflect a real world engulfed in uncertainty, betrayals, and uncontrollable events. As static models, they were but pro-forma outlines of a new society absent from the explosive forces of a military invasion and the overthrow of an existing regime. To see how the plans would be implemented required the successful occupation of Iraq by a determined international coalition willing to sponsor the State Department and Iraqi exile organizations' ambitious neo-Wilsonian goals for the Republic of Iraq.[26]

IMPLEMENTING TRANSFORMATIONAL WARFARE

Shock and Awe

The signature strategy and event of the Second Gulf War was the implementation of *Shock and Awe,* both a metaphor and a valid doctrine of the United States military in the early twenty-first century. The core of transformational warfare as understood by the Pentagon in 2003 was the imposition of Clausewitzian principles of total war according to the new precision network-centric technologies of the new age. *Shock and Awe* required the complete dominance of the battlefield by a vastly superior military force. As defined in the opening sentence of the second chapter of Harlan K. Ullman and James P. Wade's 1996 monograph by the same title, Shock and Awe was coterminous with *Rapid Dominance*. The argument was quite simple. "The basis for Rapid Dominance rests in the ability to affect the will, perception, and understanding of the adversary through imposing sufficient Shock and Awe to achieve the necessary political, strategic, and operational goals of the conflict or crisis that led to the use of force."[27]

Ullman and Wade were careful to discuss Shock and Awe in historical context. The general concept is as old as warfare. The authors described briefly different forms of the strategy as expressed in military history. Most recently, the doctrine of overwhelming or invincible force, also known as the "Powell doctrine," and used in the First Gulf War was a classic interpretation of the general theory. Other examples were the German Blitzkrieg of the Second World War and the massive bombing strategies of the Allies including the use of nuclear weapons on Hiroshima and Nagasaki. Still earlier examples of using Shock and Awe to force or break an enemy's resolve included the tactics of the legendary ancient war theorist Sun Tzu. All of these historical examples of Shock and Awe had the objective to achieve rapid and sustained dominance of an enemy. Of course, each of the variations on the strategy had limitations, including the huge political costs of causing severe damage on civilian populations. The purpose of the 1996 monograph by these two military theorists was to propose a new information age understanding of the strategy, one that would fit into the political architecture of the times.

For the authors, writing in the middle of the Clinton years, the political context over U.S. military action was a paramount concern. In a world that was so volatile, so open to local conflicts in the vacuum caused by the end of the bipolar system in the early 1990s, the United States needed to impose order or dominance on the world's peripheries, but only in ways that were politically sustainable:

> The U.S. will, nevertheless, need to maintain the capability to deter and defeat both strategic and other direct threats to its vital interests, preferably on a decisive basis. In an unsettled, less structured, and volatile world, the ability to use force with precision, effectiveness, impunity, and, when needed, rapidity, will still be a powerful influence on cooperation, stability, and, where relevant, submission.

> Imposing Rapid Dominance on a nation, group, or situation, if achievable, will be a highly desirable and relevant asset in this turbulent period.[28]

The full vision of a Clausewitzian strategy for the information age was what the authors were after in their classic 1996 text. The doctrine became the basis for the transformational net-centric warfare doctrines of the first decade of the twenty-first century, which established the framework for the Iraq or Second Gulf War as well as the ongoing transformational doctrines undergoing development in all branches of the U.S. armed services and in modern foreign military establishments as well. The crux of the 1996 vision was implementation of a level of battlefield control unknown in the history of warfare. All actions on the ground and in the air, in all the spaces of command and control would be synchronized and defined by precise technological means of limiting damage while targeting the destruction of the enemies' assets. Supremacy would be complete, control would be complete, but the appearance would be self-limiting:

> For shock to be administered with minimum collateral damage, key targets of value must be neutralized or destroyed and the enemy must be made to feel completely helpless and unable to consider a meaningful response. Furthermore, the enemy's confusion must be complete, adding to a general impression of impotence. Most importantly, strategic targets, military forces, leadership and key societal resources must be located, tracked, and targeted. This will require substantial sensor, computational, and communication technologies. Designated targets must be destroyed rapidly and with assurance. Finally, the status and position of friendly forces must be known at all times, and the logistics supporting them must be sufficiently flexible to allow for rapid movement, reconfiguration, and decentralization of location.[29]

The essence of Shock and Awe which was applied in the Second Gulf War was the application of information-based communication technologies to the delivery systems and battlefield communications of the military forces engaged in war. The enemy would be controlled and where necessary destroyed through digital electronic weapons and munitions by an integrated operational command. The political objectives of the national command authority would be met through the technocratic means of the twenty-first century U.S. armed forces.

In practice, the Shock and Awe of 2003 had many predictable effects on the Iraqi military and civilian population. In the theater of operations in March and April 2003, the demonstration of U.S. military dominance through the its hightech satellite guided missiles, showed the preeminence of American power on the battlefield. It demonstrated to demoralized Iraqi officers that any attempt to challenge the United States in conventional warfare would meet with the annihilation of their forces.

COBRA II: THE DRIVE TO BAGHDAD

Tommy Franks, the commander in chief of U.S. Central Command, an area of responsibility that covered 27 nations from East Africa to Central Asia, a land mass of 6.5 million square miles, or roughly twice the size of the continental United States. As theater commander, he was assigned the task of developing an invasion plan that would satisfy the political requirements of the White House and the Defense Department. Franks and his staff were first instructed in November 2001 to revise the operational contingency war plans for an Iraq invasion, OPLAN 1003-98 which had been developed during the Clinton years.

The revised 1998 invasion plan called for 375,000 troops. Rumsfeld made clear to Franks that the number was too large. Within a month, Franks had trimmed the invasion force to 275,000. Yet, this too was larger than what Rumsfeld had wanted. The U.S. armed forces had been nearly cut in half since the end of the Cold War. With only 1.3 million active duty forces, and an active commitment to the defense of South Korea, a war of any length involving any substantial number of troops would place a significant strain on the U.S. military.[30]

The transition to information age warfare, which had begun more than a decade before the Second Gulf War, had impressed on senior military officers the necessity of relying on the new assets available to them. Special forces equipped with net-centric communications, real time satellite intelligence, and coordinated with precision guided munitions from stealth aircraft would play a major role in the new Iraq war just as they were critical to the success of the Afghan conflict a year and a half earlier. The ground forces that Franks would commit would be equipped with heavy tanks and artillery systems, but with their overwhelming advantages vis-à-vis the Iraqi forces in mobility, air support and "situational awareness" allowed them to simply drive past Iraqi force concentrations on the way to Baghdad. This was precisely what they did. In less than three weeks, Franks's Army and Marine divisions swept over Southern and Central Iraq forming a pincer movement to take the Iraqi capital.[31]

Hussein, surprisingly, had never believed the United States would invade. From postwar interrogations and documents we know that right up till the start of the war he thought the coalition attack would be short and intensive, with the limited objectives of punishing Iraq for its alleged evasions of UN weapons inspections. Invading and occupying Iraq would cause too many U.S. casualties, or so he presumed. When the attack took place, involving a swift and devastating assault by over 100,000 troops, Hussein's generals stuck to their defensive positions, letting the Americans attack. The United States after all, had overwhelming military superiority based on its advanced weapons systems, battlefield situational awareness, and highly trained and motivated troops.

In less than a month, the post-Gulf War Iraqi army was effectively destroyed by invading United States and coalition forces. When the U.S. Third Army penetrated Baghdad's defenses in the first week of April, the disorganized and demoralized Iraqi army offered little organized resistance. Ostensibly, the war was a smashing success. Hussein disappeared from the site and quite suddenly, the United States and Great Britain had effective control of the Republic of Iraq.[32]

The invasion plans however, developed by Tommy Franks with the approval and heavy hand of his superior Donald Rumsfeld were badly flawed. While administration spokespersons including Rumsfeld believed the war was terminated in April 2003, it had barely begun. The invasion had been planned like an engineering project. It coordinated a joint warfare plan whose main objectives included the seizing of Iraq's more than 1000 operating oil wells to protect them from sabotage by the fedayeen. The plan expertly attacked military installations including Hussein's elaborate systems of palaces. The United States destroyed or disabled principal components of Iraq's military infrastructure. Care was placed in the need to occupy suspected WMD facilities to ensure their possession by the coalition. All this was accomplished with speed and alacrity by the military machine organized by CENTCOM and the Pentagon.

What the war plans left out was absolutely critical and laid the foundation for the catastrophic first years of the coalition occupation. Franks assumed that the postwar political state of Iraq would be quickly and effectively organized by other Washington institutions. The invading force was not designed as a long-term occupying army. The mission, as understood by CENTCOM was to liberate Iraq and destroy the Ba'athist regime, which would be quickly replaced by a robust and proactive postwar regime. Alas, the war strategy was premised on utterly false assumptions. It misperceived the nature of Iraqi internal politics, and the massive security problems posed by a decentralized and very potent insurgency; a resistance movement which could rely on hundreds of thousands of tons of munitions stored throughout the country in hidden caches.[33]

LIBERATION

Despite its fatal flaws, the invasion did accomplish its primary objective, the end of the rule of Saddam Hussein. Throughout much of Iraq, the fall of the dictator came with overwhelming joy. U.S. soldiers were kissed by Iraqi men, flowers were thrown, and crowds cheered as coalition tanks drove through the heart of Baghdad. The giant statues of Hussein, reminiscent of the same to those of Stalin and Mao in Russia and China were disfigured and toppled. Hussein's all-consuming personality cult, a central ideological component of his Republic of fear, evaporated, even as millions of Sunni Arabs continued to admire him. For Kurds and other non-Muslim and non-Arab minorities and for the huge Shiite population, Hussein's overthrow and the destruction of Baathism was a time of ecstasy. No amount of sanctions or internal dissidence would have removed Saddam Hussein and his evil dynasty. Without the interdiction of a supremely powerful foreign army, Hussein would never have left, his deadly regime perpetuated by his sons and his Tikriti brethren would have continued far into the future.[34]

THE INTIFADA BEGINS

The disintegration of Iraq was simply not anticipated by the Bush administration. The extensive State Department plans assumed the smooth establishment of order by the coalition forces and the immediate transition to an occupational authority with control over Iraqi territory. Yet, hundreds of thousands of angry and desperate men were living in an Iraqi state that had largely ceased to exist. The Ba'athist had not surrendered, but had merely gone underground according to the resistance that was planned before the war and invasion. Thousands of heavily armed and well-trained former soldiers, supplied with hidden weapons caches throughout the country began an insurgency campaign against the occupying forces. The attacks against the coalition multiplied with each passing month, as the reconstruction efforts of the occupational authority faltered and failed with disastrous results.

No institution in the U.S. government, despite 12 years of time to prepare for the occupation of Iraq from the end of the First Gulf War in 1991, had the training or resources to deal with a hostile occupation of a country of this size and complexity. Vast deserts, mountains, and urban landscapes inhabited by a foreign people whose language and culture were remote to U.S. soldiers and administrators. Barely a handful spoke fluent Arabic, and barely the same were at all familiar with the intricate tribal and sectarian politics of the nation. The Department of Defense had planned a transformational war, where a relatively small invasion force backed by the vast technological means of the Pentagon's net-centric warfare capabilities, would crush the inept and backward armed forces of a corrupt dictator. Hussein had no genuine military training, and with his military infrastructure weakened and damaged severely with the First Gulf War and more than a decade of sanctions, it was going to be a "cakewalk," according to Kenneth Adelman, a senior aide to the Secretary of Defense, Donald Rumsfeld.[35]

The masterful destruction of the Iraqi army in a few weeks made self-congratulations in order for Secretary of Defense, Donald Rumsfeld, and General Tommie Franks. The subsequent capture of most of the members of the most wanted Ba'athists, the notorious "Iraqi playing cards" gave more cheer to the supporters of the war who believed the performance of the U.S. military and the response to the liberation of Iraq was vindication for the policy. The beginning of the intifada did not affect the administration's optimism, nor were setbacks in reconstruction cause for worry as the main objective, the overthrow of the Iraqi regime had been accomplished.

By the end of 2003, Saddam Hussein himself was captured, and his sons killed. It looked as if the insurgency would now dissipate, and the Bush administration could claim victory. However, the Sunni uprising against the coalition authority not only survived Hussein's capture but expanded. Attacks by numerous groups throughout the Sunni dominated areas of the Iraq grew. At the same time, the Shiites built their own militias that challenged the occupation but also ended in sectarian war with the Sunnis. The occupation's problems would grow with each passing year, a cancer not only on Iraq, which saw its remaining physical infrastructure as well as its human capital destroyed.

The first years of the occupation proved an extraordinary nightmare for George Bush and his administration. Nothing seemed to work. His policies soon fell into ruins, with more than one cabinet official and several trusted aids resigning over the course of his second term.[36] It seemed as if the Iraqi intifada, planned originally by Hussein to punish the Americans for occupying Iraq, drew up millennia of Iraqi resistance to foreign occupiers. Like the Taliban in Afghanistan, the total destruction of their regime and the scattering of their forces did not mean the end of the war. In both Iraq and Afghanistan, timeless narratives of popular war against invaders fed into the dogged, fanatical resolve of Muslim rebels against a foreign enemy.[37]

Through the ensuing years, Iraq became for American society a return to the Vietnam War of the 1960s and 1970s. The planning systems that had failed in the first conflict, failed again in the twenty-first century. The methods of planning had become somewhat more sophisticated since the Tet Offensive and Invasion of Cambodia, but the information-based warfare of the 2000s still lacked the ability to truly control the battlefield. Despite exponential increases in the information content of military operations, including the precision and efficacy of armed strikes afforded by the new military systems, warfare still remained resistant to the power of the American state.

The revolution in military affairs begun during the 1990s had not conquered the tenacity and ingenuity of asymmetrical opponents, who relied on "local knowledge," and who did not obeyed conventional rules of warfare. Fighting in Iraq, in its urban centers and in the outlying villages and rural areas of the country, still required large number of troops. These forces, no matter how well protected with body armor, would take casualties on a daily basis, just as occupying armies had for centuries and millennia in the Middle East and around the world.

The effect of this reality was impressive. While Iraq was turned into a cauldron of chaos in the years following the Second Gulf War, the Bush administration was slowly de-legitimated by the process. Just as in Vietnam, and the parallels continue into the past with other wars and other countries, the Bush administration of the 2000s suffered just like the Johnson administration of the 1960s. The political costs of the war mounted, in lock step with the social and economic costs of a long-term foreign counterinsurgency.[38]

The Liberal Technocratic Order
in the Persian Gulf

On March 20, 2003, the United States, the United Kingdom and a Coalition of allies invaded Iraq and overthrew the government of Saddam Hussein. They claimed to bring peace, prosperity and democracy. But ever since, violence, civil strife and economic hardship have wracked the land. Though US President George W. Bush delivered his "mission accomplished" speech on May 2, 2003, the conflict has continued for more than four years. Thousands of innocent people are now dead and wounded, millions are displaced, several of Iraq's cities lie in ruins, and enormous resources have been squandered.

Global Policy Forum[1]

Because we acted, Saddam Hussein no longer fills fields with the remains of innocent men, women and children. Because we acted, Saddam's torture chambers and rape rooms and children's prisons have been closed for good. Because we acted, Saddam's regime is no longer invading its neighbors or attacking them with chemical weapons and ballistic missiles. Because we acted, Saddam's regime is no longer paying the families of suicide bombers in the Holy Land. Because we acted, Saddam's regime is no longer shooting at American and British aircraft patrolling the no-fly zones and defying the will of the United Nations. Because we acted, the world is better and United States of America is safer.[2]

George Bush, March 2008

THE CASE OF TWO NARRATIVES

In contemporary American culture, there have been two narratives to interpret America's role in the world and its conduct of foreign relations. On one hand, there is the legacy or memory or narrative of Munich and Pearl Harbor. On the other hand, there was the memory of Vietnam. The first script, so dominant in the decades immediately after the Second World War, imagined America as a righteous nation fighting evil. In the minds of both Bush presidents, the Gulf Wars were fought as just wars against tyranny; they were conflicts undertaken not for oil or power or revenge but to protect America and the world. This script centered the policy that mobilized the first Bush administration to go to war even in the face of powerful domestic opposition.

Yet, the second script in American culture was just as powerful if not more so than the first. The opposition to the First Gulf War and to the aftermath of the Second was grounded in the second narrative for postwar American internationalism. The legacy from the Vietnam War drove a determined opposition that saw both wars not as moral challenges but as dangerous illusions of an imagined threat. The two national traumas, one ending in victory, the other in defeat and tragedy, competed with one another in the minds of the public and of policymakers for both wars in the Persian Gulf. September 11, a third trauma, reignited the power of the first narrative, giving it a material advantage in fall 2002 against the antiwar script of the Vietnam experience. The neoconservative script, founded on the national identity of American greatness and global supremacy, took September 11 as a resurrection of American nationalism in response to "Islamo-fascism" and its allies.

In the Second Gulf War, the "Iraq War," the United States experienced both narratives. The heroic story of America showed itself in the fall of Baghdad, and the outpouring of joy among the liberated masses. Then, almost immediately, the second story, which Americans have experienced over and over again, turned history upside down. Weeks of triumph and victory turned into years of counterinsurgency war that destroyed Iraq, driving millions into exile, demolishing what had not been ravaged by decades of Saddamist rule. America as liberator and America as oppressor lived side by side in American society and culture. In the wider world, America as an unwelcome force far surpassed the image of the country as a force for freedom. While neoconservatives had long championed the expansion of democracy around the world, true to their Wilsonian traditions, the image they represented was utterly different. A significant part of the rest of the world incorporated an evil superpower into its national script; a nation of enormous military strength which threatened the international community with its clumsy and perhaps pernicious actions.

THE PROBLEM OF CONTROL

Beyond the problem of competing narratives and a damaged international image, the United States was still occupied with the management of the liberal technocratic order. America at the end of the twentieth and the beginning of the twenty-first century stood at the core of global power and modernization. The intellectual constructs of the new age are "complexity theory," "net-centric warfare," the "information age," "nanotechnology," "communications theory," "virtual communities," "distributed computing," "biotechnology," and so on. The terms themselves are rubrics for hundreds and thousands of other terms and concepts that define an exploding civilization of technocratic knowledge that has changed the nature of political economy, the nature of military science and modern warfare, and the social and cultural foundations of societies around the world. The liberal scientific civilization of the West, anchored by the interconnected technological systems of science and capitalism, has at its vortex American power and institutions. Capitalism has been in a period of extraordinary expansion; the rise of East Asia that began with Japan in the 1950s and 1960s has extended to the giant Asian nation-states of China and India. China has experienced explosive economic growth since the 1990s promising to equal and perhaps surpass the United States as an economic power by the middle of the twenty-first century. Massive expansion and technological innovations have created a global economic system of compelling power and energy that transforms the world's cultures, social, and political organizations, and scientific and industrial systems.[3]

American power, though, as evidenced in the Persian Gulf has been most dominant in the military sphere. The geometric rise of American military power continues to create an ever present colossus, whose technocratic organizations and evolving technocratic knowledge systems have maintained a massive and growing military machine. The intellectual center of this strength continues to lie in the specialized institutions of the national security state, where scientists, engineers, military professional, and policy theorists have worked for decades in a constant quest for innovation. DARPA (Defense Advanced Research Projects Agency) scientists and military theorists at various military institutes have continued the evolution of advanced weapon systems, operational, and strategic paradigms for the application of American power, and the fulfillment of America's self-defined security mission. That mission has been since the Second World War and continues far into the new century the idea of dominance. In some documents the term has been "full spectrum dominance," or the ability to establish control over any battlefield environment and to win against any possible adversary. Global dominance has been a concept that national security planners have felt comfortable with because U.S. vital interests have since the first half of the twentieth century been perceived as global in nature. To protect the country's vast global security interests, the only path had to be toward a concept of dominance on a world scale.

In the Persian Gulf, from the Iranian revolution of 1979 to the present, American power had to reestablish its dominance in the wake of the fall of the Shah and his replacement by a hostile anti-Western regime. In the Gulf, the global economic system depended upon an uninterrupted stream of oil, and this was enough to justify the projection of American power into the Gulf to a greater extent than it had in previous decades of the Cold War. Oil was the basis of the projection of U.S. power, but it was not the sole determinant. By the time of the First Gulf War, an added dimension to U.S. security interests related to nuclear proliferation by Iraq in the Gulf that promised its domination of the vital region as well as the complete destabilization of the Middle East.

The problem of stabilizing the Gulf, and ordering the societies of the Middle East to integrate into the Western metascript for world civilization became the script for U.S. foreign policy in the Gulf and the Middle East. In an ultimate sense, what the Gulf Wars and the GWOT have represented to the United States has been a problem of control. All civilizations involve developing effective systems of controlling essential areas of interest. At the end of the twentieth and the beginning of the twenty-first century, the nature of U.S. power in the Persian Gulf related fundamentally to the problem of establishing order over the political, economic and strategic dimensions of the region. Technocratic order does not require absolute domination, but it does affect a common regime for regional development and integration. Technocratic order or control entails the development of institutions and knowledge systems that establish highly efficient quantitative and quantifiable means of measuring power and information. The Gulf Wars, and especially the aftermath of the second one, demonstrated the failure of all areas of technocratic order. Neither weapons systems, which became integrated into the new information technology combat of the 2000s, nor administrative systems informed by different levels of politics, were capable of establishing an effective means of control in Iraq after the fall of the Ba'athist regime, in April 2003, nor in the remote regions of Afghanistan, Somalia, and other anarchic peripheries of the international system.

Paradoxically, establishing control for Saddam Hussein was relatively easy. His methods were the time-tested means of totalitarian rulers who used sheer force and brutality to create an enduring personalist regime. Hussein's control system would have lasted for decades more if he not challenged the liberal order of the United States. Once Hussein was overthrown by his most powerful enemy, who liberated his population from his medieval cruelty, the enemy/liberator was unwilling to use the same methods as he, thereby ensuring resistance from the substantial remnants of his fascist regime as well as other many other groups deeply opposed to the establishment of a Western-dominated state in the heart of Middle East.[4]

Military control of Iraq was achieved during the brief period of conventional war. The United States and Great Britain defeated the weakened and obsolete Iraqi armed forces in little more than a month, establishing immediate dominance in the air and sea, followed quickly by the capture of all major Iraqi cities. Military technologies developed over decades of research and development demolished conventional resistance with minimal casualties for the U.S. coalition. The United States had a full repertoire of precision guided weapon systems in 2003, far more than 1990, when it used the same technological superiority to defeat a larger Iraqi armed force. In 2003, the technocratic combat protocols destroyed entrenched Iraqi forces, making victory a certainty.

Yet, the spectacular efficiency of the U.S. war machine failed miserably once the conventional war came to an end. For years afterward, Iraqi insurgents fought savagely against the Americans and their coalition partners, using the proven tactics of insurgency warfare to impose deep political costs upon its world dominating occupying force. Despite the technical means to map every square inch of Iraq with satellite photos, to eavesdrop on every cell phone conversation, to divide Iraq up into hundreds of districts and within districts thousands of neighborhoods, control, or order was illusive for years. The various Iraqi resistance groups, fought with the same ruthlessness their ancestors had used upon occupying enemies for centuries. None of the new scientifically engineered military products, from the unmanned aerial reconnaissance vehicles, armored helicopters with guided missiles, and heavy machine guns firing thousands of rounds per minute, the 80 ton battle tanks, or the integrated real-time communication systems of the combat units were effective in ending determined and fanatical armed resistance groups. As with other counterinsurgency wars fought since 1900, superior arms did not lead to immediate victory or victory at all.[5]

Above all else, for the United States, victory in Iraq, Afghanistan and elsewhere required security for the populations of these countries, including for the elected officials and government workers of their national governments. The loss of order, at least in the short term, revealed the very real limits on organizational and technological resources to achieve control against the illusive tactics of clandestine enemies. For the new century, technocratic dimensions for control remained in their infancy. There was as yet no proven technical means to prevent the use of IED (improvised explosive devices), and to find and defeat operating cells and small groups of fighters who were indistinguishable from civilians.[6] Defeating native armed resistance in the complex and difficult urban and non-urban terrains of the war still necessitated human intelligence and human resources. This, it appeared, was the Achilles heel of the U.S. coalition. In parallel to the Vietnam War of three decades earlier, the Second Gulf War forced the First World power to sacrifice its soldiers on the battlefield. That factor alone, in the context of modern warfare, was enough to force an end to the war before the establishment of order.

Without control in Baghdad and its environs, and elsewhere in the ruined state of Iraq, the entire structure of the war effort, from Washington to the military command centers and the capitals of allied powers, all collapsed under the weight of failure. The political costs for the war were immense for the Bush administration and the Republican Party, as the mass media ran stories that illuminated the extent of the policy failures. The management systems of the American state failed in Iraq and elsewhere, triggering vociferous demands for reform. Despite a revolution in information-based technologies that promised a new world of voluminous wealth and security, the technocratic organization for asymmetric war was defeated in its first years by the human incompetence of its administrators and the human ingenuity of its Third World foes. Until the summer of 2007, there was no measurable progress against the Iraqi insurgency and the Afghan War remained an interminable nightmare. In the last year of the second term of the Bush presidency, the production of official and private reports on the conflict continued apaced.[7]

After years of bloodshed and a huge toll on the land forces of the United States, a semblance of order appeared in the late months of 2007. After so many years of intense day-to-day counterinsurgency warfare, the dynamics for at least a temporary means of political order looked in the cards. Yet, was the effective truce, which reduced dramatically the number of deaths and seriously wounded a result of effective U.S. military and political strategies inside Iraq, or were they a result of a summary cease-fire among the opposing sides in the Iraqi civil war? Was the technocratic strength of the United States, which in the early twenty-first century was without peer anywhere in the world, the factor that established "peace" in late 2007 or was it nearly irrelevant?

POLITICAL SCRIPTS

As in life, during the Gulf Wars political scripts abounded. As systems of control, scripts force actors to act unaware of the forces directing their behaviors. Scripts exist within the minds of individuals, who live in particular cultures, at particular times, and are all subject to the intricate dimensions of individual personal histories. Yet, they also exist collectively, mobilizing groups and indeed entire societies for the exigencies of a historical moment as well as for the longer patterns that have typified collective scripts of groups and societies throughout history. As cognitive systems, scripts have enormous power to determine both collective and individual behaviors. In the Middle East, historical scripts have reproduced its conflict systems, its tribal and clan relations over many centuries and even millennia. Historians have drawn parallels between the conflicts that engaged ancient Mesopotamians with those that have been central to the modern history of the Middle East. At the ground level, the present-day journalists and foreign policy analysts view actors who seem unalterable in their behaviors. It seemed no one was capable of preventing the Bush administration from pursuing its war policies in spring 2003, even though some observers understood all too well deep flaws were evident in U.S. doctrine and its implementation by military and civilian officials. Throughout the terms of the George W. Bush administration, tragedy informed public policy. Yet, the dysfunctional nature of Iraq policy and of U.S. foreign policy in general appeared in situ. Unlike his father, who had two decades of foreign policy experience prior to his assumption of office, the younger Bush had no competence in foreign policy or in presidential leadership. His administration, dominated by a fractured leadership of flawed personalities, established a collective script for the Bush administration that suggested preordained disaster. The path of the United States into the Persian Gulf in the early twenty-first century appeared predestined by a confluence of scripts.

What were those scripts? Embodied in collective scripts are group interests that are economic, political, social, and ideological in origin. The most powerful collective narrative related to the interests of the liberal technocratic order, which in turn, was a force serving the designs of cosmopolitan elites and their interests in preserving the structures of Western liberal civilization. The culminating script which was evident in public policy papers, journal articles, and monographs was the drive to maintain the liberal technocratic order against the stresses of a critical region in conflict with itself. The collective narrative expressed in speeches to "defend freedom" was in fact coded rhetoric for maintaining order against anti-Western groups, using advanced military forces to support the strategic vision of a modernizing Islamic world, by the development and diffusion of capitalism, contemporary Western culture and technological change. The American script was compelled by national security interests articulated by public intellectuals who represented the strategic interests of American political economy. The Gulf was vital to the economic health of the international economy, and its radical Islamists, a political threat to social order in the Third World and a strategic threat, through terrorism, to the social order in the developed world. In the Gulf, each group carried its collective narrative on its sleeve. The Iranian clerics circled the morass in neighboring Iraq, threatening to challenge the United States, Israel, and the remainder of its adversaries with Iranian nuclear bombs and long-range missile systems to deliver them. In Iraq, the remnants of the Ba'athists fought with fanaticism guided by the vision of a pan-Arab Sunni nation driving the foreign invaders from their homeland. Collective scripts, situated in the particular historical experiences, memories, and interests of tribes, and groups, established an anarchic swarm of violence, with reprisals and counter reprisals. By the summer of 2008, order seemed to have finally come to Iraq, but the scars of the conflict remain. History will need to judge if the war, so badly executed in so many ways, accomplished its goals.[8]

Interpreting history has always been a question of perspective. What was relevant, significant, or revealing about any subject or object of the past has always depended upon the observer. Just as Albert Einstein said about the nature of time that it was an observer-dependent phenomenon, so history only exists as an interpretation specific to the time, place, and mentality of the historian and his or her readers. It is far too early to have historical perspective on the Gulf Wars of 1991 and 2003. Nonetheless, in this monograph, I have attempted to explain the outlines of such a view, which will continue to refine itself, with new evidence and perspectives over decades and generations to come. At this moment in time, around the end of the first decade of the twenty-first century, the Second Gulf

War has dominated American foreign relations for most of the tenure of the century's first U.S. president, George W. Bush. The narrative of this second war, unlike that of the first, has been one of unremitting tragedy and abject failure. This may indeed change in years to come, but the war appears to contemporary observers as an enduring foreign policy disaster.

As Akira Iriye, the historian of modern East Asia wrote of the Pacific War, there exist two sets of relations between nations. One set has to do with cultural relations, the other with relations defined by power.[9] In this brief study of the Gulf Wars and American foreign policy, I have attempted to define the interrelationships between both "power and culture." I have related the common notions of realism and ideology to my underlying philosophy of history, which has to do with the idea of historical scripts. All history, whether individual, familial, local, institutional, national, or transnational, involves the working out of scripts. As a narrative discipline, history follows scripts as narratives, dynamically related in time and space to the substance of often messy dramas. The United States and the Gulf involved the intersection of a superpower's script with the millennial old scripts of the region's peoples. The American script of a liberal scientific Christian-based culture encountered the collective narratives of Arabs, Persians, Jews, and Turkic peoples, engaged in rivalries within and between themselves. It should have come as no surprise to anyone that the American venture in its explicit objectives, at least in the near and midterm as understood by public policy analysts, appeared to have failed.

George W. Bush, intent on defeating what he and his administration believed to be a dangerous enemy, launched a quick but decisive war with the intuitive belief in his own judgment that his actions were moral and necessary. Reflecting an ethnocentrism characteristic of American foreign relations since its origins in the eighteenth century, Bush and his advisers believed in the universal appeal of Western liberalism. Just as in the early nineteenth century, John Quincy Adams believed in spreading the virtues of American civil society throughout the Americas, and just as his successors believed equally in the vital nature of American democracy as a primal force in world affairs, George Bush, the 43rd president of the United States, continued the millenarian script. Anticipating very quick and very decisive victory, key Bush advisers expected an easy occupation and immediate geostrategic benefits.[10]

Trapped in a parochial world view, ignorant of the cultural and political complexities of Iraq and the Gulf region, their policy ignored the possibilities of clandestine resistance by the defeated Ba'athists, a guerrilla war that Saddam Hussein had planned for well in advance, issuing orders and storing vast quantities of explosives in hidden caches throughout the country. The Bush White House was blind to the intricate nature of a country with a hundred tribes divided between ethnic and sectarian groups all fully capable of waging war against each other and against the coalition. The failures of both civilian and military branches of the federal government to plan for the postwar occupation of Iraq were stunning. Despite a national security establishment whose resources were greater than those of all other defense establishments in the world combined, and despite decades and generations of international experience, the United States proved extraordinary incompetence in stabilizing a country that it had occupied with overwhelming military force.

None of this was new in U.S. foreign policy. Despite the technocratic civilization that underpinned its military might, public policy in America, nor in any other nation-state, has never been wholly rational. Politics by definition involves multiple levels of power, multiple levels of interest that are most often dependent upon the idiosyncratic needs of leaders and their attendants. In a complex political system, policies are often lost, unmoored by chaos and the absence of clear authority of ownership. This happened endlessly in Iraq as the administration's policies, poorly conceived and executed erroneously, led to one disaster after another. From the failure to protect Iraqi antiquities from rioters to the terrifying results of the Abu Ghareb scandal, to the plundering of countless billions of U.S. aid through theft and incompetence, the technocratic order collapsed in Iraq, as it has done elsewhere, terminated by incoherence.[11]

The political nature of public policy has always militated against effective continuity in diplomacy and the complex administrative tasks required of a global power. The aggressive guerrilla warfare waged against United States and coalition forces not wholly prepared for the task, imposed serious human, political, and economic costs not only on the United States but also on Iraq. The policy itself, a disaster in the eyes of the Middle East from its very beginning, became a global disaster for the international prestige of the country. America had followed its script into Iraq, and buried itself in a disastrous policy of cultural and linguistic ignorance.

The problems that faced the Bush administration after the conquest of Iraq appeared obvious. They were so obvious because they were conundrums that Americans have faced in Third World countries since the nineteenth century. Once again, similar patterns repeated through history suggest a script, a powerful one that guided American internationalism for 200 years. Ignorant of the consequences of their bold actions, Americans in 2003, just as they had done in earlier times, encountered an environment they could not control or understand. There was little or no sensitivity in the Bush administration for the dangers incipient in conquering a Muslim land in the heart of the Arab and Muslim world. The war plans, vetted through the Pentagon, the State Department, and the National Security Council, were enormously flawed, and Bush's advisers and much of the American public were just as blind to it as the senior leadership of the administration. The Americans fell into the occupation of Iraq thoroughly ensconced in an American reality defined by Americans for Americans. In Iraq, they discovered the complexity and tragedy of the nation they had conquered. They had not liberated Iraq as much as they had unleashed tribal and sectarian forces neither they nor the Iraqis could control. With each year of occupation, the state of Iraq fluctuated between factional separations and civil war and pure anarchy between rival groups, criminals and the subterranean force of Islamic terrorism.

George W. Bush had always been a risk taker. In business, he ran an independent oil company which failed with the decline in world oil prices in the 1980s. In attempting a political career in the 1990s, he appeared to do so without the endorsement of his parents. As president, he quickly went to war, trusting his advisers who failed to inform him of a coherent plan for postwar Iraq. As Iraq turned into an unmitigated disaster during his second term, and other policies met with failure, notably the disastrous response to the Katrina hurricane, Bush appeared to have reopened a script from his past. His leadership had the distinct style of a chief executive who had lost his moorings. He was in effect, following the presidential script of a failed leader. As a plethora of journalists and editorialists have written about George Bush, his management decisions were too often ill informed and ineffectual. His foreign policy and his entire administration seemed dysfunctional. Bush's failed presidency was perceived as not only a tragedy for him but for the United States, which in the space of just a few years had seen its international image change from admired global leader to in many parts of the world, a dangerous and destructive hegemon.

The failure of the Bush script translated into a cacophony of failed leaderships and institutions. Rumsfeld and his key deputies had failed at the Pentagon, and the Pentagon as an institution had failed as a manager of military resources and strategy. The same could be said of the State Department and other major national institutions, including the CIA and its affiliated intelligence agencies. Not only was the executive branch a failure, but so was the Congress, which had done nothing to stop the administration from its nightmarish war and its other public policy imbroglios, including the response to the destruction of New Orleans, the burgeoning federal deficit and entitlements crisis, and lack of an energy policy or a serious response to climate change, an international issue of equal importance as, or indeed greater than, the GWOT.[12]

The political scripts failed in the early 2000s, both for the United States and for much of the Middle East, where internecine and international war flourished. The Jews and Palestinians continued their 100-year war over the holy land, while throughout the region, a myriad of groups were either in armed conflict or nearly so over sectarian, ethnic, and nationalist issues. It appeared that despite substantive changes in world civilization in the twentieth century, where rationality and a code of universally recognized human rights were adopted in international law, violence in the form of war or terrorism had not lost its appeal as an instrument of power.

Violence, of course, has always been understood according to the particular vision of the combatants and other parties. Osama bin Laden and his radical

Islamist followers did not view the destruction of the Twin Towers in New York City to be an immoral act. Rather, they understood the actions of al Qaeda to be entirely defensive. For centuries, but most especially since the end of the last Muslim Caliphate with the dissolution of the Ottoman Empire, the West had placed the Muslim Umma under grave assault. Through colonization, occupation and imperialism the West had sought to annihilate the Muslims ending the existence of the Umma.[13] To attack the United States at its heart was to seek just retribution for the death of Muslim children and the desecration of the holy land by Israel, the United States and their allies in the West.

In postwar Iraq, the array of factions who engaged the U.S.-led multinational coalition had similar perspectives on violence against the occupiers. Waging war with all available means was just, moral and rational for Iraqi armed insurgents, just as it was viewed in similar ways by the United States and its armed forces. International war, in virtually all cases, involves an established system of armed conflict that locks antagonistic world views, ideologies, and interests into the processing of violent actions. The end of a violent or military confrontation usually comes with exhaustion and unacceptable costs, in life, money and political will. Political settlements, unfortunately, come at the very end of wars, after they have followed paths of often profound destruction. This was true of many or most wars fought in the twentieth century, and even with the advanced scientific and technical world of the twenty-first century it appears to remain so. No matter the costs of war and opportunities for peace, conflict systems create collective scripts that run their course. As long as the key elements of war remain unchanged, it will go to its logical end. In American history, the Continental Army was not going to capitulate nor were the British willing to end the war until a stunning defeat broke the British public's will to continue; in effect, ending the scripted conflict system for the American Revolutionary War.

In Iraq, both in 1990 and 2003, the wars were "locked in" by the historical frameworks that connected both Bush presidents and Saddam Hussein. Hussein could not have negotiated his way out of Kuwait in 1990–91 even if he wanted to do so. Withdrawal from land that he viewed as part of his nation, that is, Kuwait, was a cultural impossibility for a proud Iraqi Sunni. While the United States and much of the rest of the world in 1991 viewed Iraq as an aggressor, Hussein viewed his actions as justified, morally correct and vital to the Iraqi nation. Foreign powers should not and could not impose their collective will on Iraqis who had inhabited the Gulf region since time immemorial.

KNOWLEDGE AND INSTITUTIONS

For more than a century, Marxist theorists of various schools have argued that economic interests and relations have been, and are, determinants in human affairs. Alternatively, I have argued that capitalism as both an ideology and as technology relates to a larger synthesis of knowledge and institutions in industrialized societies, in which political scripts, knowledge systems, and institutions interact and codetermine each other. As a consequence, I submit that international affairs in the late twentieth and the early twenty-first century have been dominated by the synergy between complex professional knowledge systems and the institutions that have been both progenitors and creatures of them.

There was and still remains a problem of control for the United States in the Persian Gulf and globally. The same is true for the entire world community which must deal with a menu of formidable problems of control or management. The technocratic order must solve the nexus of problems related to sustainability, including climate change and other ecological crises that require the production of information, its dissemination and its intricate devolution into laws, treaties, and programs to control and stabilize the world's ecological systems. The same determinations have been required of related problems of economic development, social development, and human rights and democratization. In short, the Western metascript whose declarative principles have been enshrined in the UN Charter, have been driven by the codetermining factors of knowledge systems and their institutions. Professional knowledge has been nearly interchangeable with technology, that is, intellectual technology and government and corporate institutions arguably technologies in and of themselves.

Modern wars have been driven by military institutions and the nexus of advanced technical disciplines that generate both military doctrines and technologies. Quintessentially, they have been technology-driven events. The Gulf Wars and their aftermath have been exemplars of this pattern. The entire modern period, from 1990 to the present has in fact been a generative one for military technology founded on the knowledge and institutional systems of the U.S. national security state. The wars were showcases for the latest innovations in military weapon systems, including the advanced communications systems that have defined net-centric warfare.[14] During the First Gulf War, GPS-guided missiles from ships, submarines, and combat aircraft were a demonstration of American power, both a technological achievement and a political statement to the world broadcast on live satellite television. The advances in military technology continued at a rapid pace through the 1990s and into the first decade of the twenty-first century, along a wide spectrum of technologies and military systems. The "Shock and Awe" doctrine deployed in the Second Gulf War represented the maturation of satellite-directed missile systems as tactical and strategic weapons of enormous lethality with little collateral damage. In larger political terms, once again, they demonstrated an image of the United States as a near omnipotent force capable of projecting its might halfway around the world with only a fraction of its national resources.

The institutions and professional knowledge systems of the United States and the West appeared triumphant in 2003 and far less so in 2004 and 2005 and later. Nonetheless, the wars accrued resources for the development of advanced military systems which have continued to revolutionize the nature of warfare. The wars have been a catalyst for a new generation of military forces, where robotic systems and unmanned vehicles and aircraft have advanced as successors to the costly use of human soldiers against insurgents armed with deadly IEDs and other unconventional weapons. While United States and the coalition forces were driven to exhaustion in both Iraq and Afghanistan, the next generation of military technology was being designed, developed, and tested by the same military-industrial system that has been in place since 1940.[15]

DARPA's institutional mission or script has driven military and civilian institutions to create generations of technologies that have transformed not only war but civilization. By the early 2000s, a NASA study projected a world in the 2020s and 2030s where technological advances had completely transformed the nature of world civilization. NASA envisioned a near future where advanced technological systems had established not only a superabundance of wealth but a society where the normative characteristics of the twentieth-century civilization had lost or were quickly dissolving in relevance. This was not a Pollyanna vision of the future, but rather a sophisticated analysis based upon existing projections for advances in information technology, biotechnology, and material sciences.[16]

How does the NASA study relate to the narrative of the Gulf Wars? The study and U.S. military intervention in Iraq were coterminous, and reflected the same force of history that appeared to be elemental to both. Along with political scripts, the other force in history that orders the modern world relates to the expansion of formal systems of knowledge and institutional systems as coterminous structures to its production and dissemination. The political scripts drove the physical systems of modern warfare in the Gulf, the enormous aircraft carrier groups, B-2 bombers, and many thousands of coordinated tanks, armored vehicles, and artillery systems, gigantic in themselves but in fact connected to an incomparably vast and global military infrastructure. Those scripts, however, were incorporated into institutions and professional knowledge systems, deep repositories of power and information that in turn have a fundamental impact on human affairs.

Scientific and policy institutions have created the environments in which ideas have been created and ultimately legitimated. In the post–World War II institutional environment for national security, a vast system of knowledge production and institutionalization brought together universities, private policy institutes, and governmental organizations that funded and employed the scientists and intellectuals who developed the vast web of scientific and applied knowledge that created the modern technocratic state.

Institutionally, the most salient characteristics of the Gulf Wars involved the expansion of the American technocratic state. This was consistent with the outcome of every war since the beginning of the twentieth century. Although the size and scope of the U.S. military declined between the first and second World Wars, the technocratic infrastructure for global war quickly became operational. The same renewal of the state occurred during the Korean War and continued with the same pattern for the Gulf Wars and their associated conflict, the GWOT.

This leads to the final conclusion about the Gulf Wars. These related conflicts as well as the war on terror were catalytic events for the liberal technocratic order. Together, they accelerated the knowledge technologies that are at the core of twenty-first-century power. In this respect, there was far more continuity than discontinuity between the foreign policies of George H. Bush, Bill Clinton, and George W. Bush. Perpetuating the drive for global dominance that began in the early years of the Second World War, these administrations maintained the institutional and knowledge-based structure for the expansion of U.S. political, economic, and military power.

The occupation of Iraq did not go the way the administration had hoped. From the start, the profound deficits in the Bush administration's postwar management led to nearly catastrophic results. For a country that had fallen in weeks, and most of whose population welcomed American troops as liberators, the ensuing months and years of U.S. military and civilian administration fell into an abyss of sectarian violence and Ba'athist resistance. In the space of three years, the entire Bush foreign policy appeared to fall into an utterly disastrous cycle of bad public policy. Like the early post–Cold War period, the world's political system appeared to fly out of control, as American diplomacy and military actions lost the initiative not only in the Middle East but in Northeast Asia and Africa as well.

Despite the massive apparatus of the national security system, and the enormous resources of American society and its allies in the First World, the liberal order appeared impotent in the face of incipient anarchy in parts of Africa, the Middle East, and Asia. The technocratic designs of the advanced nations, to create self-sustaining and rapidly developing societies in the Third World, were tragically ineffective. The Iraqi debacle of the first decade of the new century represented the ongoing failures, political, and managerial, in the design of a modern egalitarian international system, where poverty, disease, violence, and political repression were finally eliminated. George W. Bush, like all his predecessors had a vision of an American peace in the Middle East, fashioned according to the liberal principles of Western civilization. In the wake of September 11, and the successful wars against the Taliban, al Qaeda, and Saddam Hussein, he and his advisers believed, if only temporarily, in the fulfillment of a neo-Wilsonian future of Iraq, the Arab world, and ultimately, the entire globe. After several of years of failure, the promise remained, but reality pressed for a reconstitution of the American script in international affairs.[17]

From the moment that U.S. troops occupied Baghdad, the stunning failure of the postwar occupation was there for the entire world to see. In the months prior to the invasion, extensive public policy papers were written outlining the nature of postwar Iraqi society as the United States envisioned it. The vision for a new Iraq was in line with the schemes proposed for the reconstruction of Germany and Japan in the late 1940s. Post-Ba'athist Iraq would be a peaceful demilitarized society, where the rule of law was respected and new democratic institutions were to immediately replace the totalitarian instruments of the Ba'athist state. Indeed, within the first year of the occupation thousands of reconstruction projects were begun in every region of the country. The United States and its coalition partners were prepared to rebuild Iraq from the ground up. There was funding and man-power allocated to repairing and expanding the country's public infrastructure for the generation of electricity, sewage systems, water supplies, hospitals, roads, and schools. The coalition under U.S. leadership intended to cancel or restruc-ture Iraq's massive external debts. They expected to rebuild the oil industry that had been devastated by war and sanctions. New political institutions, including a new constitution, and a thoroughly reformed and retrained Iraqi government were intended for this new society that would reconcile Sunni, Shiite, and Kurd-ish interests.[18]

Some five years after the end of the first phase of the Iraq war, namely, the successful defeat of Saddam Hussein's military, the high ambitions for the reconstruction of Iraq lay in grotesque ruin. The extent of the debacle was unthinkable prior to the war. In the first instance, the very reason for going to war by the international coalition led by the United States quickly evaporated. Despite months of intensive investigation throughout the country, the UN weapon inspectors could not find any indication that Saddam Hussein's brutal regime possessed WMD of any kind. In the cruelest of ironies, Hussein was toppled by his enemies for being a threat to regional and world peace. Yet, the premise for his defeat and overthrow was completely erroneous. While he had thousands of WMDs in the recent past, when his regime was finally confronted by his nemesis, the United States, he had none, making the invasion of his coun-try in retrospect unjustified and in some observers' eyes, illegal.[19]

The postwar insurrections by Iraqi tribal militias, former Ba'athists and the par-ticipation of foreign jihadists proved an unmitigated disaster for the coalition and, especially the Bush administration. The technological superiority of U.S. forces was unquestioned in spring 2003, as they were also unquestioned several decades in the past in Indochina. Yet, the power and precision of U.S. arms, whether deliv-ered by aircraft or ground forces, were completely ineffective in deterring the tactics of the Iraqi resistance. Instead of retaining the appellation of "liberator," George Bush became a tragic figure, like his predecessor and fellow Texan, Lyndon Johnson. He once thought he would bring democracy to the Islamic Middle East, instead he was trapped presiding over a catastrophe. His lieutenants had walked the country into a grinding war of suicide bombers and IEDs.

The broader outlines of the Gulf Wars relates to changes in the international system, and world and American civilization, in the two decades after the Cold

War. The rate of change, technological especially but also social and political was breathtaking. The most recent period in modern history has unleashed the extraordinary forces of capitalism and science-based technology. The Persian Gulf was a vital strategic theater for the United States and the world during and after the Cold War. The collapse of communism resulted in the primacy of Islamism and nationalism as transcendent forces in the Islamic world from Indonesia across the entire southern rim of Asia and Saharan Africa. U.S. power converged on the Gulf first because of Saddam Hussein, then because of al Qaeda and the apparent threat from Iran. These indigenous forces that opposed the United States and its regional and extraregional allies set the political framework for the Gulf Wars and its related conflict in Afghanistan. The other regional conflicts, especially the Arab-Israeli conflict fed into the conflict system that trapped the United States and its fellow combatants.

In the larger scheme of world history, the Gulf Wars of 1990–91 and 2003 to the present, have been tortuous and ultimately minor wars to stabilize the international system by the world's predominant power. That power, energized by the perceived threat environment posed by the anti-Western forces of radical Arab nationalism and Islamism, accelerated the technological expansion of the post–Cold War American national security system. The rhetoric and the reality of anti-American forces and especially the critical events of September 11, 2001, triggered the mobilization of financial and intellectual resources to expand the national security state. With combat in Afghanistan and Iraq, the Pentagon was given hundreds of billions of dollars to innovate; to create the "transformational warfare" with intent to establish "full-spectrum dominance" on the global battlefield. The declining defense budgets of the Clinton era were swept aside by the new mandates for revolutionizing the military and intelligence establishments of the United States. In the wake of the failed Iraqi occupation and the prewar intelligence failures, institutional resources focused on modernizing both military and civilian aspects of war.

The broader lessons of the Gulf Wars relate to the nature of U.S. foreign policy as an agent in the international system. The force of American power, economic, military, and political cannot be underestimated. In the first decades after the Cold War, the institutional systems that drove American influence in the world were at their apogee. Yet the irony remained that just as U.S. institutions have been paragons of innovation, they have also been the epitome of bureaucratic failure. On the one hand, the systematization of advanced knowledge by modern technocratic institutions, both corporate and public sector, suggests an abiding order in American and modern world civilization. On the other hand, the irrationality and chaos of so many public policies, suggest that the world has been far more anarchic in its design than planned.

The continuing challenge of the American, the Western and now global meta-script must be the management of order in a protean age. The Gulf Wars were at the heart of the conflicts that have stressed the international system and the institutions and systems required to govern it. The complex messages from these conflicts, bearing upon ethnic, religious, economic, and political differences, reflected the continuity of historical scripts both in U.S. foreign relations and international affairs in general. The nature of the world may be larger and more intriguing, but its fundamental characteristics should be the same.

Notes

CHAPTER 1

1. Dwight D. Eisenhower, "Eisenhower Doctrine" (January 5, 1957), Miller Center, University of Virginia online archive, http://millercenter.org/scripps/digitalarchive/speeches/spe_1957_0105_eisenhower.

2. Benjamin Shwadran, *The Middle East, Oil, and the Great Powers* (New York: Praeger, 1955), 443

3. Apple, Jr., "The Iraqi Invasion; Invading Iraqis Seize Kuwait and its Oil; U.S. Condemns Attack, Urges United Action," *New York Times,* August 3, 1990, 1

4. "Confrontation in the Gulf; Excerpts from Iraqi Document on Meeting with U.S.," *New York Times,* September 23, 1990; James A. Baker, *The Politics of Diplomacy, Revolution, War and Peace, 1989–1992* (New York: G.P. Putnam and Sons, 1995), 2–3.

5. For the First Gulf War, annotated bibliographies exist from the 1990s, see Andrew Orgill, *The 1990–91 Gulf War: Crisis, Conflict, Aftermath: An Annotated Bibliography* (London: Mansell, 1995); The best military history of the First Gulf War is Anthony Cordesman and Abraham Wagner, *The Lessons of Modern War: The Gulf War* vol. 4 (Lessons of Modern War) (Boulder, CO: Westview Press, 1996); For the Second Gulf War or Iraq War, there a numerous contemporary accounts which may or may not be dated. The Global War on Terror has a very large and growing literature but it has no real center among authors other than basic ideas of where al Qaeda originated. Indeed, it is such a vast concept, that it defines an age.

6. Orrin Schwab, *Redeemer Nation: America and the World in the Technocratic Age, 1914 to the Present* (Salt Lake: ABP, 2004), 1–70.

7. ibid, 325–34. The institutional literature on American national security begins with the "warfare state" of the 1950s and 1960s. See C. Wright Mills, *The Power Elite* (New York: Oxford University Press, 1956); Fred Cook, *The Warfare State* (New York: Collier Books, 1962); Adam Yarmolinsky, *The Military Establishment: Its Impact on American Society* (New York: Harper and Row, 1972); Gene M. Lyons and Louis Morton, *Schools for Strategy,*

Education and Research in National Security Affairs (New York: Praeger, 1965); Paul Dickson, *Think Tanks* (New York: Atheneum, 1971); Marcus G. Raskin, *The Politics of National Security* (New Brunswick, NJ: Rutgers University Press, 1979); Richard J. Barnet, *The Economy of Death* (New York: Atheneum, 1969) and *Roots of War* (New York: Atheneum, 1972); Franz Schurmann, *The Logic of World Power: An Inquiry into the Origins, Currents and Contradictions of World Politics* (New York: Pantheon Books, 1974).

8. In addition to *Redeemer Nation,* a newer institutional literature includes Michael Hogan, *A Cross of Iron, Harry S. Truman and the Origins of the National Security State, 1945–1954* (Cambridge: Cambridge University Press, 1998); Aaron L. Friedberg, *In the Shadow of the Garrison State, America's Anti-statism and its Cold War Grand Strategy* (Princeton, NJ: Princeton University Press, 2000); Amy Zegart, *Flawed by Design: The Evolution of the CIA, JCS and NSC* (Stanford: Stanford University Press, 1999); Gregory Hooks, *Forging the Military-Industrial Complex: World War II's Battle of the Potomac* (Chicago: University of Illinois Press, 1991); Benjamin Franklin, *Cooling, Complex Gray Steel and Blue Water Navy: The Formative Years of America's Military-Industrial Complex, 1881–1917* (Hamden, CT: Archon Books, 1979); Harvey M. Sapolsky, *Science and the Navy: The History of the Office of Naval Research* (Princeton, NJ: Princeton University Press, 1990); Stuart W. Leslie, *The Cold War and American Science: The Military-Industrial-Academic Complex at MIT and Stanford* (New York: Columbia University Press, 1993).

9. Full Spectrum Dominance has been a strategic and tactical doctrine for all branches of the U.S. armed forces since the 1990s. "The Army seeks to achieve full-spectrum dominance— the ability to defeat any adversary and control any situation across the full range of military operations." Major Frank L. Andrews, *A Stability Force: The Missing Link in Achieving Full-Spectrum Dominance* (Fort Leavenworth, KS: School of Advanced Military Studies, 2004), ii. "Command and Control (C2) is the key enabler allowing U.S. forces to achieve Full Spectrum Dominance in the Ground, Air, and Space mediums. A key to this supremacy is Information Dominance." Lt. Col. Paul W. Phister, *C2 of Space: The Key to Full Spectrum Dominance* (Rome, NY: Air Force Research Laboratory, 1999), 1. The most comprehensive mission for full spectrum dominance is defined in the mission statement for the U.S. Strategic Command:

> USSTRATCOM combines the synergy of the U.S. legacy nuclear command and control mission with responsibility for space operations; global strike; Defense Department information operations; global missile defense; and global command, control, communications, computers, intelligence, surveillance, and reconnaissance (C4ISR), and combating weapons of mass destruction. This dynamic command gives National Leadership a unified resource for greater understanding of specific threats around the world and the means to respond to those threats rapidly.

United States Strategic Command, http://www.stratcom.mil/organization.html.

10. Schwab, *Redeemer Nation,* 53–68; Friedberg, *Garrison State,* 199–244.

11. Jimmy Carter, *State of the Union Address,* January 23, 1980, http://jimmycarterlibrary .org/documents/speeches/su80jec.phtml. This policy was later formalized in national security directive 63. White House, "Persian Gulf Security Framework," *Presidential Directive/NSC 63,* January 15, 1981, Washington, DC, www.jimmycarterlibrary.org/documents/pres _directive.phtml.

12. William Shepard, *Energy Studies* (London: Imperial College Press, 2003), 131.

13. White House, *U.S. Policy Response to the Iraqi Invasion of Kuwait,* NSD 45, August 20, 1990, Washington, DC, http://bushlibrary.tamu.edu/research/nsd.php.

14. Baker, *The Politics of Diplomacy,* 280.

15. Stephen J. Randall, *The United States Oil Policy Since World War One, for Profits and Security* (Montreal: McGill-Queen's University Press, 2005), 299.

16. ibid., 295–331; the literature on U.S. energy security is too large for one footnote, however, an important contemporary study that addresses is this issue has been issued by Council on Foreign Relations; see *National Security Consequences of U.S. Oil Dependency,* Report of Independent an Task Force (New York: Council on Foreign Relations Press, 2006).

17. Orrin Schwab, *Defending the Free World: John F. Kennedy, Lyndon Johnson and the Vietnam War, 1961–1965* (Westport, CT: Praeger, 1998), 13–14; Schwab, *Redeemer Nation,* 228–40.

18. For a detailed understanding of Kennan's thought, see Giles D. Harlow and George C. Maerz, eds., *Measures Short of War,* The George F. Kennan lectures at the National War college, 1946–47 (Washington, DC: National Defense University Press, 1991).

19. Baker, *Politics of Diplomacy,* 410; George Bush and Brent Scowcroft, *A World Transformed* (New York: Knopf, 1998), 489.

20. Schwab, *Defending the Free World,* 192–95; Orrin Schwab, *A Clash of Cultures, Civil Military Relations During the Vietnam War* (Westport, CT: Praeger Security International, 2006), 10–15.

21. The "Powell Doctrine" was premised on the "Weinberger Doctrine" formulated in a speech by Secretary of Defense Caspar Weinberger in 1984. Essentially, the Powell-Weinberger doctrine was a summary of the principles of war followed by major national armies for the past 200 years. See Caspar Weinberger, *The Uses of Military Power,* remarks at the National Press Club, Washington, DC, November 28, 1984, http://www.pbs.org/wgbh/pages/frontline/shows/military/force/weinberger.html; Colin Powell, *U.S. Forces: The Challenges Ahead, Foreign Affairs* (Winter 1992/93), http://www.cfr.org/publication/7508/us_forces.html.

22. Michael R. Gordon and Bernard E. Trainor, *The Generals' War: The Inside Story of the Conflict and the Gulf* (New York: Little Brown, 1995), 130–31.

23. For the intellectual roots of Wilsonian Internationalism; See Schwab, *Redeemer Nation,* 131–42; Lloyd E. Ambrosius, *Woodrow Wilson and the American Diplomatic Tradition: The Treaty Fight in Perspective* (New York: Cambridge University Press, 1990); John Milton Cooper, Jr., *Breaking the Heart of the World: Woodrow Wilson and the Fight for the League of Nations* (New York: Cambridge University Press, 2001); Thomas J. Knock, *To End All Wars: Woodrow Wilson and the Quest for a New World Order* (Princeton, NJ: Princeton University Press, 1995).

24. The neoconservative movement in the United States began in the early 1970s as a response to the anti-Cold War activism of the left wing of the Democratic party and the rise of the "counterculture." See Irving Kristol, *Neoconservatism: The Autobiography of an Idea* (Chicago: Ivan Dee, 1999); Jeanne J. Kirkpatrick, *Dictatorships and Double Standards: Rationalism and Reason in Politics* (New York: Simon and Schuster, 1982); Norman Podhoretz, *Breaking Ranks: A Political Memoir* (New York: Harper and Row, 1979); David Horowitz, *Left Illusions: An Intellectual Odyssey* (Dallas, TX: Spence Publishing, 2003); David Frum and Richard Norman Perle, *An End to Evil: How to Win the War on Terror* (New York: Random House, 2003).

25. John McNaughton, *Action for South Vietnam,* March 10, 1965, Washington, DC, *Foreign Relations of the United States,* 1964–1968, vol. 2, Vietnam January–June 1965 (Washington, DC: GPO, 1996), No. 193, http://www.state.gov/www/about_state/history/vol_ii/192_194.html.

26. Schwab, *Defending the Free World,* 206–10; Schwab, *Redeemer Nation,* 191–204.

27. Schwab, *Redeemer Nation,* 33–46. The idea of scripts or narratives cuts a broad swath over the intellectual disciplines of the humanities and the social sciences. The psychoanalytic tradition and cultural anthropology developed these ideas before they cross fertilized other fields. See Sherry B. Ortner, ed., *The Fate of Culture: Geertz and Beyond* (Berkeley: University of California Press, 1999); Clifford Geertz, *The Interpretation of Cultures* (New York: Basic Books, 1973), 7, and *Local Knowledge: Further Essays in Interpretive Anthropology* (New York: Basic Books, 1983). Victor Turner, *Dramas, Fields and Metaphors: Symbolic Action in Human Society* (Ithaca, NY: Cornell University Press, 1974); Victor Turner and Edward Bruner, eds., *The Anthropology of Experience* (Urbana: University of Illinois Press, 1986). My concept of scripts is from the psychoanalytic tradition. The post-Freudian psychiatrist Eric Berne and his school of transactional analysis originated the concept of the script as the center of human behavior and cognition. See Eric Berne, *The Structure and Dynamics of Organizations and Groups* (New York: Grove Press, 1963); Eric Berne, *Intuition and Ego States: The Origins of Transactional Analysis: A Series of Papers* (San Francisco: TA Press, 1977); Eric Berne, *Beyond Games and Scripts* (New York: Grove Press, 1976); Eric Berne, *What Do You Say after You Say Hello? The Psychology of Human Destiny* (New York: Grove Press, 1972); Claude Steiner, *Scripts People Live: Transactional Analysis of Life Scripts* (New York: Grove Press, 1974). Since the 1970s, the concept expanded through the field of psychodynamic psychology and beyond. See James M. Glass, *Psychosis and Power: Threats to Democracy in the Self and the Group* (Ithaca, NY: Cornell University Press, 1995); M.P. Freeman, *Rewriting the Self: History, Memory, Narrative* (New York: Routledge, 1993); R. Langs, "Psychoanalysis: Narrative Myth or Narrative Science," *Contemporary Psychoanalysis* 29, no. 4 (1993): 555–94; K.M. Hunter, *Doctors' Stories: The Narrative Structure of Medical Knowledge* (Princeton, NJ: Princeton University Press, 1991); M.F. Hanley, "'Narrative,' Now and Then: A Critical Realist Approach," *International Journal of Psycho-Analysis* 77, no. 3 (1996): 445–57; O.F. Goncalves, "Cognitive Narrative Psychotherapy: The Hermeneutic Construction of Alternative Meanings," *Journal of Cognitive Psychotherapy* 8, no. 2 (1994): 105–25; P. Van den Broek and R. Thurlow, "The Role and Structure of Personal Narratives," *Journal of Cognitive Psychotherapy* 5, no. 4, special issue (1991): 257–74.

28. There is a substantial literature of the messianic idea in American history, see Ernest Lee Tuveson, *Redeemer Nation: The idea of America's Millennial Role* (Chicago: University of Chicago Press, 1968); Ruth H. Bloch, *Visionary Republic: Millennial Themes in American thought 1756–1800* (Cambridge: Cambridge University Press, 1985); Terry Givens, *By the Hand of Mormon: The American Scripture that Launched a New World Religion* (New York: Oxford University Press, 2003); *Millenarian Piety of Roger Williams* (Chicago: University of Chicago Press, 1979); Jonathan Edwards, "The End for Which God Created the World." In *The works of Jonathan Edwards,* vol. 1 (Carlisle, PA: Banner of Truth Trust, 1995), 94–121; Charles R. Watson, *God's Plan for World Redemption: An Outline Study of the Bible and Missions* (Philadelphia, PA: United Presbyterian Church of N.A., 1911); Grant Underwood, *The Millenarian World of Early Mormonism* (Urbana: University of Illinois Press, 1993); James H. Moorehead, *American Apocalypse: Yankee Protestants and the Civil War, 1860–1869* (New Haven, CT: Yale University Press, 1978); Michael Hunt, *Ideology and U.S. Foreign Policy* (New Haven, CT: Yale University Press, 1987); Ninkovich, *The Wilsonian Century: U.S. Foreign Policy Since 1900* (Chicago: University of Chicago Press, 2001); Knock, *To End All Wars.*

29. Schwab, *Redeemer Nation,* 303–22; Alfred B. Evans, Jr., *Soviet Marxist-Leninism: The Decline of an Ideology* (Westport, CT: Praeger, 1993), 193–210.

30. There is a huge literature on the idea of nations as "imagined communities." See Benedict Anderson, *Imagined Communities: Reflections on the Origin and Spread of Nationalism*

(London: Verso, 1983); Michael Berkowitz, ed., *Nationalism, Zionism and Ethnic Mobilization of the Jews in 1900 and Beyond* (Boston: Brill Leiden, 2004); Yingjie Guo, *Cultural Nationalism in Contemporary China, the Search for National Identity Under Reform* (New York: Routledge Curzon, 2003); John Fousek, *To Lead the Free World: American Nationalism and the Cultural Roots of the Cold War* (Chapel Hill: University of North Carolina Press, 2000).

31. Iran is the center of Shiite Islam, see Graham Fuller, *The Center of the Universe: The Geopolitics of Iran* (Boulder, CO: Westview Press, 1991); Joyce N. Wiley, *The Islamic Movement of Iraqi Shi'as* (London: Lynne Riley, 1992); Roger Owen, *State, Power and Politics in the Making of the Modern Middle East* (New York: Routledge, 2004).

32. If there is a region of the world where tribal, ethnic, and religious bonds run long and deep, it is the Persian Gulf. See Vali Nasr, *The Shia Revival, How Conflict Within Islam Will Shape the Future* (New York: Norton, 2007), 229–54; Writing in the mid-1990s, one Middle East scholar summarized the state of Arab politics as one that had to confront the most existential questions:

> This Arab crisis confronts the Arab world—that is, its people and its leaders—with disquieting concrete questions, the answers to which can only be formulated in political terms. Regarding the nature of Arab society, these include various fundamental questions: What is, or should be, the relationship between Arabism and religion, between individual freedom and communal responsibility, between rich and poor sectors of the Arab world, between society and state, between government and citizenry, and among the existing Arab polities?

Dan Tschirgi, "The Arab World and the Rest of the World," in *The Arab World Today*, ed., Dan Tschirgi (Boulder, CO: Lynne Reiner, 1994), 247–64, 247.

33. Leadership theory is now a science, which explores the social and psychodynamics characteristics of leaders in business, politics, and other institutional and group processes. See John Adair, *Inspiring Leadership: Learning from Great Leaders* (London: Thorogood, 2002); Thomas Preston, *The President and His Inner Circle: Leadership Style and the Advisory Process in Foreign Affairs* (New York: Columbia University Press, 2001); Jane Whitney Gibson, John C. Hannon, and Charles W. Blackwell, "Charismatic Leadership: The Hidden Controversy," *Journal of Leadership Studies* 5, no. 4 (1998): 11–29; Kathy B. Smith and Craig Allen Smith, *The White House Speaks: Presidential Leadership as Persuasion* (Westport, CT: Praeger Publishers, 1994), 1–28.

34. Archie Brown, *The Gorbachev Factor* (Oxford: Oxford University Press, 1996), 306–18; Robert D. English, *Russia and the Idea of the West: Gorbachev, Intellectuals, and the End of the Cold War* (New York: Columbia University Press, 2000), 206–29.

35. Smith, *The White House Speaks,* 229–34; Preston, *The President and His Inner Circle,* 190–250.

36. Claudia Posch *This World He Created is of Moral Design: The Reinforcement of American Values in the Rhetoric of George W. Bush* (Wien: Praesens, 2006); Bill Sammon, *The Evangelical President: George Bush's Struggle to Spread a Moral Democracy Throughout the World* (Washington, DC: Regency, 2007); Stefan Halper and Jonathan Clarke, *America Alone: The Neo-conservatives and the Global Order* (New York: Cambridge University Press, 2004).

CHAPTER 2

1. William Kristol and Robert Kagan, *Present Dangers: Crisis and Opportunity in American Foreign and Defense Policy* (San Francisco, CA: Encounter Books, 2000), 5.

2. Edward Said, speech, *Culture and Imperialism,* York University, Toronto, February 10, 1993, at www.zmag.org/zmag/articles/barsaid.htm.

3. The idea of "energy security" dates from the 1980s. Since the consolidation of OPEC power in the aftermath of the Yom Kippur war, all major Western world powers have had to confront the idea of securing sufficient oil to meet vital economic needs. The strategic emphasis on the Persian Gulf for the United States and its allies has been a sine qua non of post 1973 foreign policy. Robert Belgrave, Charles K. Ebinger, and Hideaki Okino, eds., *Energy Security to the Year 2000* (Boulder, CO: Westview Press, 1987); Stephen Pelletière, *Iraq and the International Oil System: Why America Went to War in the Gulf* (Westport, CT: Praeger, 2001), 197–232.

4. See John H. Maurer and Richard H. Forth, eds., *Military Intervention in the Third World: Threats, Constraints, and Options* (Westport, CT: Praeger, 1984); Odd Arne Westad, *The Global Cold War: Third World Interventions and the Making of Our Times* (New York: Cambridge University Press, 2005).

5. Jerry W. Sanders, *Peddlers of Crisis: The Committee on the Present Danger and the Politics of Containment* (Boston: South End Press), 235–76; Drew Middleton, "Report on Soviet Nuclear Strategy Says Moscow Emphasizes Victory," *New York Times,* June 29, 1977, 7; Drew Middleton, *House Study Warns of Soviet Arms Gain;* Rep. Stratton Says That the Report Predicts Deterioration of U.S. Deterrent Role by 1980, *New York Times,* December 21, 1977, 7; Richard Burt, "Nuclear Gains by Russians Prompt a Reaction by U.S.; Defense: Is the U.S. Prepared? Soviet Advances in Weapons Prompt U.S. Reaction Capacity to Retaliate Weapons Production Studied Controversy Over MX A Submarine Alternative Criticism From the Right," *New York Times,* September 22, 1980, A.1.

6. Brzezinski was quite candid in a 1998 interview that he was instrumental in establishing the critical U.S. role in aiding the Afghan resistance against the Soviet Union:

> According to the official version of history, CIA aid to the Mujahadeen began during 1980, that is to say, after the Soviet army invaded Afghanistan, 24 Dec 1979. But the reality, secretly guarded until now, is completely otherwise. Indeed, it was July 3, 1979 that President Carter signed the first directive for secret aid to the opponents of the pro-Soviet regime in Kabul. And that very day, I wrote a note to the president in which I explained to him that in my opinion this aid was going to induce a Soviet military intervention.

Zbigniew Brzezinski, interview, Le Nouvel Observateur, Paris, January 15–21, 1998.

7. Edward N. Luttwak, "A 'Hands-Off' U.S. Policy On Afghanistan? No," *New York Times,* January 6, 1980, E19; James Reston, "Washington Moscow's Costly 'Victory,'" *New York Times,* January 6, 1980, E19.

8. Jimmy Carter, State of the Union Address, January 23, 1980, http://jimmycarterlibrary.org/documents/speeches/su80jec.phtml; Report, House Committee on Foreign Affairs, An Assessment of the Afghanistan Sanctions: Implications for Trade and Diplomacy in the 1980s (Washington, DC: GPO, 1981), 11–97.

9. Babak Ganji, *Politics of Confrontation: The Foreign Policy of the USA and Revolutionary Iran* (London: Taurus, 2006), 101–46; Ofira Seliktar, *Failing the Crystal Ball Test: The Carter Administration and the Fundamentalist Revolution in Iran* (Westport, CT: Praeger, 2000), 125–72.

10. For MIRV technology, see Ted Greenwood, *Making of the MIRV: A Study of Defense Decision-making* (New York: Ballinger, 1975). For Soviet nuclear forces, see www.fas.org/irp/dia/product/smp_index.htm, Nuclear statistics. General data on both United States, Soviet, and other nuclear powers is maintained by the Natural Resources Defense Council,

http://www.nrdc.org/nuclear/nudb/datainx.asp; Robert Norris, William Arkin, and William Burr, *United States Secretly Deployed Nuclear Bombs In 27 Countries and Territories During Cold War* (October 20, 1999), www.gwu.edu/~nsarchiv/news/19991020/index.html; Ken Alibek and Stephan Handelman, *Biohazard: The Chilling True Story of the Largest Covert Biological Weapons Program in the World* (New York: Delta, 2000); Lev Aleksandrovich Fedorov, *Chemical Weapons in Russia: History, Ecology, Politics* (July 27, 1994), Moscow Center of Ecological Policy of Russia, www.fas.org/nuke/guide/russia/cbw/jptac008_l94001.htm.

11. U.S. sponsorship of the Pahlavi dynasty from 1953 through its fall in 1978 has been well documented. Stephen Kinzer, *All the Shah's Men: An American Coup and the Roots of Middle East Terror* (Hoboken, NJ: Wiley, 2003); Ganji, *Politics of Confrontation,* 147–68; David Patrick Houghton, *US Foreign Policy and the Iran Hostage Crisis* (New York: Cambridge University Press, 2001).

12. The Reagan era national security system was heavily funded and expansionist by design. See Kenneth A. Oye, ed., *Eagle Resurgent? The American Foreign Policy* (Boston: Little, Brown and Co., 1987); Janne E. Nolan, *Guardians of the Arsenal: The Politics of Nuclear Strategy* (New York: Basic Books, 1989); Steven Kull, *Minds at War: Nuclear Reality and the Inner Conflicts of Defense Policymakers* (New York: Basic Books, 1988); Mark P. Lagon, *The Reagan Doctrine: Sources of American Conduct in the Cold War's Last Chapter* (Westport, CT: Praeger, 1994).

13. David Newsom, "America Engulfed," *Foreign Policy,* no. 43, Summer 1981, 17–32; Kenneth Waltz, "A Strategy for the Rapid Deployment Force," *International Security,* 5, no. 4, Spring 1981, 49–73, 53; Flora Lewis, "Carter Step Seems to Please Europeans; Dependence on Oil Bonn May Hold Key Germans Move Toward U.S.," *New York Times,* January 25, 1980, A.8; Michael M. Yoshitsu, "Japan and the Mideast," *New York Times,* February 2, 1981; "U.S. Vulnerability to Oil Cutoff Seen," *New York Times,* September 18, 1983; Leslie H. Gelb, "Oil-X in a Strategic Equation," *New York Times,* October 7, 1983.

14. Dilip Hiro, *The Longest War, the Iran-Iraq Conflict* (London: Grafton Books, 1989), 7–39; W. Thom Workman, *The Social Origins of the Iran-Iraq War* (Boulder, CO: Lynne Reiner, 1994).

15. Stephen J. Randall, *United States Foreign Oil Policy Since World War I, For Profits and Security* (Montreal: Mcgill-Queens's University Press, 2004), 253–318; Simon Bromley, *American Hegemony and World Oil, The Industry, State and the World Economy* (University Park, PA: Pennsylvania State University, 1991), 117–62.

16. A range of writers discussed the military, economic, and political decline of the United States. Lester Thurow, *The Zero-Sum Society: Distribution and the Possibilities Force Economic Change* (New York: Basic Books, 1980) and *Zero-Sum Solution: Building a World-class American Economy* (New York: Simon and Schuster, 1985); Paul Kennedy, *The Rise and Fall of the Great Powers: Economic Change and Military Conflict From 1500 to 2000* (New York: Random House, 1987); Paul Kennedy, *Preparing for the Twenty-first Century* (London: HarperCollins, 1993); Colin S. Gray and Jeffrey G. Barlow, "Inexcusable Restraint: The Decline of American Military Power in the 1970s," *International Security,* 10, no. 2, Autumn, 1985, 27–69.

17. The U.S. Department of Defense had a budget of $273 billion in 1986. Adjusted for inflation this number was approximately $440 billion in 2008. While this is substantially below combined defense spending for the current era, it was an exceptional amount far above previous defense spending levels during the Cold War. See "Table 3.1: Outlays by superfunction and function: 1940–2009," in *Office of Management and Budget, Historical Tables, Budget of the United States Government, Fiscal Year 2005* (Washington, DC: GPO, 2004), 45–52.

18. See Joyce Battle, ed., "Shaking Hands with Saddam Hussein: The U.S. Tilts Toward Iraq, 1980–1984," *National Security Archive Electronic Briefing Book* No. 82, March 27, 2003, www.gwu.edu/~nsarchiv/NSAEBB/NSAEBB82.

19. Nasr, *The Shia Revival,* 125. Ulama are the "learned of Islam" or Islamic religious leaders; see Muhammad Qasim Zaman, *The Ulama in Contemporary Islam: Custodians of Change* (Princeton, NJ: Princeton University Press, 2007).

20. Geoff Simons, *From Sumer to Saddam* (New York: MacMillan, 1996), 275–6; Reeva Spector Simon and Eleanor H. Tejirian, eds., *The Creation of Iraq, 1914–1922* (New York: Columbia University Press, 2004).

21. Marvin Zonis Daniel Brumberg, "Shi'ism as Interpreted by Khomeini: An Ideology of Revolutionary Violence," in *Shiism, Resistance and Revolution,* ed., Martin Kramer (Boulder, CO: Westview Press, 1987), 47–66; Babak Ganji, *Politics of Confrontation: The Foreign Policy of The USA and Revolutionary Iran* (London: Taurus Academic Studies, 2006), 62–99; Dariush Zahedi, *The Iranian Revolution Then and Now: Indicators of Regime Instability* (Boulder, CO: Westview Press, 2000).

22. R.K. Ramazani, *Revolutionary Iran: Challenge and Response in the Middle East* (Baltimore: Johns Hopkins University Press, 1986); Mark Gasiorowski and Nikki Keddie, eds., *Neither East nor West: Iran, the Soviet Union and the United States* (New Haven, CT: Yale University Press, 1990).

23. Phebe Marr, "The Iran-Iraq War: The View from Iraq," in *The Persian Gulf War: Lessons for Strategy, Law and Diplomacy* ed., Christopher C. Joyner (Westport, CT: Greenwood, 1990), 59–73, 59–64; Naid El-Sayed El-Shazly, *The Gulf Tanker War: Iran and Iraq's Maritime Swordplay* (New York: St. Martin's Press, 1998), 73–81.

24. It should be noted at no point did the Reagan administration end its moral objections to Iraq's use of chemical weapons. NSC, National Security Decision Directive (NSDD 139) Measures to Improve U.S. Posture and Readiness to Respond to Developments in the Iran-Iraq War, April 5, 1984 at www.gwu.edu/~nsarchiv/NSAEBB/NSAEBB82/; ibid., State Department, Cable, George P. Shultz to the U.S. Embassy in Iraq. "Memcon: Secretary's Meeting with Iraqi DepPrimMin Tariq Aziz, November 26, 1984, 10:00 a.m.," November 29, 1984. at http://www.gwu.edu/~nsarchiv/NSAEBB/NSAEBB82/iraq60.pdf; Amin Saikal, "Soviet Policy Toward Southwest Asia," *Annals of the American Academy of Political and Social Science* 481 (September 1985): 104–16.

25. The Malta Summit of December 1989, just after the East European revolutions, established the idea of a "New World Order" under the partnership of the United States and the Soviet Union. As the USSR collapsed, this idea transitioned to unipolarity. R. W. Apple Jr., "The Malta Summit: Destiny in Air, Leaders Arrive For the Summit," *New York Times,* December 2, 1989. Robert W. Tucker and David C. Hendrickson, *The Imperial Temptation: The New World Order and America's Purpose* (New York: Council on Foreign Relations, 1992).

26. For fiscal year 1990, the United States possessed 7,314 nuclear warheads on ballistic missiles in addition to a fleet of 324 nuclear capable long-range bombers. See www.fas.org/nuke/guide/usa/forces.htm; A dissident view on the preponderance of U.S. military power as the determining factor in the Gulf War was made by Stephen Biddle, "Victory Misunderstood: What the Gulf War Tells Us about the Future of Conflict," *International Security,* 21, no. 2, Autumn, 1996, 139–79.

27. In 1990, the world was awash in political and social change and foreign policy problems for the United States. Howard Wiarda, *The Democratic Revolution in Latin America: History, Politics, and U.S. Policy* (New York: Holmes and Meter, 1990); Robert A. Pastor,

"Preempting Revolutions: The Boundaries of U.S. Influence," *International Security,* 15, no. 4, Spring, 1991, 54–86; President's News Conference on Foreign and Domestic Issues, *New York Times,* January 25, 1990; Nicholas D. Kristof, "Ominous Embers from the Fires of 1989," *New York Times,* April 15, 1990; Bill Keller, "Li Peng Says Soviet Ideas of Change Do Not Apply to China," *New York Times,* April 26, 1990.

28. Shahram Chubin, and Charles Tripp, *Iran and Iraq at War* (Boulder, CO: Westview Press, 1988), 84–122; Abbas Alnasrawi, *The Economy of Iraq Oil, Wars, Destruction of Development and Prospects, 1950–2010* (Westport, CT: Greenwood Press, 1994), 79–104.

29. The military losses suffered by the Iranian army at the end of the war were dramatic:

> While Iran's exact losses are in dispute, it is clear that Iran clearly lost over half of its operational armor between February and July, 1988. Iraq seems to be correct in claiming to have captured some 1,298 Iranian tanks and heavy armored fighting vehicles, 155 other armored fighting vehicles, 512 armored personnel carriers, large amounts of artillery, 6,196 mortars, 8,050 RPGs and recoilless rifles, 60,694 rifles, 322 pistols, 501 pieces of heavy engineering equipment, 6,156 pieces of communications gear, 16,863 items of chemical warfare defense equipment, and 24,257 caskets. 78 The disintegration of Iran's armed forces at the end of the Iran-Iraq War is reflected in the fact that much of this captured equipment showed no sign of combat damage or wear. Much was abandoned in the field, either out of panic or because of supply problems.

Anthony H. Cordesman, *Iran and Iraq: The Threat from the Northern Gulf* (Boulder, CO: Westview Press, 1994), 45.

30. Fuller, *Iran: the Center of the Universe,* 34–84. Writing in the mid-1990s, one Western-based Iranian political scientist summarized Iran's relations with its Arab neighbors as follows:

> Iran has proposed its own security system for the Persian Gulf, one composed exclusively of regional powers. The Arab states consider this proposal to be an act of indirect Iranian hegemony and thus reject it altogether. Arabs continue to mistrust Iran; and since the beginning of the revolution, Iran has condemned the petro-monarchies as corrupt mercenaries of the United States. Rhetoric and accusations on both sides have reinforced this mistrust, which complicates any rapprochement between Iran and its Arab neighbors. In such circumstances, only the American military umbrella holds back a credible system for the defense of the six states in the GCC.

Houchang Hassan-Yar, "Iranian Foreign Policy in the Postwar Era," in *Iranian Perspectives on the Iran-Iraq War,* ed. Farhang Rajaee (Gainesville, FL: University Press of Florida, 1997), 144.

31. Bengio, *Saddam's Word,* 171.

32. Thomas Friedman, "Confrontation in the Gulf; U.S. Courts Syria and Iran To Join Anti-Iraq Coalition," *New York Times,* August 9, 1990; Alan Colwell, "War in the Gulf: Syria; Official Syrian Paper Urges Iraqis to 'Liquidate' Hussein," *New York Times,* February 10, 1991; Eberhard Kienle, "Syria, the Kuwait War and the New World Order," in *The Gulf War and the New World,* eds., Ismael and Ismael (Gainesville, FL: University of Florida Press, 1994), 383–98. Assad's willingness to join the Gulf War coalition has also been attributed to Assad's pragmatism in light of the decline of the Soviet Union and the rise of the United States at the end of the Cold War, see Raymond Hinnebusch, *Syria: Revolution* (New York: Routledge, 2001), 157–60.

33. Sheri Laizer, *Martyrs, Traitors and Patriots, Kurdistan after the Gulf War* (London: Zed Books, 1996); Michiel Leezenberg, "The Anfal Operations in Iraqi Kurdistan," in *A Century*

of Genocide: Critical Essays and Eyewitness Accounts, eds. Samuel Totten, William S. Parsons, and Israel W. Charny (New York: Routledge, 2004), 375–94.

34. Hussein's extensive anti-Israeli terrorism has been documented by the Pentagon massive declassification project of captured Iraqi documents. See *Iraqi Perspectives Project Saddam and Terrorism: Emerging Insights from Captured Iraqi Documents* (redacted) Institute for Defense Analyses, November 2007 (released March 2008), 5 vols.

35. Sabra Chartrand, "War In The Gulf: The Palestinians; Palestinians Are Buoyed By the Attacks on Israel," *New York Times,* January 21, 1991; Joel Brinkley, "War In The Gulf: Israel; 3 From Jordan Hit Israeli Bus, Then Are Killed by Soldiers," *New York Times,* February 9, 1991.

36. There are many excellent histories of the Jewish People and of Zionism, the latter subject of extraordinary contention among contemporary academics. Modern Jewish attachment to Palestine has been documented for the mid-Eighteenth century, 150 years prior to the establishment of the modern Zionist movement. A group of Sephardic pilgrims to Palestine in the 1740s expressed deep fervor in returning to the land of their ancestors:

> [W]e had to wait for the ship which the community of Istanbul hires every year...since every Sephardi Jew who fears God and has the means goes to Eretz Israel once in his lifetime, and goes around to the graves of our forefathers, to the righteous and the pious men, and also the women go around, and devote themselves with all their heart and soul. And it should be counted for them as an atonement of sins, as it is said, "And the land will atone for its people," and they return to their cities and their houses, and there are some who go to settle there until the day of their death. Therefore even though there are other ships to be found which go to Egypt and from there to Eretz Israel...we waited for them...and when they hire a ship, they announce it in all the synagogues.

Jacob Barnai, *The Jews in Palestine in the Eighteenth Century: Under the Patronage of the Istanbul Committee of Officials for Palestine* trans. Naomi Goldblum (Tuscaloosa, AL: University of Alabama Press, 1992), 28

37. Bengio, *Saddam's Word,* 197–201; Philip Shenon, "Standoff In The Gulf; Pentagon Calls Israel Likely Iraqi Target," *New York Times,* December, 27, 1990; Alan Cowell, "War In The Gulf: Jordan; In Jordan, the Iraqis Regain Respect by Striking at Israel," *New York Times,* January 19, 2001; Joel Brinkley, "Confrontation in the Gulf, Palestinians Give Passionate Support To Hussein as a Hero and a Liberator," *New York Times,* August 12, 1990.

38. Cheryl A. Rubenberg, "The Gulf War, the Palestinians and the New World Order," in *The Gulf War and the New World Order,* eds., Ismael and Ismael, 317–46; and ibid., Kamel S. Abu Jaber, *Jordan and the Gulf War,* 366–82; John Kifner, "Confrontation in the Gulf; Champion of Arab Poor? Hussein Grasps for Nasser's Revolutionary Mantle," *New York Times,* August 9, 1990; John Kifner, "Confrontation in the Gulf; Mirage of Arab Unity," *New York Times,* August 12, 1990; Martin Tolchin, "After The War; Congress Withholds $55 Million in Aid To Jordan," *New York Times,* March 23, 1991.

39. For Egypt's role in the Gulf War, some $10 billion in foreign debt was forgiven. Steven Greenhouse, "Half of Egypt's $20.2 Billion Debt Being Forgiven by U.S. and Allies," *New York Times,* May 27, 1991.

40. Stephen Page, "New Political Thinking and Soviet Policy Toward Regional Conflict in the Middle East: The Gulf Wars," in *The Decline of the Soviet Union and the Transformation of the Middle East* eds., David H. Goldberg and Paul Marantz (Boulder, CO: Westview Press, 1994), 28–52; Graham E. Fuller, "Moscow and the Gulf War," *Foreign Affairs,* Summer 1991.

41. Judith Miller, "War In The Gulf: Iraq's Leader; Hussein's Driving Force: Mission to Save Arab World," *New York Times,* February 25, 1991; Saddam Hussein, "Call for Jihad

in Turi Munthe" *The Saddam Hussein Reader* (New York: Thunder Mouth Press, 2002), 239–46.

42. George Bush speech, Address Before a Joint Session of the Congress on the State of the Union January 29, 1991, Public Papers of the Presidents, George Bush, vol. 1, 1991 (Washington, DC: GPO, 1992), 74–80, 74.

CHAPTER 3

1. George H.W. Bush, Address to the Nation on the Invasion of Iraq (January 16, 1991), Miller Center, University of Virginia, http://millercenter.org/scripps/digitalarchive/speeches/spe_1991_0116_bush.

2. Saddam Hussein, remarks, *Baghdad Observer,* July 19, 1990, http://saddamhusseinblog.blogspot.com/2007/05/president-saddam-husseins-speech-at.html.

3. S.N. Eisenstadt, *The Political Systems of Empires* (New York: Free Press, 1969); Lawrence Keppie, *The Making of the Roman Army: From Republic to Empire* (New York: Routledge, 1998); Clifford Ando, *Imperial Ideology and Provincial Loyalty in the Roman Empire* (Berkeley: University of California Press, 2000); T. Corey Brennan, *The Praetorship in the Roman Republic* (New York: Oxford University Press, 2000); Nicola Di Cosmo, *Ancient China and its Enemies: The Rise of Nomadic Power in East Asian History* (Cambridge: Cambridge University Press, 2003); Gang Deng, *The Premodern Chinese Economy: Structural Equilibrium and Capitalists Sterility* (New York: Routledge, 1999).

4. The use of historical imagery and analogies by Saddam Hussein and his fellow Ba'athists is explored by Ofra Bengio, *Saddam's Word: Political Discourse in Iraq* (New York: Oxford, 1998); Eric Davis, *Memories of State: Politics, History, and Collective Identity in Modern Iraq* (Berkeley: University of California Press, 2003), 200–70.

5. There is an extensive literature on war and national memory in American history. See Reginald Horsman, *Race and Manifest Destiny The Origins of American Racial Anglo-Saxonism* (Cambridge, MA: Harvard University Press, 1981); Robert W. Johannsen, *To the Halls of the Montezumas: The Mexican War in the American Imagination* (New York: Oxford University Press, 1988); Yuen Foong Khong, *Analogies at War: Korea, Munich, Dien Bien Phu, and the Vietnam Decisions of 1965* (Princeton, NJ: Princeton University Press, 1992); David Ryan, *US Collective Memory, Intervention and Vietnam, The Cultural Politics of US Foreign Policy Since 1969* (London: Routledge, 2008).

6. *All the Best, George Bush: My Life and Other Writings* (New York: Scribner's, 1999), 23.

7. Timothy J Christmann, Vice President Bush Calls World War II Experience "Sobering," *Naval Aviation News,* 67, March–April, 1985, 12–15.

8. Despite the primitive organizational methods of the 1860s, the U.S. Army managed to find 2.8 million men to serve in the Civil War, out of a prewar population in the Northern states of 22 million people. This would be equivalent to 40 million volunteers and draftees in the United States of the early twenty-first century; Fred Shannon Albert, *The Organization and Administration of the Union Army, 1861–1865* vol. 2 (New York: Arthur H. Clark, 1965), 277–78; Mark R. Wilson, *The Business of Civil War: Military Mobilization and the State, 1861–1865* (Baltimore: Johns Hopkins University, 2006).

9. Cordesman, Wagner, *The Gulf War,* 94; Daniel S. Papp, "The Gulf War Coalition: The Politics and Economics of a Most Unusual Alliance," in *The Eagle in the Desert: Looking Back on U.S. Involvement in the Persian Gulf War,* eds., William Head and Earl H. Tilford, Jr. (Westport, CT: Praeger, 1996), 21–46.

10. Anh Nga Longva, *Walls Built on Sand: Migration, Exclusion, and Society in Kuwait* (Boulder, CO: Westview Press, 1997); Jacqueline S. Ismael, *Kuwait: Social Change in Historical Perspective* (Syracuse, NY: Syracuse University Press, 1982), 129–52.

11. The total financial burden on Saudi Arabia was enormous relative to the size of its economy:

> The fiscal impacts of Desert Storm upon the well-being of Saudi Arabia were as monumental as their geopolitical counterparts. Its costs in military operations, operations reimbursements, and regional aid commitments are estimated at $64 billion, in an economy whose 1991 GDP was just over $100 billion.

C.A. Woodson, *Saudi Arabian Force Structure Development in a Post Gulf War World,* U.S. Army, Foreign Military Studies Office, Fort Leavenworth, KS, June 1998, www .globalsecurity.org/military/library/report/1998/saudi.htm. In addition to its huge financial support, the Saudis made the second largest contribution in military forces to the war as well. Cordesman, and Wagner, *The Gulf War,* 173–95.

12. Saudi inadequacies were quite apparent. Despite huge arms purchases the army was grossly ineffective:

> Undermanning, deployment problems, lack of total force strength, lack of maneuver experience, and political concerns were all factors that helped shape a relatively static and defensive force. They were reinforced by the fact that the Saudi Army was largely a garrison army that operated out of fixed major bases ("military cities") that rarely deployed long distances from its casernes or engaged in large-scale training and exercises. The Saudi Army had no significant helicopter contingent and rarely exercised with the air force in any kind of serious air support exercises.

Cordesman and Wagner, *The Gulf War,* 177.

13. Baker, *The Politics of Diplomacy,* 300–25; Human Rights Watch, *Genocide in Iraq, the Anfal campaign against the Kurds, a Middle East Watch Report,* July 1993, Washington, DC, www.hrw.org/reports/1993/iraqanfal.

14. R.W. Apple Jr., "Confrontation in the Gulf; Oil, Saddam Hussein and the Reemergence of America as the Superpower," *New York Times,* August 20, 1990; Editorial, Tokyo's Share of World Leadership, *New York Times,* August 31, 1990; Richard Spellman, "The Emerging Unipolar World," *New York Times,* August 21, 1990.

15. Youssef M. Ibrahim, "Confrontation in the Gulf; Paris adding 84000 to Force in Gulf; Bonn's Aid to Rise," *New York Times,* September 16, 1990; Thomas L. Friedman, "The World: Running the Gulf Coalition is Tricky Business," *New York Times,* September 23, 1990; Cordesman and Wagner, *Lessons of Modern War,* 156–210.

16. Michael R. Gordon, "Mideast Tensions: Nunn, Citing 'Rush' to War, Assails Decision to Drop Troop Rotation Plan," *New York Times,* November 12, 1990; R.W. Apple, *Standoff in the Gulf: The Collapse of a Coalition,* December 6, 1990; Eric Schmitt, *Mideast Tensions: Fighting the Iraqis, Four Scenarios, All Disputed,* November 19, 1990.

17. Michael R. Gordon, "Mideast Tensions: Democrats Press Bush to Put Off Military Action," *New York Times,* November 28, 1990; Susan F. Rasky, "Tactical Positions; Congress Asks What It Should Do In the Gulf, and How," *New York Times;* "Confrontation in the Gulf; Day 2: Lawmakers Debate War and More Time for Sanctions," *New York Times,* January 12, 1991.

18. James Reston, "Too Early for Bush to Dial 9/11," *New York Times,* November 13, 1991; Thomas L. Friedman, *Mideast Tensions; Selling Sacrifice: Gulf Rationale Still Eludes Bush,*

November 16, 1990; Michael R. Gordon, *Mideast Tensions; 2 Ex-Military Chiefs Urge Bush to Delay Gulf War,* November 29, 1990.

19. Gordon and Trainor, "The Generals' War," 153; H. W. Brands, "George Bush the Gulf War of 1991," *Presidential Studies Quarterly,* 34, no. 1 (2004): 113–31.

20. Ted Thornton, *History of the Middle East Database, The Gulf Wars, Iraq occupies Kuwait, 1990–91,* www.nmhschool.org/tthornton/mehistorydatabase/gulf_war.php.

21. Bush and Scowcroft, *A World Transformed,* 435.

22. Cordesman and Wagner, *Lessons of Modern War,* 227–27; Robert H. Scales, *Certain Victory: The U.S. Army in the Gulf War* (New York: Brassey's, 1994), 46–154.

23. ibid., 94; Chris Hedges, "War in the Gulf: Combat; Town regained, Morale of Arab Allies is Lifted," *New York Times,* February 2, 1990; Youseff M. Ibrahim, "War in the Gulf: Arabs; Arab Allies Reaffirm Unity Despite Iraqi Proposal," *New York Times,* February 17, 1991; "War in the Gulf: Allies and Adversaries; Anti-Iraq Nations Firmly Reject Offer, Calling It 'Insincere' and an 'Obstacle'," *New York Times,* February 16, 1991.

24. The Arab coalition against Iraq was conflicted but it worked. John Kifner, "Confrontation in the Gulf; Mubarak's Stand Against Iraq Wins Praise From His People," *New York Times,* August 15, 1990; Alan Cowell, "Standoff in the Gulf; Arabs of the Gulf Mosaic: Artful Tactics but Quite Different Goals," *New York Times,* December 17, 1990; Hamidi A. Hassan, *The Iraqi Invasion of Kuwait, Religion, Identity and Otherness in the Analysis of War and Conflict* (London: Pluto, 1999), 137–71.

25. Scales, *Certain Victory,* 115–58; Eliot A. Cohen, "The Mystique of U.S. Air Power," in *Turning Point: The Gulf War and U.S. Military Strategy,* ed., L. Benjamin Ederington and Michael J. Mazarr (Boulder, CO: Westview Press, 1994), 53–64; C. Kenneth Allard, "The Future of Command and Control: Toward a Paradigm of Information Warfare" in ibid., 164–92.

26. Saddam Hussein's speech of withdrawal from Kuwait, February 26, 1991, www.globalsecurity.org/wmd/library/news/iraq/1991/irqkwt900226.htm.

27. Bush and Scowcroft, *A World Transformed,* 489.

28. Daniel L. Byman and Matthew C. Waxman, *Confronting Iraq: U.S. Policy and the Use of Force Since the Gulf War* (Santa Monica, CA: Rand, 2000), 43–53; Nicholas J. Weaver, *Saving Strangers: Humanitarian Intervention in International Society* (New York: Oxford University Press, 2002), 139–71.

29. UNSC 687 outlines the terms of the 1991 cease-fire against Iraq. See *United Nations Security Council Resolution* 687, April 8, 1991, http://www.fas.org/news/un/iraq/sres/sres0687.htm; Jean E. Krasno and James S. Sutterlin, *The United Nations and Iraq: Defanging the Viper* (Westport, CT: Praeger, 2003); Anthony H. Cordesman, *Iraq and the War of Sanction: Conventional Threats and Weapons of Mass Destruction* (Westport, CT: Praeger, 1999); Michael V. Deaver, *Disarming Iraq: Monitoring Power and Resistance* (Westport, CT: Praeger, 2001).

30. James Piscatori, "Religion and Realpolitik: Islamic Responses to the Gulf War," *Bulletin of the American Academy of Arts and Sciences,* 45, no. 1, October 1991, 17–39; Abdullah Al-Shayeji, "Dangerous Perceptions: Gulf Views of the U.S. Role in the Region," *Middle East Policy,* 5, no. 3, 1997, 1–13; Kenneth L. Vaux, *Ethics and the Gulf War: Religion, Rhetoric, and Righteousness* (Boulder, CO: Westview Press, 1992), 63–86.

CHAPTER 4

1. President Clinton, Address to the Nation, December 16, 1998, transcript, *PBS Newshour,* www.pbs.org/newshour/bb/middle_east/july-dec98/clinton_12-16.html.

2. The two term Clinton presidency has established a much larger literature than his immediate predecessor George H. Bush (with the exception of the Gulf War), or his successor whose term of office has not ended. See Todd G. Shields, Jeannie M. Whayne, Donald R. Kelley, eds., *The Clinton Riddle: Perspectives on the Forty-second President* (Fayetteville: University of Arkansas Press, 2004); William Hyland, *Clinton's World: Remaking American Foreign Policy* (Westport, CT: Praeger, 1999); Nigel Hamilton, *Bill Clinton: Mastering the Presidency* (New York: Public Affairs, 2007); Mark Katz, *Clinton and Me* (New York: Hyperion, 2003); Charles O. Jones, *Clinton and Congress, 1993–1996: Risk, Restoration, and Reelection* (Norman, OK: University of Oklahoma Press, 1999); James MacGregor Burns, *Dead Center: Clinton-Gore Leadership and the Perils of Moderation* (New York: Scribner's, 1999); Hanes, Walton, Jr., *Reelection: William Jefferson Clinton as a Native-son Presidential Candidate* (New York: Columbia University Press, 2000); Sally Bedell Smith, *For Love of Politics: Bill and Hillary Clinton: The White House Years* (New York: Random House, 2007); Stanley A. Renson, *High Hopes: The Clinton Presidency and The Politics of Ambition* (New York: New York University Press, 1996); Bill Clinton, *My Life* (New York: Knopf, 2004); Meredith Oakley, *On the Make: The Rise of Bill Clinton* (Latham, MD: Regnery, 1994); *No Surprises: Two Decades of Clinton-watching* (Washington, DC: Brassey's, 1996).

3. During his first year in office, a Democratic foreign policy adviser described Clinton's foreign policy advisers as "hijacking American foreign policy in the name of neo-Wilsonian internationalism." In the end, however, his foreign policy was not "reoriented" from its core principles. Hyland, *Clinton's World*, 197.

4. David Halberstam, *War in a Time of Peace: Bush, Clinton and the Generals* (New York: Knopf, 2002); William Jefferson Clinton, Address Before a Joint Session of Congress (February 17, 1993), http://millercenter.org/scripps/digitalarchive/speeches/spe_1993 _0217_clinton.

5. The White House, *National Security Strategy for a New Century* (December 1999): 3. Defense Strategy Review Page: http://www.comw.org/qdr/offdocs.html#nss.

6. The Russians were quite transparent in the mid-1990s detailing the drastic decline of their military forces. Regarding the navy:

> Not a single surface vessel has been begun in the last five years Of the four ships lying incomplete at various shipyards, work has stopped on all but one (Petr Velikiy). At current building rates, perhaps one new nuclear submarine will be delivered every three years. The aircraft carrier building program is effectively dead; it will not be revived without serious overhaul efforts directed at existing Russian shipyards. The production of guided naval missiles is in jeopardy, with the collapse of the old development-production system.

Naval Construction Programs, prepared (October 24, 1995), http://webcom.com/ ~amraam/build.html. Andrei Kortunov, "Demilitarization and Defense Conversion," in *The New Russia: Troubled Transformation*, ed., Gail W. Lapidus (Boulder, CO: Westview Press, 1995), 153–92.

7. U.S. Defense Department, *1995 Annual Defense Report*, Executive Summary www.dod.mil/execsec/adr95/roles.html.

8. By some estimates, Clinton's overall foreign policy achievements were modest. Richard Haas viewed his economic foreign policy much stronger than his policies that addressed international peace and security. See Richard N. Haas, "The Squandered Presidency: Demanding More from the Commander in Chief," *Foreign Affairs*, May/June 2000. William J. Taylor, "Pax Clintonia—the Clinton Foreign Policy Was Marked by an Unwillingness to

Devote Adequate Resources to Sustain the Major Instruments of American Diplomacy and an Inability to Set Priorities and Develop a Coherent Strategy," *World and I,* 16, no. 7 (July 2001): 26–34; The critical literature on Clinton's limited use of force in largely humanitarian interventions includes a number of treatments, see Karen Von Hippel, *Democracy by Force US Military Intervention in the Post–Cold War World* (New York: Cambridge University Press, 2000).

9. Clinton's commitment to economic internationalism stands out as a lasting achievement fully consistent with the modern ideology of American foreign relations. Bernhard Speyer and Klaus Gunter Deutsch eds., *The World Trade Organization Millennium Round: Freer Trade in the Twenty-First Century* (New York: Routledge, 2001); Gary P. Sampson, *The Role of the World Trade Organization in Global Governance* (New York: United Nations Press, 2001).

10. The first years of Clinton's foreign policy were especially distressing to foreign policy professionals. As Thomas Lippman wrote:

> Clinton's indecisiveness and his penchant for hedging his foreign policy bets to avoid political damage at home were only the most obvious causes of the administration's early foreign policy distress. Another was that it had inherited some very difficult problems: Bosnia, Haiti, Somalia, Iraq, a truculent North Korea, and a fragile, unstable Russia. Moreover, Clinton and his advisers initially had no theoretical or conceptual framework for managing post–Cold War world affairs. Not until September 1993 did they lay out a comprehensive policy framework, and by that time events in Bosnia and Somalia had fostered a widespread impression of ineptitude.

Thomas Lippman, *Madeleine Albright and the New American Diplomacy* (Boulder, CO: Westview Press, 2000), 310.

11. Barbara Crossette, "The United Nations: The Overview; Clinton Urges World Action on Terror," *New York Times,* August 22, 1998. The ovation was followed by a "listless speech" which according to the *New York Times* did not impress many of the delegates. Nonetheless, other contemporary observers approved the broad outlines of Clinton's foreign policy. See Stephen M. Walt, "Two Cheers for Clinton's Foreign Policy," *Foreign Affairs,* March/April 2000; "Clinton's Foreign Policy," *Foreign Policy,* November 2000, 18.

12. In U.S. military doctrine, transformational warfare includes a wide range of concepts including "net-centric warfare" and other technical constructs that were only conceivable after the invention of interactive computer networks in the 1980s and 1990s. See David S. Alberts, John J. Garstka, and Frederick P. Stein, *Network Centric Warfare: Developing and Leveraging Information Superiority* (Washington, DC: CCRP, 1999); Joint Chiefs of Staff, *Joint Vision 2010* (Washington, DC: Joint Chiefs of Staff, 1996); Martin Burke, *Thinking Together: New Forms of Thought for a Transformation in Military Affairs* (Washington, DC: Defense Science and Technology Organization, 2000), DSTO RR-0173.

13. The lodestone for the neoconservative critique of the Clinton administration was the founding of the Project for a New American Century in June 1997 (www.newamericancentury.org). The signature publication for this critique: William Kristol, and Robert Kagan, eds., *Present Dangers: Crisis and Opportunity in American Foreign and Defense Policy* (New York: Encounter Books, 2000).

14. James McKinley, Jr., "Bombings in East Africa: the Overview; Bombs Rip Apart 2 U.S. Embassies in Africa; Scores Killed; No Firm Motive or Suspects," *New York Times,* August 8, 1998; Steven Lee Myers, "U.S. Fury On 2 Continents: The Weapons; Dozens of Ship-Launched Cruise Missiles Strike at Same Moment, 2,500 Miles Apart," *New York Times,*

August 21, 1998; Jane Perlez, "After The Attacks: In Sudan; A Moderate Thinks U.S. Shot Itself in the Foot," *New York Times,* August 25, 1998; Tim Weiner, "Missile Strikes Against bin Laden Won Him Esteem in Muslim Lands, U.S. Officials Say," *New York Times,* February 8, 1999.

15. Richard Perle, "Iraq: Saddam Unbound" in *Present Dangers: Crisis and Opportunity in American Defense Policy,* eds., William Kristol, and Robert Kagan (New York: Encounter Books, 2000), 99–110, 106.

16. Two Web sites run by the United Nations archive the documents for the two UN commissions who administered the UN mandated inspections regime for Iraq. See www .unmovic.org and www.un.org/Depts/unscom/unscmdoc.htm.

17. Steve Bowman, "Iraqi Chemical and Biological Weapons (CBS) Capabilities," *CRS Report to Congress,* 98-129 F, updated September 4, 1998 (Washington: Library of Congress, 1998), 2–3.

18. ibid, 5. Also "Iraq Weapons of Mass Destruction Programs," *U.S. Government White Paper* (February 13, 1998): 11, www.fas.org/irp/threat/whitepap.htm.

19. Saddam's army was held at bay in the north, but little else. Katherine Wilkins, "How We Lost the Kurdish Game," *Washington Post,* September 15, 1996, C01; Steven Erlanger, "U.S., Warily Eyeing Iraq, Urges Warring Kurds to Make Peace," *New York Times,* October 15, 1996. CIA operations to aid Kurdish rebels was crushed by Hussein's army in September 1996. Tim Weiner, "Iraqi Offensive Into Kurdish Zone Disrupts U.S. Plot to Oust Hussein," *New York Times,* September 7, 1996.

20. The Jewish response to Saddam Hussein has been explored in John J. Mearsheimer and Stephen M. Walt, *The Israel Lobby and U.S. Foreign Policy* (New York: Farrar, Straus and Giroux, 2007), 229–62; Masoud Kazemzadeh, "Thinking the Unthinkable: Solving the Problem of Saddam Hussein for Good," *Middle East Policy* 1, no. 1(1998): 74–87.

21. Iran was a problem but not a very serious one. See Anthony H. Cordesman and Ahmed S. Hashim, *Iran, the Dilemmas of Dual Containment* (Boulder, CO: Westview Press, 1997); Anoushiravan Ehteshami and Raymond A. Hinnebusch, *Syria and Iran, Middle Powers in a Penetrated Regional System* (New York: Routledge, 2001).

22. As a national priority, terrorism was given less than a page by Warren Christopher. Warren Christopher, *In the Stream of history, Shaping Foreign Policy in a New Era* (Stanford: Stanford University Press, 1998), 464–65. Writing after 9/11, Madeleine Albright devoted one thin chapter out of twenty-nine to the subject. Madeleine Albright, *Madame Secretary* (New York: Miramax Books, 2003), 361–77.

23. U.S. Commission on National Security/21st Century, *Hart-Rudman Commission,* July 1998–February 2001 at www.au.af.mil/au/awc/awcgate/nssg.

24. Hart Rudman, "New World Coming: American Security in the 21st Century," *Major Themes and Implications in The Phase I Report on the Emerging Global Security Environment for the First Quarter of the 21st Century,* July 1998, 1–11, www.au.af.mil/au/awc/awcgate/nssg.

25. Elizabeth M. Cousens and Charles K. Cater, *Toward Peace in Bosnia: Implementing the Dayton Accords* (Boulder, CO: Lynne Reiner, 2001); Kathleen Hill Hawk, *Constructing the Stable State: Goals for Intervention and Peace Building* (Westport, CT: Praeger, 2002).

26. The Clinton pursued Israeli-Palestinian conflict resolution throughout his presidency with ultimately modest success. Robert O. Freedman, ed., *The Middle East and the Peace Process: The Impact of the Oslo Accords* (Gainesville, FL: University of Florida Press, 1998); Andrew S. Buchanan, *Peace with Justice: A History of the Israeli-Palestinian Declaration of Principles on Interim self-Government Arrangements* (New York: MacMillan, 2000).

CHAPTER 5

1. Harry Truman, remarks, *Columbia Scholastic Press Association* (March 15, 1952), Miller Center Archives, University of Virginia, http://millercenter.org/scripps/digitalarchive/speeches/spe_1952_0315_truman.

2. Peter Novick, *That Noble Dream: The 'objectivity question' and the American Historical Profession* (New York: Cambridge University Press, 1988).

3. Stanford Encyclopedia of Philosophy, *Time Travel and Modern Physics,* rev. entry June 10, 2005, at http://plato.stanford.edu/entries/time-travel-phys/.

4. Historians have been enormously creative in producing alternative or counterfactual historical interpretations. The exercises can be viewed as mind or thought experiments. No matter how convincing the analysis, the alternative scenarios will never be proven, they can only serve as teaching tools or by some as "parlor games." Bunzl, Martin, "Counterfactual History: A User's Guide," *The American Historical Review* 109, no. 3 (2004); Robert Cowley, ed., *What If? The World's Foremost Military Historians Imagine What Might Have Been* (New York: Putnam, 1998); Philip E. Tetlock, Richard Ned Lebow, and Geoffrey Parker, eds., *Unmaking the West: "What-If?" Scenarios That Rewrite World History* (Ann Arbor, MI: University of Michigan Press, 2006).

5. James Mann, *The Rise of the Vulcans: The History of Bush's War Cabinet* (New York: Penguin Books, 2004).

6. The locus of control on matters of war and peace has always been the presidency. Bob Woodward's investigative journalism of the Bush presidency confirmed the continuation of this principle, see Bob Woodward, *Bush at War* (New York: Simon and Schuster, 2002–2006), 3 volumes.

7. Two reporters for the *New York Times* spent years investigating the alleged biological warfare programs of Saddam Hussein. Their work, outside the neoconservative orbit, was significant evidence for U.S. efforts to overthrow or remove Hussein and his regime from power. William J. Broad and Judith Miller, "The Deal on Iraq: Secret Arsenal: The Hunt for the Germs of War—A Special Report; Iraq's Deadliest Arms: Puzzles Breed Fears," *New York Times,* February 26, 1998; "The World: Live Ammo; The Threat of Germ Weapons Is Rising. Fear, Too," *New York Times,* December 27, 1998; William J. Broad, *Stephen Engelberg and Judith Miller, Germs: Biological Weapons and America's Secret War* (New York: Simon and Schuster, 2001), 98–150; The "Iraq Liberation Act" of 1998 committed the United States at least formally, to regime change premised on the concept of Saddam Hussein as a strategic threat see http://www.iraqwatch.org/government/US/Legislation/ILA.htm.

8. The "butterfly effect" first hypothesized by a mathematician in the 1960s has become a popular motif in science fiction. It is also a well-used metaphor for describing how complex systems, such as the weather or human societies are sensitive to very small events. Hence, the flapping of a butterfly's wings may randomly produce enormous long-term system wide effects that will produce a tornado on the other side of the world. Analogously, the random luck of an assassination attempt, i.e., JFK in Dallas in November 1963, may have had enormous effects on the course of world history. See the butterfly effect, at www.cmp.caltech.edu/~mcc/chaos_new/Lorenz.html; Yaneer Bar Yam Concepts in Complex Systems at http://necsi.org/guide/concepts/butterflyeffect.html.

9. Perhaps the finest piece of investigative journalism to date on the origins of the Second Gulf or Iraq War is Ron Suskind's "One Percent Solution." According to Suskind, the Iraq War was launched to "make an example" of Saddam Hussein and his defiance of American power. Ron Suskind, *The One Percent Doctrine, Deep Inside America's Pursuit of its Enemies Since 9/11* (New York: Simon and Schuster, 2006), 80–81.

10. Among the significant literature that critiques Bush's war policies are Suskind, *The One Percent Solution;* Woodward, *State of Denial, Bush at War,* part 3; Ali A. Allawi, *The Occupation of Iraq: Winning the War, Losing the Peace* (New Haven: Yale University Press, 2007); George Packer, *The Assassins' Gate, America in Iraq* (New York: Farrar Straus, 2005); Stefan Halper and Jonathan Clarke, *America Alone: The Neo-conservatives and the Global Order* (New York: Cambridge University Press, 2004).

11. In the months following September 11, The *New York Times* covered the new war on terrorism intensively as it unfolded as a national and international mission. Michael R. Gordon, "After The Attacks: The Strategy; A New War And Its Scale," *New York Times,* September 17, 2001; David E. Rosenbaum and David Johnston, "A Nation Challenged: The Alert; Ashcroft Warns of Terror Attacks Soon Against U.S.," *New York Times,* October 30, 2001; William J. Broad, Stephen Engelberg, and James Glanz, "A Nation Challenged: The Threat: Assessing Risks, Chemical, Biological, Even Nuclear," *New York Times,* November 1, 2001; Thom Shanker, "A Nation Challenged: The Allies; Rumsfeld Asks NATO to Shift To Wide Fight Against Terror," *New York Times,* December 19, 2001.

12. Said K., Aburish, *Saddam Hussein: The Politics of Revenge* (London: Bloomsbury, 2000), 1.

13. During the 1990s during the period of Clinton's downsizing of the U.S. armed forces, neoconservatives voiced the strident opinion that the U.S. needed to restore its military capabilities. This would be accomplished after September 11. See Thomas Donnelly, *Rebuilding America's Defenses, Strategy, Forces and Resources for a New Century* (Washington, DC: Project for a New American Century, September 2000).

14. In addition to the sources already cited, Cheney and Rumsfeld's critical roles were illustrated in the investigative journalism of the PBS series Frontline. See Bush's War, Part 2, Frontline documentary at www.pbs.org/wgbh/pages/frontline/bushswar. Several hundred oral history interviews are part of the film's online archive.

15. Paul Wolfowitz, "Statesmanship in the New Century," in *Present Dangers,* ed., Kagan and Kristol, 307–36, 335.

16. In addition to works cited previously see Walter MacDougall, *Promised Land, Crusader State: The American Encounter with the World Since 1776* (Boston: Houghton Mifflin, 1997); Edward M. Burns, *The American Idea of Mission: Concepts of National Purpose and Destiny* (New Brunswick, NJ: Rutgers University Press, 1957).

17. The Iraq Liberation Act, i.e., Public Law 105–235 was cited in the 2002 legislation that provided Congressional authorization for the Second Gulf War:

> Whereas in Public Law 105–235 (August 14, 1998), Congress concluded that Iraq's continuing WMD programs threatened vital United States interests and international peace and security, declared Iraq to be in "material and unacceptable breach of its international obligations" and urged the President "to take appropriate action, in accordance with the Constitution and relevant laws of the United States, to bring Iraq into compliance with its international obligations".

Public Law 107–243, 107th Congress Joint Resolution, To authorize the use of United States Armed Forces against Iraq, October 16, 2002, 1 at http://thomas.loc.gov/cgi-bin/query/z?c107:H.J.RES.114.ENR.

18. House, Committee on International Relations, Hearing, *Human Rights Violations Under Saddam Hussein: Victims Speak Out,* 108th Cong., 1st sess., November 20, 2003 (Washington, DC: GPO, 2003); A newly declassified report shows the international scope of Saddam Hussein's international terrorism, aimed primarily at enemies of his regime both

inside and outside Iraq. See Institute for Defense Analyses, *Iraqi Perspectives Project Saddam and Terrorism: Emerging Insights from Captured Iraqi Documents* (redacted) 5 volumes, November 2007 at www.fas.org/irp/iraqi/index.html.

19. Hart Rudman, *Road Map for National Security: Imperative for Change*. The Phase III Report of the U.S. Commission on National Security/21st Century, February 15, 2001, Washington D.C., vol. 1: 8, http://www.au.af.mil/au/awc/awcgate/nssg/phaseIIIfr.pdf.

20. ibid., 2–3.

21. Robert T. Marsh, *Critical Foundations: Protecting America's Infrastructure*, Center for Policy Research, Harvard University, June 2000; Clark L. Staten, *Asymmetric Warfare, the Evolution and Devolution of Terrorism; The Coming Challenge For Emergency and National Security Forces*, Emergency Response and Research Institute, April 27, 1998 at http://www.d-n-i.net/fcs/asymmetric_warfare_staten.htm; Douglas C. Johnson and Steven Metz, *Asymmetry and U.S. Military Strategy: Definition, Background, and Strategic Concepts* (Carlisle Barracks, PA: U.S. Army War College, 2001); Ivan Arreguin-Toft, *How the Weak Win Wars: A Theory of Asymmetric Conflict* (New York ; Cambridge University Press, 2005); Roger W. Barnett, *Asymmetrical Warfare: Today's Challenge to U.S. Military Power* (Washington, DC: Brassey's, 2003).

22. The threat from global modernization related to America's relative decline in social and educational institutions which remain the critical backbone for the country to maintain its leadership status. Hart Rudman, *Road Map for National Security*, Phase III, vol. 1: 30–38.

23. A detailed summary and chronology summary of Saddam Hussein's biological warfare program can be found at http://www.iraqwatch.org/profiles/biological.html and http://cns.miis.edu/research/wmdme/iraq.htm, including an overall analysis of his WMD programs.

24. Hart Rudman, *Roadmap for National Security*, Phase III, 5.

25. Neal Gabler, "This Time, the Scene was Real," *New York Times*, September 16, 2001; Mike Wallace, "The Fragile City: 'These Fantasies Have Been Horribly Realized,'" *New York Times*, September 16, 2001.

26. Steve Coll paints a portrait of an al Qaeda prior to September 11 that struck fear in the hearts of the Central Intelligence Agency. Steve Coll, *Ghost Wars: The Secret History of the CIA, Afghanistan, and bin Laden, from the Soviet Invasion to September 10, 2001* (New York: Penguin, 2004), 453–542.

27. The Sixteenth Conference on International Defense Cooperation, National Press Club, Washington, DC, September 5, 2001; http://www.ideea.com/comdef01/program.htm.

28. Testimony Before the House Armed Services Committee: Fiscal Year 2002 National Defense Authorization Budget Request, *As Delivered by Secretary of Defense Donald H. Rumsfeld, Chairman of the Joint Chiefs of Staff General Hugh Shelton, Rayburn House Office Building, Washington, DC*, Thursday, June 28, 2001, http://www.defenselink.mil/speeches.

29. Advance Questions and Answers—Dr. Paul Wolfowitz confirmation hearing before The Senate Armed Services Committee, February 27, 2001, 6, http://www.comw.org/qdr/01 qdr.html.

30. Michele A. Flournoy, ed., *QDR 2001: Strategy Driven Choices for America's Security* (Washington, DC: National Defense University, November 2000), 41–42, 75–106.

31. ibid.

32. "After The Attacks: Reaction From Around the World," *New York Times*, September 13, 2001; Steven Erlanger, "A Nation Challenged: The Alliance; So Far, Europe Breathes Easier Over Free Hand Given the U.S.," *New York Times*, September 29, 2001.

33. John Burns, "A Nation Challenged: On the Move; Reports Swirl Out of Afghanistan Of Panic and Taliban Defections," *New York Times*, October 4, 2001; Michael R. Gordon

and Steven L. Myers, "A Nation Challenged: The Tactics; U.S. Shifts Focus Of Attack in Afghanistan By Bombing Ground Forces of Taliban," *New York Times,* October 11, 2001.

34. But al Qaeda, like the Taliban survived in the mountains of the Pakistani borderlands. Bruce Reidel, "Al Qaeda Strikes Back," *Foreign Affairs,* May/June, 2007. An in-depth Congressional Hearing in 2007 documented the depth of al Qaeda's strength in Pakistan, a nation of more than 150 million people. U.S. House, Subcommittee on U.S. National Security and Foreign Affairs, Extremist Madrassas, Ghost Schools, and U.S. Aid To Pakistan: Are We Making The Grade On The 9/11 Commission Report Card? 110 Cong., 1st sess., May 9, 2007 (Washington, DC: GOP, 2007).

35. The classic work on U.S. nuclear strategy during the Cold War was published in 1980 by then Ohio University historian John L. Gaddis. John L. Gaddis, *Strategies of Containment: A Critical Appraisal of American National Security Policy during the Cold War* (New York: Oxford University Press, 1980); with the coining of the term asymmetric warfare, its antithesis became "symmetric warfare."

36. United States Military Academy, at Westpoint, The Center for Combating Terrorism at www.ctc.usma.edu. From obscurity, asymmetric warfare has now supplanted earlier terms and has become a central aspect of U.S. national security strategy, http://www.ctrasymwarfare .org/resources.htm.

37. An ever futuristic concept, net-centric warfare quickly became military doctrine throughout the Department of Defense. At the level of the JCS, Joint Warfare doctrine using "net-centric" design showed a thoroughly institutionalized framework for information-based warfare:

> The Net-Centric Environment Joint Functional Concept is an information and decision superiority-based concept describing how joint forces might function in a fully net-worked environment 10 to 20 years in the future. Within this concept, the networking of all Joint Force elements creates capabilities for unparalleled information sharing and collaboration, adaptive organizations, and a greater unity of effort via synchronization and integration of force elements at the lowest levels.

Defense Department, Net-Centric Environment Joint Functional Concept 1.0, April 7, 2005, executive summary, 5. DOD, Arlington, Virginia.

38. Donald H. Rumsfeld, "Guidance and Terms of Reference for the 2001," *Quadrennial Defense Review,* Department of Defense, Washington, DC, June 22, 2001, 7.

39. Department of the Navy, Office of Naval Research, Continuing the Revolution in Military Affairs (RMA), Proceedings of Workshop held on June 5–7, 2001, Quantico, VA, September, 2001.

40. Michael Zang, *The Architecture of a Case Based Reasoning Application* in ibid., 131–42, 131.

41. Kim J. Pohl, "Perspective Filters as a Means for Interoperability Among Information-Centric Decision-Support Systems in Continuing the Revolution in Military Affairs (RMA)," *Proceedings of Workshop held on June 5–7, 2001,* 125–9, 125, 129.

42. George W. Bush, *The Global War on Terrorism: The First 100 Days,* White House, December 2001, www.whitehouse.gov/news/releases/2001/12/100dayreport.html; Norman Podhoretz, *World War IV: The Long Strong Against Islamo-fascism* (New York: Doubleday, 2007).

43. NSC, National Strategy for Combating Terrorism, February 14, 2003, at www.fas.org/ irp/threat/terror.htm; ibid., U.S. Army Training and Doctrine Command, A Military Guide to Terrorism in the Twenty-First Century, February 15, 2007.

44. The famous "Axis of Evil" speech was in fact George W. Bush's 2002 State of the Union Address, www.whitehouse.gov/news/releases/2002/01/20020129-11.html. The term was subsequently defended and elaborated on by the Bush Administration extending the Axis to more countries. Powell, "Rice Defend Bush's 'axis of evil' Speech," *CNN,* February 18, 2002; John R. Bolton, remarks, Heritage Foundation, *Beyond the Axis of Evil: Additional Threats from Weapons of Mass Destruction,* Washington, DC, May 6, 2002 at www.state.gov/t/us/rm/9962.htm. For a spirited critique of the doctrine see Bruce Cumings, Ervand Abrahamian, and Moshe Ma'oz, *Inventing the Axis of Evil the truth about North Korea, Iran, and Syria* (New York: Free Press, 2004).

45. U.S. claims against Iran were quite modest prior to the Second Gulf War. John Bolton, among the most hawkish of U.S. officials, detailed his charges, which were indeed relatively limited:

> Iran's biological weapons program began during the Iran-Iraq war, and accelerated after Tehran learned how far along Saddam Hussein had progressed in his own program. The Iranians have all of the necessary pharmaceutical expertise, as well as the commercial infrastructure needed to produce—and hide—a biological warfare program. The United States believes Iran probably has produced and weaponized BW agents in violation of the Convention. Again, Iran's BW program is complemented by an even more aggressive chemical warfare program, Iran's ongoing interest in nuclear weapons, and its aggressive ballistic missile research, development, and flight testing regimen.

Bolton, *Beyond the Axis of Evil,* 2002.

46. Iran was designated a state sponsor of terrorism by the U.S. State Department in 1984. In a year 2000 report, the Clinton administration described Iran's terrorist activities as follows:

> Iran's involvement in terrorist-related activities remained focused on support for groups opposed to Israel and peace between Israel and its neighbors. Statements by Iran's leaders demonstrated Iran's unrelenting hostility to Israel. Supreme Leader Khamenei continued to refer to Israel as a "cancerous tumor" that must be removed; President Khatami, labeling Israel an "illegal entity," called for sanctions against Israel during the intifadah; and Expediency Council Secretary Rezai said, "Iran will continue its campaign against Zionism until Israel is completely eradicated." Iran has long provided Lebanese Hizballah and the Palestinian rejectionist groups—notably HAMAS, the Palestine Islamic Jihad, and Ahmad Jibril's PFLP-GC—with varying amounts of funding, safehaven, training, and weapons. This activity continued at its already high levels following the Israeli withdrawal from southern Lebanon in May and during the intifadah in the fall. Iran continued to encourage Hizballah and the Palestinian groups to coordinate their planning and to escalate their activities against Israel. Iran also provided a lower level of support—including funding, training, and logistics assistance—to extremist groups in the Gulf, Africa, Turkey, and Central Asia.

State Department, *Patterns of Global Terrorism,* 2000, April 30, 2001, http://www.state.gov/s/ct/rls/crt/2000/2441.htm.

47. Foreign assistance was one antidote, see Steven Radelet, "Bush and Foreign Aid," *Foreign Affairs,* September/October 2003; Ambassador Cofer Black, Coordinator for Counterterrorism, Foreign Assistance and International Terrorism, Testimony before the Senate Appropriations Subcommittee on Foreign Operations, Washington, DC, April 21, 2004 at merln.ndu.edu/merln/pfiraq/archive/state/31672.pdf; Jennifer L. Windsor, "Promoting Democratization can Combat Terrorism," *The Washington Quarterly,* 26, no. 3, Summer

2003: 43–58. The idea of democratic societies remained the core principle of Bush's counter-terrorism policy:

> The long-term solution for winning the War on Terror is the advancement of freedom and human dignity through effective democracy. Elections are the most visible sign of a free society and can play a critical role in advancing effective democracy. But elections alone are not enough. Effective democracies honor and uphold basic human rights, including freedom of religion, conscience, speech, assembly, association, and press. They are responsive to their citizens, submitting to the will of the people. Effective democracies exercise effective sovereignty and maintain order within their own borders, address causes of conflict peacefully, protect independent and impartial systems of justice, punish crime, embrace the rule of law, and resist corruption. Effective democracies also limit the reach of government, protecting the institutions of civil society. In effective democracies, freedom is indivisible. They are the long-term antidote to the ideology of terrorism today. This is the battle of ideas.

The White House, National Strategy for Combating Terrorism, September 2006 at www.state.gov/s/ct/rls/wh/71803.htm#long.

CHAPTER 6

1. White House Press Release, President Bush Outlines Iraqi Threat: Remarks by the President on Iraq Cincinnati Museum Center—Cincinnati Union Terminal Cincinnati, Ohio, October 7, 2002, www.whitehouse.gov/news/releases/2002/10/20021007-8.html.

2. A time honored subject studied by historians and analyzed by political scientists, sociologists, anthropologists, and other behavioral scientists. See Hidemi Suganami, *On the Causes of War* (Oxford: Clarendon Press, 1996); Arthur Porritt, ed., *The Causes of War: Economic, Industrial, Racial, Religious, Scientific, and Political* (London: Macmillan, 1932); Reginald Horseman, *The Causes of the War of 1812* (Philadelphia: University of Pennsylvania Press, 1962); Camille Bloch, *The Causes of the World War: An Historical Summary* (London: George Allen and Unwin, 1935); Isabelle Duyvesteyn and Jan Angstrom, eds., *Rethinking the Nature of War* (London: Frank Cass, 2005).

3. Iraq attempted to seize Kuwait with the nation's separation from Great Britain in 1961. UPI, "Sheik of Kuwait Vows To Combat Any Iraqi Attack; Declares His Land Is Free-Use of Force by Kassim to Press Claims Doubted. Kuwait To Fight Any Iraqi Attack," *New York Times,* June 27, 1961. Not only did Iraq claim Kuwait but the Trucial States of the Gulf as well. AP, "Wider Iraqi Claims on Oil Lands Along Persian Gulf Are Hinted," *New York Times,* June 28, 1961.

4. Richard Perle, "The U.S. Must Strike at Saddam Hussein," *New York Times,* December 28, 2001; Todd S. Purum, "The Brains Behind Bush's War Policy," *New York Times,* February 1, 2003; Richard Perle and David Frum, *An End to Evil: How to Win the War on Terror* (New York: Random House, 2003); Jane Perlez, "Capitol Hawks Seek Tougher Line on Iraq," *New York Times,* March 7, 2001; Elaine Sciolino, "In a Humble World, Defense Deputy Stands Firm," *New York Times,* April 2, 2001; Editorial, "War Without Illusions," *New York Times,* September 15, 2001; Elaine Sciolino and Patrick E. Tyler, "A Nation Challenged: Saddam Hussein; Some Pentagon Officials and Advisers Seek to Oust Iraq's Leader in War's Next Phase," *New York Times,* October 12, 2001; Clyde Haberman, "The Nation: Past Ground Zero; The Distance Traveled in a Month of War," *New York Times,* October 14, 2001; Patrick

E. Tyler, "The World; In Washington, a Struggle to Define the Next Fight," *New York Times,* December 2, 2001; Elaine Sciolino and Allison Mitchell, "Calls for New Push Into Iraq Gain Power in Washington," *New York Times,* December 3, 2001.

5. Kenneth M. Pollack, *The Threatening Storm: The Case for Invading Iraq* (New York: Random House, 2002); Suskind, *The One Percent Solution,* 163–91; Mann, *Rise of the Vulcans,* 294–358.

6. Congressional Research Service, "Iraq: Differing Views in the Domestic Policy Debate," CRS RL31607, October 16, 2002.

7. Middle East Policy Council, *Thirtieth in the Capitol Hill Conference Series on U.S. Middle East Policy War with Iraq: A Cost-Benefit Analysis* at www.mepc.org/forums_chcs/30.asp.

8. ibid., Cordesman remarks.

9. The mobilization process was extremely broad and predated the October 2002 National Intelligence Estimate by some months. See John Prados, ed., "PR Push for Iraq War Preceded Intelligence Findings," at http://www.gwu.edu/~nsarchiv/NSAEBB/NSAEBB254/index.htm.

10. Editorial, "George W. Bush's Moment," *New York Times,* January 30, 2003; David Sanger, "A Nation Challenged: The Rogue List; Bush Aides Say Tough Tone Put Foes on Notice," *New York Times,* January 31, 2002.

11. U.S. Senate, Select Committee on Intelligence, On the U.S. Intelligence Community's Prewar Intelligence Assessments on Iraq, together with additional views, Report 108-301, 108th 2nd Session, July 9, 2004 (Washington, DC: GPO, 2004), 18.

12. ibid., 148–60. This heavily redacted testimony does not identify German intelligence but other sources do. Erich Follath, John Goetz, Marcel Rosenbach, and Holger Stark, "The Real Story of 'Curveball': How German Intelligence Helped Justify the US Invasion of Iraq," *Spiegel Online International,* www.spiegel.de/international/world/0,1518,542840,00.html; CBS News, Sixty Minutes, Faulty Intel Source "Curve Ball" Revealed 60 Minutes: Iraqi's Fabricated Story Of Biological Weapons Aided U.S. Arguments For Invasion, November 4, 2007 at www.cbsnews.com/stories/2007/11/01/60minutes/main3440577.shtml.

13. Craig Smith, "Threats And Responses: The Allies: Europeans Try to Stem Anti-U.S. Anger," *New York Times,* January 24, 2003.

14. The Gulf's hostility toward Hussein was deep. See Alan Munro, *Arab Storm: The Politics and Diplomacy Behind the Gulf War* (London: I.B. Taurus, 2006), 44; Azadeh Moaveni, "Iranians Eager for Hussein to Be Ousted," *Los Angeles Times,* February 23, 2003, A7.

15. Mearsheimer and Walt, *Israel Lobby,* 229–62.

16. Michael R. Gordon, "Threats and Responses: Readiness; U.S. is Preparing Base in Gulf State to Run Iraq War," *New York Times,* December 1, 2002; months before the war, regional support was tepid but still almost automatic:

> America's allies in the Arab world are positioning themselves to go along with a United States-led war against Iraq, driven by their need for American strategic and economic assistance, officials and diplomats in the region said.
>
> Each country is maneuvering to signal enough acquiescence to allow them to preserve good relations with Washington but at the same time not provoke new levels of anger in the streets, they said.
>
> In the important Persian Gulf nations where American forces are based—Saudi Arabia, Kuwait, Bahrain, Oman, the United Arab Emirates and Qatar—officials acknowledge that their facilities would be used for a war against Iraq.

Jane Perlez, "Threats and Responses: Iraq's Neighbors; Arab Leaders Glumly Brace for Inevitable War, With an Eye to Anger in the Streets," *New York Times,* October 8, 2002.

17. Trevor Stanley, "Perspectives on World History and Current Events," *Coalition of the Willing* at www.pwhce.org/willing.html; White House, Operation Iraqi Freedom, Coalition Members, March 27, 2003 at www.whitehouse.gov/news/releases/2003/03/20030327 -10.html.

18. Tyler F. Parker and Felicity Barringer, "Threats And Responses: United Nations; Annan Says U.S. Will Violate Charter if It Acts Without Approval," *New York Times,* March 11, 2003.

19. Project for a New American Century, The Clinton Administration's Public Case Against Saddam Hussein, www.newamericancentury.org/iraq-20040623.htm; White House, Containing Saddam Hussein's Iraq, December 16, 1998 at http://clinton5.nara.gov/WH/ EOP/NSC/html/nsc-11.html.

20. White House, Remarks by the Vice President to the Veterans of Foreign Wars 103rd National Convention, August 26, 2002, http://www.whitehouse.gov/news/releases/2002/08/ 20020826.html.

21. David E. Sanger, "The World: First Among Evils? The Debate Over Attacking Iraq Heats Up," *New York Times,* September 1, 2002.

22. The White House, *Iraq: Denial and Deception,* U.S. Secretary of State Colin Powell addresses the UN Security Council, Press Release, February 5, 2003, www.whitehouse.gov/ news/releases/2003/02/20030205-1.html.

23. Fred Kaplan, "The Tragedy of Colin Powell: How the Bush Presidency Destroyed Him," *Slate Magazine,* February 19, 2004, www.slate.com/id/2095756/; Derrick Z. Jackson, "Too Much the Good Soldier," *Boston Globe,* November 17, 2004; Editorial, "Cabinet Shuffle, Good Soldier Powell," *New York Times,* November 16, 2004; Joseph Levyfeld, "The Good Soldier," *New York Review of Books,* 53, no. 17, November 2, 2006.

24. State Department, The Future of Iraq Project, Civil Society Building Working Group, Iraq Institute for Democracy, September 8, 2003, Washington, DC, 7, http://www.gwu.edu/ ~nsarchiv/NSAEBB/NSAEBB198/index.htm.

25. ibid., 8.

26. State Department, The Future of Iraq Project, Overview, Washington, DC, May 12, 2003, http://www.gwu.edu/~nsarchiv/NSAEBB/NSAEBB198/index.htm.

27. Harlan K. Wade and James P. Wade, *Shock and Awe,* achieving rapid dominance (Washington, DC: National Defense University, Institute for Strategic Studies, 1996), 19.

28. ibid., 40.

29. ibid., 75.

30. Michael R. Gordon and Bernard E. Trainor, *COBRA II: The Inside Story of the Invasion and Occupation of Iraq* (New York: Random House, 2006), 29–42.

31. ibid., 394–456; Michael Knights, *Cradle of Conflict, Iraq and the Birth of the Modern U.S. Military* (Anapolis, MD: Naval Institute Press, 2005), 280–357.

32. Elisabeth Bumiller and Douglas Jehl, "A Nation at War: Washington; Bush Tunes In And Sees Iraqis In Celebrations," *New York Times,* April 10, 2003; David Sanger and Steven R. Weisman, "A Nation At War: Iraq's Neighbors; Bush's Aides Envision New Influence in Region," *New York Times,* April 10, 2003; R. W. Apple Jr., "A Nation At War: News Analysis; A High Point in 2 Decades of U.S. Might," *New York Times,* April 10, 2003.

33. Michael R. Gordon, "'Catastrophic Success,' Poor Intelligence Misled Troops About Risk of Drawn-Out War," *New York Times,* October 20, 2004; John F. Burns, "Troops, Shadow of Vietnam Falls Over Iraq River Raids," *New York Times,* November 29, 2004. The arsenals available to insurgent forces were formidable:

During their patrol, Soldiers from 2nd Battalion, 8th Field Artillery Regiment discovered huge stockpiles of weapons and munitions, including an anti-aircraft gun, 15,000 anti-aircraft rounds, 4,600 hand grenades, 144 VOG-17M anti-personnel grenade launchers, 25 SA-7 surface-to-air missiles, 44 SA-7 battery packs, 20 guided missile packs, 21 120 mm mortar rounds, two 120 mm mortar tubes, 10 122 mm rockets, six 152 mm artillery rounds and two 57 mm artillery rounds. Soldiers also discovered a building full of explosive-making materials.…

U.S. Army, Huge weapons cache unearthed in northern Iraq, Army News Service, November 22, 2004.

34. The impenetrable heart of Saddam Hussein's regime were his fedayeen militia. Composed of 40,000 loyalists, they and the Iraqi Republican Guard formed regime protection structures that were impossible to defeat internally. See John Pike, Saddam's Martyrs ["Men of Sacrifice"] Fedayeen Saddam, Federation of American Scientists, at www.fas.org/irp/world/iraq/fedayeen/; CNN, Gruesome videotape allegedly shows brutal Fedayeen Saddam punishment, CNN, October 30, 2003 at www.cnn.com/2003/world/meast/10/30/sprj.irq.torture.tape/. The massive terror apparatus of Hussein's Baath Party should be revealed in coming years with processing, analysis and publication of million of pages of central party records now at Stanford University. Kanan Makiya, "All Levels of the Iraqi Government Were Complicit," *Middle East Quarterly* 12, no. 2 (September 2005) at www.meforum.org/article/718.

35. Adelman was among the most prominent of neoconservative mid level officials in the Department of Defense. His argument was that Iraq would be a cakewalk because:

1) It was a cakewalk last time; 2) they've become much weaker; 3) we've become much stronger; and 4) now we're playing for keeps.

Kenneth Adelman, "Iraq would be a Cakewalk," *Washington Post,* February 13, 2002, A.27.

36. Of the many books written on the postwar occupation of Iraq, one of the most informed and analytical to date is Ali A. Allawi, *The Occupation of Iraq, Winning the War, Losing the Peace* (New Haven, CT: Yale University Press, 2007). Extensive analytical reports on all aspects of Iraqi postwar reconstruction are required by U.S. law. The Special Inspector General for Iraqi Reconstruction issues quarterly reports to Congress, detailed project assessments and lessons learned reports at www.sigir.mil/Default.aspx. Further reports have issued by Congressional committees and private public policy institutes, notably Johns Hopkins' CSIS. In addition to extensive waste, corruption and war damage, the success of reconstruction efforts has been obviated by the ongoing political divisions and sectarian war. Among many fatalist critiques were: Pauline H. Baker, *From Failed State to Civil War: The Lebanonization of Iraq, 2003–2006* (Washington, DC: Fund for Peace, 2006).

37. Christopher Alexander, Charles Kyle, and William McCallister, *The Iraqi Insurgency Movement,* U.S. Army, November 14, 2003, http://www.comw.org/warreport/fulltext/03alexander.pdf; Bruce Hoffman, *Insurgency and Counterinsurgency in Iraq,* OP-127-IPC/CMEPP, June 2004, Rand Corporation at www.rand.org/pubs/occasional_papers/2005/RAND_OP127.pdf; Anthony Cordesman, *New Patterns in the Iraqi Insurgency: The War for a Civil War in Iraq,* Working Draft, September 27, 2005, CSIS, Washington, DC, www.comw.org/warreport/fulltext/0509cordesman.pdf and Anthony Cordesman, The Quarterly Report on "Measuring Stability and Security in Iraq:" Fact, Fallacy, and an Overall Grade of "F," January 2, 2006, CSIS, Washington, DC at www.comw.org/warreport/fulltext/0606cordesman.pdf.

38. Political costs of the war to the Bush administration and the Republican Party were incalculable. Linda J. Blimes, and Joseph E. Stiglitz, *The Three Trillion Dollar War: The True*

Cost of the Iraq Conflict (New York: W.W. Norton, 2008); By 2008, Bush's approval rating had plunged forty points since the start of the Iraq War in March 2003. CNN, Poll: Bush's popularity hits new low, March 19, 2008.

CHAPTER 7

1. James Paul and Céline Nahory, *War and Occupation in Iraq* (New York: Global Policy Forum, June 2007), i. at www.globalpolicy.org/security/issues/iraq/occupation/report/index.htm.

2. White House, Press Release, *President Bush Discusses Global War on Terror: The Pentagon,* March 19, 2008, www.whitehouse.gov/news/releases/2008/03/20080319-2.html.

3. IMF and World bank data shows World real per capita GDP growth has averaged over 4 percent since the early 2000s, see *World Economic and Financial Surveys World Economic Outlook,* October 2007, 1, www.imf.org/external/pubs/ft/weo/2007/02/index.htm. Such massive growth will raise average world living standards 5000 percent if sustained through the end of the twenty-first century; Robert J. Barro and Xavier Sala-i-Martin, *Economic Growth,* 2nd ed. (Cambridge: MIT Press, 2003), 1–21.

4. Neil MacFarquhar, "A Nation At War: The Islamic World; For Arabs, New Jihad Is in Iraq," *New York Times,* April 2, 2003; Editorial, "The War Americans Don't See," *New York Times,* April 4, 2003; Elizabeth Becker, "A Nation At War: The Message; Portrayal of a War of Liberation Is Faltering Across the Arab World," *New York Times,* April 5, 2003; Andrew Borowiec, "Impotence, Rage Fuel Opinions in Arab press; Anti-Americanism Drowns Out Occasional Self-criticism," *Washington Times,* April 9, 2003; Adeed Dawisha, *The Arab Radicals* (New York: Council on Foreign Relations, 1986); Sigrid Faath, ed., *Anti-Americanism in the Islamic World* (London: Markus Weiner Publishers, 2006).

5. A hard critique of America's transformational warfare in Iraq came from the military historian and public policy analyst who was to become the father of the "surge." Frederick W. Kagan, *Finding the Target: The Transformation of American Military Policy* (New York: Encounter Books, 2006), 323–59.

6. The IED has had a devastating and unique effect on the long-term military deployment in Iraq. The lethality of this low tech weapons was described in a 2005 Congressional Research Service Report:

> Insurgents have constructed IEDs powerful enough to kill soldiers inside 22-ton Bradley Fighting Vehicles. In one incident in 2004, after a Bradley ran over a large IED, the armored bottom plate of the vehicle was reportedly found some 60 yards from the site of the explosion.

Clay Wilson, "Improvised Explosive Devices in Iraq: Effects and Countermeasures," *Congressional Research Service,* November 23, 2005 (Washington, DC: GPO, 2005), 2.

7. Anthony Cordesman, "Understanding the Fighting in Southern Iraq Between Sadr and the Iraqi Forces," *CSIS Report,* March 26, 2008; Anthony Cordesman, "The Cost of the Iraq War CRS, GAO, CBO, and DoD Estimates," *CSIS Report,* March 31, 2008; Anthony Cordesman, "Commentary: The NATO Summit and Afghanistan: Cosmetics and the Slow Road to Defeat," *CSIS Report,* April 4, 2008; Daniel Serwer and Sam Parker, *Iraq After the Surge: Options and Questions* (Washington, DC: United States Institute of Peace, April 2008) at www.usip.org/pubs/usipeace_briefings/2008/iraq_surge.pdf; U.S. Senate Committee on Foreign Relations, Hearings, *Iraq After the Surge: Military Prospects,* April 2, 2008,

110th Cong., 1st sess. (Washington, DC: GPO, 2008), www.senate.gov/~foreign/hearings/
2008/hrg080402a.html.

8. Jeff Zeleny, "Leading Democrat in Senate Tells Reporters, 'This War Is Lost,'" *New York Times,* April 20, 2007.

9. Akira Iriye, *Power and Culture, The Japanese American War, 1941–1945* (Cambridge, MA: Harvard University Press, 1981), iii.

10. Packer, *Assassin' Gate,* 114–20; Two scholars of the modern Middle East, Bernard Lewis of Princeton and Fouad Ajami were major figures supporting the war as a feasible project. Fouad Ajami, *Iraq and the Arabs' Future, Foreign Affairs* (January/February, 2003); Bernard Lewis, *What Went Wrong? The Clash Between Islam and Modernity in the Middle East* (New York: Harper, 2003); David Sanger and James Dao, "Threats and Responses: The White House; U.S. Is Completing Plan To Promote A Democratic Iraq," *New York Times,* January 6, 2003; Editorial, "President Bush's Nation-Building," *New York Times,* February 27, 2003; Alessandra Stanley, "A Nation At War: The TV Watch; Images of Victory Obscure Reality," *New York Times,* April 4, 2003.

11. Allawi, *The Occupation of Iraq,* 114–31; Peter W. Galbraith, *The End of Iraq, How American Incompetence Created a War Without End* (New York: Simon and Schuster, 2006); Mark Danner, *Torture and Truth: America, Abu Ghraib, and the War on Terror* (New York: New York Review of Books, 2004).

12. Jed Horne, *Breach of Faith: Hurricane Katrina and the Near Death of a Great American City* (New York: Random House, 2006); Christopher Cooper and Robert Block, *Disaster: Hurricane Katrina and the Failure of Homeland Security* (New York: Times Books, 2006); Chris Mooney, *Storm World: Hurricanes, Politics, and the Battle Over Global Warming* (New York: Harcourt, 2007); Dowling Campbell, ed., *A Bird in the Bush: Failed Domestic Policies of the George W. Bush Administration* (New York: Algora Publishing, 2005).

13. Juan Cole, *Osama bin Laden's Scary Vision of a Grand Muslim Super State,* October 4, 2004 at http://hnn.us/articles/7378.html.

14. Operation Iraqi Freedom became a living laboratory for military theorists and planners. U.S. Army War College, *Network Centric Warfare Case Study Network Centric Warfare Case Study Volume I 'Operations': U.S. V Corps and 3rd Infantry Division (Mechanized) during Operation Iraqi Freedom* (March–April 2003), June 2006, vol. 2: A View of Command, Control, Communications and Computer Architectures at the Dawn of Network Centric Warfare; Network Centric Warfare Case Study Volume III: Network Centric Warfare Insights, October 2006 at www.au.af.mil/au/awc/awcgate/awc-forc.htm#netcentric.

15. See the Office of the Secretary of Defense Advanced Concepts Technology Demonstrations (ACTD) at www.acq.osd.mil/jctd/descript.htm for an overview of emerging technological systems.

16. See DARPA's public domain Web site for its advanced research at www.darpa.mil/sto/programs/index.html; John Edwards, *The Geeks of War: The Secretive Labs and Brilliant Minds Behind Tomorrow's Warfare Technologies* (New York: AMACOM, 2005); Ann Finkbeiner, *The Jasons: The Secret History of Science's Postwar Elite* (New York: Viking, 2006); Alex Roland and Philip Shiman, *Strategic Computing: DARPA and the Quest for Machine Intelligence, 1983–1993* (Cambridge, MA: MIT Press, 2002).

17. The Bush administration believed its strongest claim to humanitarian relief was its Africa policy, which included a $10 billion pledge for AIDS education, treatment and prevention in Africa. White House, Press Release, *U.S. Africa Policy: An Unparalleled Partnership*

Strengthening Democracy, Overcoming Poverty, and Saving Lives, February 14, 2008, www
.whitehouse.gov/infocus/africa.

18. As cited earlier, Iraqi reconstruction remains formally under the supervision of a temporary U.S. federal agency, the Office of the Special Inspector General for Iraq Reconstruction
(SIGIR), www.sigir.mil/Default.aspx. The paper trail has been immense, the number of
successes few.

19. CBS News, *Interrogator Shares Saddam's Confessions Tells 60 Minutes Former Iraqi
Dictator Didn't Expect U.S. Invasion,* Sixty Minutes, broadcast transcript for January 27, 2008,
www.cbsnews.com/stories/2008/01/24/60minutes/main3749494.shtml.

Index

About the Author

ORRIN SCHWAB is a visiting scholar at the University of Chicago. He is the author of *Clash of Cultures: Civil Military Relations During the Vietnam War* (PSI, 2006) and *Defending the Free World: John F. Kennedy, Lyndon Johnson and the Vietnam War, 1961–1965* (Praeger, 1998). He has taught at Purdue University Calumet and the University of Chicago.